Conversations with Shelby Foote

Literary Conversations Series

Peggy Whitman Prenshaw
General Editor

Sylvia Martin

Conversations with Shelby Foote

Edited by
William C. Carter

University Press of Mississippi
Jackson and London

Books by Shelby Foote

Tournament. New York: Dial Press, Inc., 1949. (Second edition, Summa Publications, Birmingham, Alabama, 1987)
Follow Me Down. New York: Dial Press, 1950.
Love in a Dry Season. New York: Dial Press, 1951.
Shiloh. New York: Dial Press, 1952.
Jordan County: A Landscape in Narrative. New York: Random House, 1954.
The Civil War: A Narrative. Vol. 1: *Fort Sumter to Perryville.* New York: Random House, 1958.
The Civil War: A Narrative. Vol. 2: *Fredericksburg to Meridian.* New York: Random House, 1963.
The Civil War: A Narrative. Vol. 3: *Red River to Appomattox.* New York: Random House, 1974.
September September. New York: Random House, 1978.

Manufactured in the United States of America
5th printing, 1998

The paper in this book meets the guidelines for permanence and durability of the Committee on Production Guidelines for Book Longevity of the Council of Library Resources.

Library of Congress Cataloging-in-Publication Data

Foote, Shelby.
Conversations with Shelby Foote / edited by William C. Carter.
p. cm. — (Literary conversations series)
Includes index.
ISBN 0-87805-385-9 (alk. paper). — ISBN 0-87805-386-7 (pbk. : alk. paper)
1. Foote, Shelby—Interviews. 2. Novelists, American—20th century—Interviews. I. Carter, William C. II. Title. III. Series.
PS3511.0348Z465 1989 88-37292
813'.54—dc19 CIP

British Library Cataloguing in Publication data is available.

Contents

Introduction

"Writing is a religion with me," Shelby Foote told Harvey Breit in 1952. To the exclusion of other hobbies or interests, Foote has remained constant in his devotion to his vocation, a writer seeking the truth about the human experience, in fiction and in history. The portrait that emerges from these interviews, which begin with the publication of Foote's first novels in the late 1940s and early '50s and span thirty-seven years of his career, is that of an artist of the narrative, a writer determined to get his facts right and to tell a good story.

Foote grew up in Greenville, Mississippi, a Delta town located on the Mississippi River that was also home to another well-known literary figure, William Alexander Percy, author of *Lanterns on the Levee.* When Percy's young cousins Walker, Leroy, and Phinizy came to live with him, Shelby Foote and the young Walker Percy began a lifelong friendship. Their relationship was crucial to Foote's decision to become a writer. As he admitted to Evans Harrington in 1971, "It's probable that if those Percy boys hadn't moved to Greenville, I might never have become interested in literary things."

Foote rejected formal education after high school, although he did spend a couple of years enrolled at the University of North Carolina at Chapel Hill, mostly in the library reading in the stacks. The independent-minded Foote explained to Harrington how he had created his own curriculum: "I did try to read everything I had any notion was a classic, ancient or modern. That was where my schooling was."

Early in his career, even without a certain source of income, Foote maintained a regular writing schedule seven days a week, keeping hours from morning until late afternoon. In an amazingly productive period just after World War II, writing in a garage apartment behind his mother's house in Greenville, he produced five novels—

Tournament, Follow Me Down, Love in a Dry Season, Shiloh, and *Jordan County: A Landscape in Narrative.* During this stretch, Foote once finished writing a book in the morning and began a new one that same afternoon. In 1954, shortly after the publication of *Jordan County,* Foote moved to Memphis, the city he describes as the capital of the Mississippi Delta, where he began work on his history of the Civil War.

Foote accepts the label "Southern writer" or "regional writer" as a compliment, believing that great writers belong to a region they succeed in making real to an audience far beyond Yoknapatawpha and Jordan County lines. Foote's favorite authors have a strong sense of place, and, as he observed to W. Hampton Sides, he believes that the books have made the locations special and not the other way around: "That holds for Dostoyevsky in St. Petersburg, for Proust in Paris, for Faulkner in Yoknapatawpha."

Foote's stories are set in the Delta, or his characters are Deltans. The Delta is not typical of the South, according to Foote, because of the immigrants from many different countries who settled there. His own maternal grandfather was a Viennese Jew who somehow—Foote says his own family doesn't understand how the grandfather carried it off—married the daughter of a planter. In his remarks about life in the Delta, Foote blames the planter for much that has gone wrong. Autocratic and reluctant to release his hold on his own kin, not to mention the hired hands, the planter makes no room for those around him. This practice is especially tough on sons and sons-in-law, as Foote pointed out graphically to Richard Tillinghast in 1983, "The old man's got a plantation, you've married his daughter. . . . But you're the person who runs after cigarettes all the rest of your life."

The novel is the literary genre that Foote prefers and has spent his life practicing. Despite his great admiration for Faulkner, Foote told Evans Harrington that he disagrees with Faulkner and many other writers who see poetry as the highest form of literature. He credits Hemingway's example with teaching him how to develop his own prose style by roughing it up: "I learned from Hemingway that roughness should be part of the smoothness. . . . Prose rhythms are to me infinitely more interesting than poetical rhythms." In our time the novelist is superior to the poet, Foote believes. Further, he sees no distinction at all between novel writing and history writing, both making the same demands upon the narrative skill of the writer.

At the beginning of his writing career, before he began work on *The Civil War: A Narrative,* Foote had formulated his definition of a historical novel. Foote had defined for himself the boundaries between fiction and history when he wrote the transitional novel *Shiloh,* in which fictional characters appear along with historical figures while all the facts about the actual battle, including the weather, and the actions and dialogue of the real participants, are based on documentation. Foote laid down his ground rules for writing a historical novel in a 1952 interview with Harvey Breit: "In this one [*Shiloh*], no historical character says or does anything except what I have accurate evidence of his having said or done."

Foote described his absolute respect for facts to John Griffin Jones: "I've never known a modern historical instance where the truth wasn't superior to anybody's distortions." But facts alone will not suffice in the telling of a story, whether imagined or documented, and Foote condemns the "unskilled historian's history. . . . I'm not saying what they do has no validity; I am saying it has no art." Comparing history and fiction, he explained to James Newcomb that the craft of a good storyteller may be even more important for the historian than for the novelist: "I think plotting is more important in history than in fiction. . . . The whole thing ought to be telling a glowing story or it won't be true."

Foote summarized for John Graham the similarities in a writer's use of *story* in fiction and history: "In one case, he has gotten [the story] out of his head, in the other he has gotten it out of documents. In both cases, plotting is necessary." In the same interview, Foote maintained that the techniques of a novelist can only benefit the historian who is trying to breathe life into his material. "I'm not talking about making it livelier than it was, I'm just talking about some attempt to make it as lively as it was." Hemingway is again the great example, as Foote told James Newcomb: "If any historian in this country wrote a single page of history that had the clarity of a single page of Hemingway, that page of history would live forever." Critical of the historian who writes without plot, Foote has quick praise for the historian whose style fits the subject, as for Douglas

Southall Freeman in the interview with Graham: "Style is the way a man is able to communicate to you the quality of his mind. And this does communicate to me the quality of Freeman's mind when he turns it on Robert E. Lee. . . ."

While critics and readers alike have found Foote's novels highly readable, significant contributions to the genre in American literature, his undisputed masterpiece is *The Civil War: A Narrative.* Foote's reading as a young man—he says he read books about the Civil War the way some people read detective stories—and his early writing prepared the way for publication of his *War.* He would later realize, as he told John Graham, that the writing of the first five novels was an ideal apprenticeship: "I don't know of anything I learned about the writing of novels in the course of practicing my craft that's not applicable to the writing of history." To Foote, the Civil War is our great national tragedy. In his lengthy 1979 interview with Jones, Foote spoke of the effect of the war on the South specifically: "We were really beaten in that war; we were beaten far worse than the Germans were in either of the world wars." Foote has emphasized the importance of the Civil War in shaping our nation and our national conscience and in distinguishing the South from the rest of the country as the only region to have lost a war—an important distinction that held until Vietnam.

Foote readily acknowledges his debt to other writers and his eagerness to learn from them, but he remains distinctly his own man as an artist. Aware that he gave up much as a novelist to write *The Civil War,* Foote is convinced he made the right decision. He admits, however, that he would never have done it if he had known completing it would take two decades. Professors Helen White and Redding Sugg asked Foote whether *The Civil War* had turned out to be more than he bargained for. In response, Foote compared the narrative to a special kind of French soup: "it's a job of compression and, as you move your spoon through it, the soup swells, and if you don't eat fast enough it overflows your bowl."

Not only has *The Civil War: A Narrative* been an acclaimed critical success, but it has done extremely well in sales in the United States. Abroad, however, it is virtually unknown because of limited funds to subsidize translations of foreign books. Even so, Foote enjoys a substantial reputation as a novelist in certain European countries. In

France, for example, Maurice-Edgar Coindreau and other leading critics consider him to be the successor of William Faulkner. While Foote's novels in general have been unjustly neglected in this country, four of his six have recently been reissued in new paperback editions in France. The French journal *Delta,* devoted to critical studies of writers of the American South, published an entire issue on Foote's novels. When Foote was invited to read from his works at a Paris university in 1985, *Le Monde* printed a conversation with him in its book section.

Despite the many lucrative offers that followed the publication of his *War,* Foote has put nonfiction behind him forever. As he told W. Hampton Sides in 1986, "The day I finished that book I stopped having anything to do with the Civil War. And I've done my best to forget it." At the same time, Foote has no plans to write about anything that happened after the late 1950s. In the television interview with James Newcomb, Foote declared that the appearance of the Hippies on the scene around 1960 marks the end of time so far as his writing is concerned: "I stopped listening."

After the long journey across the historical battlefields had ended, Foote returned to the novel in the mid-seventies and produced the thriller *September September.* Lessons learned from writing *The Civil War* show themselves in his setting the story in the Memphis of September 1957, the historically significant month of the Little Rock School integration crisis and Sputnik. Helen White has observed that although *September September* is an action novel, it is "based as firmly on painstaking research as *Shiloh* was." Foote elaborated on the two key historical events that frame the suspenseful tale of the kidnapping of a black Memphis boy: "I wanted to examine that month of September which included the Little Rock trouble over at Central High and ended on the 4th of October with the Russians throwing up the Sputnik." Foote found it alarming that such a technological feat had been accomplished by "slave labor in a slave country and quite literally by men who were almost convicts—captured German scientists—and it was a great shock to me. I wanted to look at what the world was like on the immediate eve of that."

September September is notable for, among other things, its depiction of a black bourgeois family at a crucial point in the history of race relations in the South. Foote blames the violence of civil rights demonstrations on the passiveness of responsible, decent white people who let the "riffraff" take over. In several interviews, he has related his own confrontations with the Klan in South Alabama and his rejection of the segregated and unjust society that he knew as a young man. If Shelby Foote has any regrets, it may be that he did not play a more active role in reforming the social ills of his native region. He confessed to interviewer James Newcomb that he had been struck by Bobby Kennedy's statement that if he had not gone into politics, he would have gone to the Mississippi Delta and worked for the Negro: "it hurt me to think that I had turned my back on something that Bobby Kennedy had been willing to devote his whole life to."

Since early in his career, Foote has had plans for a long Delta novel called *Two Gates to the City*. Indeed, remarks about this work in progress recur throughout the interviews like a leitmotiv. Occasionally he gives hints about the novel's contents, its plot outline, and the characters he has been developing for years. In spite of his inability so far to finish the projected work, Foote points with satisfaction to the more than two million words he has in print and the fact that his big gamble of spending a major portion of his career on his vast and complex history of the Civil War has paid off, both in terms of critical acclaim and readers.

Foote, perhaps more successfully than any writer since Voltaire, has mastered both fictional and historical narrative. He has in fact earned the professional title he prefers: a narrative artist.

These interviews come from a variety of sources. The brief, early pieces from local newspapers are more like records of conversations than formal interviews, in contrast to the long and wide-ranging later interviews that appeared in scholarly journals and trade magazines.

Of the twenty-nine interviews located, the eighteen most representative conversations are presented here, including two previously unpublished television interviews. The transcriptions of these television appearances by Foote on *The Dick Cavett Show* and in a special interview, *Shelby Foote Is a Novelist,* produced by public radio station WKNO in Memphis appear in their entirety, edited only for the sake of intelligibility.

The previously published interviews are also reprinted in full and in chronological order. While the presentation of the interviews in their original, uncut version necessarily results in some repetition, the editors believe this is preferable to cutting. The value to scholars of unedited interviews is clear in that a valuable archive is created for future students of literature and history. Furthermore, Foote's patience with his interviewers in answering the same questions more than once often results in answers that offer additional remarks, refinements of previous explanations, and other interesting variations. Often a pertinent, telling anecdote, forgotten the first time, will accompany the reply to a repeated question.

Above all, from these interviews we gain a number of insights into the creative process of an original artist, as well as Foote's observations about himself as a writer and those authors whom he especially admires. Taken as a whole, the interviews make up a delightful and informative master class on a major writer's development as a novelist and historian.

I am deeply grateful to Shelby Foote and all those who interviewed him and who have written about the man and his works. My heartfelt thanks go to those publishers and producers who have granted us permission to reprint the interviews.

I would like to express my sincere thanks to Tinker B. Dunbar, of the Reference Department of Sterne Library at the University of Alabama at Birmingham, for her invaluable aid in locating and obtaining interview material. I would also like to thank Josephine Carter for her aid in transcribing the videotapes of the television interviews.

Finally, I wish to thank my editor, Seetha Srinivasan, for her faith in this project and for answering all my questions so thoroughly and promptly.

WCC
September 1988

Chronology

1916 17 November: Shelby Dade Foote, Jr., born to Shelby Dade and Lillian Rosenstock Foote in Greenville, Mississippi

1917-22 The Footes live successively in Jackson, Vicksburg, Pensacola, and Mobile as father is promoted by Armour and Company.

1922 Father, Shelby Dade Foote, dies.

1922-25 Lillian Foote and her son return to Greenville; SF attends school through the third grade.

1925-28 Lillian Foote returns to Pensacola as a secretary with Armour and Company; SF completes the sixth grade.

1928-30 Lillian Foote returns to Greenville as a legal secretary. SF completes seventh and eighth grades and is admitted to Greenville High School.

1931 Beginning of friendship with Walker Percy and his brothers; SF becomes a frequent visitor at the home of William Alexander Percy, guardian of the Percy boys.

1935-39 Newspaper work, on an intermittent basis, for Hodding Carter's *Delta Star,* which became the *Delta Democrat-Times*

1935-37 SF attends the University of North Carolina at Chapel Hill where he contributes stories to *Carolina Magazine.*

1938 Meets William Faulkner in Oxford in June

1940-44 Begins military service with the Mississippi National Guard; commissioned and serves as captain of artillery with the Fifth Division in Northern Ireland. Tried by court-martial and dismissed, Foote returns to the States and works for the Associated Press (A.P.) in New York.

1944 Marries Tess Lavery of Belfast, Ireland, in New York

1945 Serves in the United States Marine Corps, January to November

1945-46 Employed by radio station WJPR, Greenville

1946 Publication of short story "Flood Burial" in the *Saturday Evening Post*; Foote quits job to write full time. Divorced from Tess Lavery Foote

1947 Private publication of *The Merchant of Bristol* in Greenville. Visits New Mexico with Walker Percy

1948 Marries Marguerite Dessommes

1949 Publication of *Tournament.* Daughter, Margaret Shelby Foote, is born.

1950 Publication of *Follow Me Down*

1951 Publication of *Love in a Dry Season*

1952 Publication of *Shiloh*; on 6 April, Foote attends ceremonies at Shiloh battlefield with William Faulkner.

1953 Divorced from Marguerite Dessommes Foote

1954 Publication of *Jordan County: A Landscape in Narrative.* Foote moves to Memphis and begins work on a history of the Civil War.

1955-57 Guggenheim fellow

1956 Marries Gwyn Rainer

1958 Publication of *Fort Sumter to Perryville* (Volume I of *The Civil War: A Narrative*)

1961 Son, Huger Lee Foote, II, is born.

1963 Publication of *Fredericksburg to Meridian* (Volume II of *The Civil War: A Narrative*)

1963-64 Ford Foundation fellow and playwright-in-residence at the Arena Stage, Washington

1964 *Jordan County: A Landscape in the Round* (a play adapted by Foote from his novel, *Jordan County: A Landscape in Narrative*) produced by the Arena Stage

1966-67 Lectures at Memphis State University

1968 Writer-in-residence at Hollins College, Virginia

1969 Mother, Lillian Rosenstock Foote, dies.

1974 Publication of *Red River to Appomattox* (Volume III of *The Civil War: A Narrative*)

1978 July, tours Sharpsburg and Gettysburg battlefields with President Carter. Publication of *September September*

1981 Delivers Franklin Lecture, Auburn University

1986 Publication of *The Civil War: A Narrative* by Vintage Books

Conversations with Shelby Foote

Shelby Foote, Greenville Author, Says Writing Is His Hardest Job

Edwin Vincent/1950

From the *Delta Democrat-Times* [Greenville, Miss.] 25 June 1950, 1-2. Reprinted by permission.

With the publication Friday of his second novel, *Follow Me Down,* in two years and another now being written for publication next year, Shelby Foote is rapidly turning into one of the South's most productive young writers.

On the surface, it looks like he is a book-a-year man. But as a matter of fact, *Tournament,* which came out in September, was actually begun several years ago, survived complete abandonment during the war and still provided the necessary material and many untouched pages for Mr. Foote's first novel.

It had also in the meantime provided "Flood Burial" for the *Saturday Evening Post* and "Merchant of Bristol" for the Levee Press. In addition, it had furnished Greenvillians many hours pastime trying to "figure out the people."

Since the locale of *Follow Me Down* is Mr. Foote's "Jordan County"—which bears a remarkable (and admitted) similarity to Washington County, people will possibly be tempted to try a similar pastime on this book. The author advises against it.

"Jordan County is in most respects Washington County," he said. But using another name allowed certain liberties with fact that would otherwise be impossible. However, "if anybody starts trying to identify the characters with people they know they'll go crazy. There are no portraits in it."

The book is based on fact "only in the vaguest sort of way," he said. A story of murder, it is the first time Mr. Foote has used a crime of violence as his central theme. In reality, the book is a study of evil and there is "no mystery."

He was particularly pleased with the review of the book by Elizabeth Spencer which appears today on the Critic's Page of the *Delta Democrat-Times.* "Leaving out the flattering part, she has done a remarkably good study and has understood what the book was all about," he said. Miss Spencer is the author of *Fire in the Morning* which won the Southern Literary Award in 1948—"Something I'll never do," Mr. Foote observed.

At present he is working on a collection of seven short novels and stories, *Child by Fever,* which will probably be out next year. This, too, is a history of Jordan County, "in reverse, working backward from 1950 to an Indian tale of 1798," he said.

All of these will be completely new except "Ride Out," which appeared in the *Post* as "Tell Them Goodbye."

Shelby Foote didn't really get started until he decided that the only way to write was to settle down and write. So he quit his job as radio copy-writer and got down to serious business.

"I may not have eaten dry cereal, but I didn't have nickels for coffee either," he said. Declaring that money is still short, he hasn't yet fulfilled the average reader's idea of Authors in Big Cars.

"When I ride around in that old convertible of mine without a top winter and summer most people don't know it's because the car hasn't got a top," he said. "They think I'm trying to show off."

He has definite hours for working, getting to his desk at 9 a.m. At 12:30 he stops for lunch and returns to work at 1:30. Then he knocks off about four in the afternoon. "I find if I stay away from writing for any length of time it is just as if I had never written a line before."

Sometimes he finishes a novel in the morning and begins another in the afternoon. While he was working on the first he would have been making notes on the next. "I write from a very complete outline—what I call 'a scenario,' " he said. "So the actual writing is just a question of sweating. I do a lot of that."

The idea that most people have that turning out books and stories is a "soft job" has proved entirely wrong in his case. "Every book is a separate problem. I think I'll sweat as much over the fiftieth as over the first," he said. "It may be simple for someone who keeps on writing the same novel over and over. But I never want to write one like I've done before."

Shelby Foote has held down a variety of jobs ranging from construction work to newspaper reporting, but this is the hardest. Still, "I've been writing all my life and I guess I'll write for the rest of it," he said.

Talk with Shelby Foote

Harvey Breit/1952

From the *New York Times Book Review*, 27 April 1952, p. 16.

The author of the recently published novel, *Shiloh,* is an attractive, tough-minded fellow of 35. Shelby Foote is his name and his grandfather fought at Shiloh. He himself was born and raised in Greenville, Mississippi, and attended the University of North Carolina. He was five years in the Army and Marine Corps. When his interviewer exclaimed at the amount of time he'd put in, Mr. Foote rejoined somewhat dryly. "Yeah, plus one year in the Mississippi National Guard."

How had it happened—the Army and Marines both? "I was mobilised in 1940 as a sergeant," Mr. Foote said, "and rose to captain and then got court-martialed and got kicked completely out of the Army. It was in Northern Ireland. I went to see my girl in Belfast when I shouldn't have. I later married that girl. I came back and worked as an A. P. reporter for six months because I couldn't go home in disgrace. Then the Marine Corps let me in. Yes, they know all about it."

Mr. Foote's three previous novels had been contemporary. Why had he gone back in time—ninety years to be exact—for his fourth book? "I was animated in part by revulsion to the historical novel," he said. "In this one, no historical character says or does anything except what I have accurate evidence of his having said or done. That not only applies to the historical characters but to the fictional ones. For example, when a fictional character is put into a unit, what happens to that unit really did happen."

Didn't Mr. Foote experience severe restrictions? "No," he said, "it helped me. It gave the book its form. And, after all, Shiloh is a tremendous thing. People know so little about it. They call Iwo Jima 'bloody Iwo.' That lasted nine days. Shiloh lasted two days. The same number of men were engaged in the two battles, but there were more casualties at Shiloh. And the weapons were all muzzle-loading. There were more casualties at Shiloh than in the first six months of the Korean War."

Shiloh sounded like something to get off one's chest. What about now, what was Mr. Foote up to? "I'm now ready to write my first big book," he said. "After having promised myself three moderate, modest novels. This, the fourth, is a sport, a castoff. Now I'm ready to write a big book."

Considering Mr. Foote's youthful age, the six years of fighting and preparation for fighting, he had accomplished considerable. How had he managed? "I work straight through the day, every day," he said. "I get up to New York maybe about twice a year. The rest of the time I'm working straight through, eight hours, twelve hours, it doesn't matter. And I don't have any hobbies or any other interests. Writing is a religion with me."

Obviously, there were no distractions for Mr. Foote, but what about temptations? "Temptation," Mr. Foote said, "is a lot of tripe. I believe you can't tempt talent while it's real. Not *even* talent. If a man only believes he's got talent, why, then he's incorruptible." What about the economic argument? "All I've got to say about that," Mr. Foote said, "is that it's foolishness."

Mr. Foote certainly seemed aware of what was going on around him. He was undoubtedly conscious of the hue and cry that was being raised on all sides about the failure of nerve and the absence of talent and the perversity of taste in the young writer today. Mr. Foote was conscious of it. "We appear to be in bad shape," he said, "because criticism is running in the wrong direction. They're selling authors by the tens of thousands when they should be selling in the hundreds. Critics place emphasis on the lack of vitality and then they select writers who haven't any. For instance, there's a Southern writer today who has plenty of vitality but the critics run the other way. That's Calder Willingham."

Didn't Mr. Foote think a writer needed more than vitality? "That's true," he said. "I still stick to Willingham's case. He's a humorist, he has a sense of the ridiculous. He's unquestionably the best of the young writers."

What about Mr. Foote himself? "I'm a very eclectic writer," he replied, "Stephen Crane, Stendhal, Tolstoy all helped me. I'm not afraid of what writers did before me. Writing is a progressive thing. It's ridiculous not to use them. Take Faulkner. He has true originality but he went to Sherwood Anderson and Conrad. They mainly helped him get a style. I, on the other hand, am more fortunate. I've got Faulkner and Proust and I think they're greater writers than Anderson and Conrad."

There was still the question of individual talent—that was crucial in the equation. "That's the trouble," Mr. Foote said. "There is a third party here. There's Anderson and Conrad, but there's also Faulkner. And there's Faulkner and Proust, but there's also Foote. That's the trouble."

Shelby Foote Hopes to Put Flesh and Blood of Memphis on Paper

Robert Richards/1954

From the *Memphis Press-Scimitar,* 22 March 1954, second section, p. 15.

A certain man may look tall to a boy, taller than all others. And it's the same with a boy and a city. A boy may dream of a city until the dream is big enough to last the rest of his life—and no other city ever will be larger; or more fascinating.

"In the Delta," said Shelby Foote, "this is the way it is with almost all boys and Memphis. I can go to to New York, to London, to Paris—but none of these places will be more moving to me than Memphis. Memphis is the capital of the Delta. It's the place we've dreamed about and talked about all of our lives, and we never quite recover from it."

Foote is an author from Greenville, Mississippi. At 37, he has four novels behind him and a fifth, *Jordan County* (pronounced Jer-dan), will be released by Dial Press late in April. It consists of one short novel, two novellas, two short stories and two sketches—all built around a mythical county in Mississippi. Foote's books are always about the South. He is good enough for the *New Yorker* to comment recently that his proof of talent is established. His *Follow Me Down* was recommended as among the best fiction by both the *New Yorker* and critics for the *New York Times* book magazine.

He has moved to Memphis from Greenville and at present lives in a brick duplex perched on the great bluff above the Mississippi River, on Arkansas Street. From his screened back porch he can see the broad sweep of the Mississippi—either to the south toward his native Greenville, or up-river toward Cairo, St. Louis and Pittsburgh.

"It's the same river I knew at Greenville," said Foote. "I like living near it. That's why I chose this spot."

When he says such things, you have a right to suspect that he's kidding a bit. If you've read Foote's books you know that he is no romantic—he's a realist through and through—but in conversation, almost constantly, the sound of the romantic is in his talk. It's the same thing, I think, that makes the Southerner almost a natural storyteller, that makes him love a story for its dramatic impact. The storyteller who never quite ceases to clothe even the commonplace around him with more than its ordinary dimensions.

Shelby Foote wants to write a book about Memphis. And he's going to do it. Will it be in the past, or in the present day? "I don't know yet," he answered. "But I'll say this, I find it hard to think of Memphis without thinking in terms of its past. Probably it'll be about both past and present."

Foote always speaks of Memphis as if it were his home.

"I think Memphis is on the edge of growing into something," he said. "It is much too straitlaced now. Too tightened up. I'd like to see it become the city it should be, with some of these modern ideas of censorship put behind it. And I believe the time will come when it will."

After all, said Foote, Memphis is a city with a wonderful, colorful past—but few of its citizens know anything about it. They can't see Memphis beyond the corner drugstore.

"I would give almost anything to be able to go back to 1830 and sit on the corner of Market and Main, and see what was happening then," said Foote. "If you speak to people about the Pinch Gut now, they have no idea what you're talking about."

Everyone in Memphis wants to believe that he's from some fine old family with silver on the table and cotton in the warehouse, said Foote. And no one wants to spring from those gaunt-faced muscular men who came downriver on great rafts and filled the town with fighting noises.

But these men were a living part of the beginning city. They gave it new blood. They gave it imagination and courage and a desire to do something.

Foote, himself, comes from an old Southern family. His father, Shelby Foote, Sr., was a Greenville businessman. His grandfather, Huger Foote, owned a plantation in Washington County. The character of Hugh Bart in *Tournament,* Foote's first novel, is based largely upon the author's grandfather. Gov. Isaac Shelby, governor of Kentucky in its early years and a fighter at the Battle of Cowpens in the Revolution, is an ancestor of Foote's. Shelby County was named for him.

Foote first began writing while an undergraduate at the University of North Carolina at Chapel Hill—the alma mater also of Thomas Wolfe. After leaving the university he joined the Mississippi National Guard when Hitler marched into Poland. He saw five years of war service with the Army artillery and the Marines. After the war he wrote a short story called "Flood Burial" and sold it to the *Saturday Evening Post.* Then he wrote a novelette which the *Post* also bought, called "Tell Them Good-by." Foote also turned out a short experimental novel and several publishing houses liked it, but not well enough to publish it. Dial Press took a look and said, "Look, this is a good book but we would lose money on it. Why don't we just give you the money we would lose and you go home and write another book." So that's what Foote did and *Tournament* was published in 1949. He has also written *Follow Me Down, Love in a Dry Season,* and *Shiloh.* Foote said *Follow Me Down* has been praised highest by critics. He added that he has no favorite among his novels, but when he speaks of *Shiloh* it is in the tones of a proud father.

At present he is working on a big family novel called *Two Gates to the City.* It is laid in 1948 and tells of the Lundy family. In the telling, however, it goes back into the past in the mythical city of Bristol, Mississippi (which might well be Greenville).

"I plan to do a novel a year for the rest of my life," said Foote.

Twice married, he lives alone and works from 9 a.m. to 3 p.m. Around 11 in the morning he knocks off to cook some eggs (usually fried), but then he goes back to his writing. He writes in longhand and never uses a typewriter. Some people claim that he writes standing up and moving around.

"I may be in Memphis a year, and maybe longer," said Foote.

He thinks this leaving Greenville may be good for his creative impulses. The changes brought by the war stirred up five novels, and he feels this change to Memphis may be good for five new ones.

After a time, he may move on to Rome.

"Will he go back to Greenville?"

"I don't know," said Foote. "Sometimes, you know, you can't go back."

Foote believes the area where he is living in Memphis—on Arkansas Street—may well become the "Sutton Place" of Memphis. Sutton Place in New York City was once a slum area jammed against the side of the East River. However, it has been taken over by the very rich and now is probably the most expensive real estate site in Manhattan.

"It's going to be a nice neighborhood," said Foote.

And you can tell that he has a real feeling for Memphis.

"Only it's too antiseptic now. It almost has a split personality. But I think the time will come when it'll grow up."

But whether this happens or not, it'll always be the Big Town to the boy from the Delta country.

And he hopes to put down what he feels—in black and white—on paper.

Foote-Note on Faulkner

Edwin Howard/1965

From *Delta Review* 3 (July-August 1965), 37, 80. Reprinted by permission.

The sun burned down between the leaves of the two white oaks guarding the raw grave in the bare new part of St. Peter's Cemetery. Will Huston, stripped to the waist and streaming sweat, stood waist-deep in the grave, cutting into the hard red clay beneath the sandy topsoil. Resting a moment on the hand-smoothed pick handle, he looked up the hill toward the old part of the cemetery. "Too bad they didn't have no room left in the family lot," he mused. "They's three generations of Faulkners buried back there."

Back in town near the square, Richard Patton, manager of Douglas Funeral Home, grumbled sleepily at the umpteenth inquiry about the services. "I oughtn't to tell you," he said. "I been up all night on this Faulkner funeral. Folks from all over wantin' to know about it."

And on the square where Saturday shoppers lean against parking meters and store-fronts, talking in muffled voices, three of us sat at the soda fountain in the Rexall Drug Store, silently sipping steaming coffee. We were just down from Memphis and still stunned by the sudden death the day before. Finally we talked, trying to put our thoughts about the man, William Faulkner, and his passing into some kind of perspective.

Joan Williams, whose first short story Faulkner personally persuaded *Atlantic* to publish and whose first novel, "The Morning and the Evening," had just won the John P. Marquand award, spoke first: "I'll miss just knowing that he's here. It's so hard to realize that there'll be no more books from him. And yet he has left us a great body of work. I think his stature will grow."

"It's a curious thing," said Shelby Foote, who never made any bones about Faulkner being both an idol and a model, "but a man's death seems to give shape to his whole life. The four great writers of our time—Faulkner, Fitzgerald, Wolfe and Hemingway—are gone now, and I don't think there is any question that Faulkner stands above them all, both for the volume and quality of his work.

"He always reached beyond himself. He was not always successful, but his work was greater because of the things he was willing to try."

The Bermuda grows thick on the grave in the "new part" of St. Peter's Cemetery now, and the shade from the white oaks lengthens, but Faulkner is still, in Foote's view, reaching beyond himself, from beyond the grave, into literary history.

Living and working in Memphis again (after a year's fellowship with the Arena Stage in Washington and eight months on a beach in southern Alabama during which he discovered that he is "an urban person" and gained a new appreciation of Memphis), Foote sucked on a Faulknerian briar and measured again the Faulkner stature and influence.

"I think we may be in for some kind of superficial reaction now against the extreme popularity his work has enjoyed since he died," Foote said. "But I've been thinking a lot about him lately, and I don't think we've produced any writers that rank with him except Whitman, maybe, and Henry James and Mark Twain.

"There are people in history who epitomize what an artist should be. Not just in what they produce, but in what they were. Shakespeare is an obvious example. Beethoven is another. Faulkner was that kind of writing figure.

"Writing, to him, was what living was all about. It was hard on the people close to him, but I don't think any of them regret it now. He even came through a seven-year dry spell and never lost sight of what was important, what a writer should be.

"He was not only a great writer, he was a great example to other writers in the way he lived his life and went about doing his work.

"His talent, just to talk about that for a minute, was a great one because it was so varied, so many-faceted. One time you would say, what he could really do was tell a story. Another time you would say, no, what he could do best was capture the texture of things. Then you would say the thing that made him great was the way he could create characters. And you could say all these things, at different times, with justice, because they were all the things he did best.

"He had a curious paradoxical approach to things. I always sent my books to him. I don't know if he ever read the first one, but I saw him shortly after sending him the second (*Follow Me Down*) and he said, 'I liked your book. Do better next time.'

"A few years ago when Stanley Kubrick asked me to come out to Hollywood and write a script about James Mosby, I asked Faulkner's advice. He said, and I remember his exact words: 'Go if you want to. But let me give you a piece of advice. If you go, never take the work seriously, but always take the people seriously. Hollywood is the only place where you can get stabbed in the back while you're climbing a ladder.'

"I didn't go, because I knew I'd do just the opposite. I would have taken the work seriously and not the people. I told Kubrick I'd do the script if I could do it in Memphis. That was all right with him and I did it, but nothing ever came of it because he got mixed up with *Lolita* about that time.

"A lot of what Faulkner said seemed paradoxical, but there was always a crazy kind of truth in it.

"His style—his early style, anyway, from which his later style evolved—was deliberately put together, I think, from Joseph Conrad and Sherwood Anderson. I once told him that, and I said, 'I'll be a better writer than you are, because my models are Proust and you—both better writers than Conrad and Anderson.' He said I might be right.

"A lot of us have been influenced by Faulkner, but nobody has ever come anywhere near him yet. I think it was Flannery O'Connor who said, when somebody asked if the Faulkner influence bothered her: 'When you hear the Dixie Special coming down the line, you'd better get off the track.' "

Writer's Home Has Windows on Past, Present

Jimmie Covington/1966

From the *Commercial Appeal* [Memphis] 21 August 1966, 15.
Reprinted by permission of the *Commercial Appeal*.

"The more I study the war, the stupider I think everybody was. It was a terrible mistake on the part of everybody, especially the South."

Civil War historian and novelist Shelby Foote spoke quietly but intensely as he relaxed and smoked his pipe in the study of his home at 542 East Parkway South.

Persons who study the war have an opportunity "to see people under tremendous pressure, acting as Americans do act," said Mr. Foote, 49, who was born and reared in Greenville, Mississippi.

The highly acclaimed author has lived most of the time since 1952 in Memphis. His present project is the third volume of his massive three-volume history, *The Civil War: A Narrative*. The first was completed in 1958 and the second in 1963. He hopes to finish the third in 1968 or 1969.

Mr. Foote in 1964 moved with his wife, the former Gwyn Rainer of Memphis and their son, Huger, now 4½, to the Alabama coast and planned to build a home there.

"Because of the Ku Klux Klan's effect on me and the effect of the salty air on all the steel in the house, I decided to come back to Memphis."

The Klan difficulty stemmed from his speaking out against racial discrimination and extremism. "I got the sort of feeling that I ought to carry a pistol (for protection)."

The extremism he has encountered, Mr. Foote said, "helped me a lot to understand the extremists in the period (Civil War) I'm writing about."

Sharply critical of Govs. George Wallace of Alabama, Orval Faubus of Arkansas and former Gov. Ross Barnett of Mississippi, he said, "They had their counterparts in the Civil War . . . but their relationship to the Confederacy is about as remote as it can be."

Mr. Foote said he has always read Civil War material "like other people read detective stories." His chief source material is 128 volumes of records on the war.

He reads a great deal during his spare time and especially likes old fiction. He says he has no hobbies. He often hunted as a youth in Mississippi, but doesn't now.

"I take no exercise whatsoever. I think it will kill you. Doctors tell me this is the opposite from the truth . . . I enjoy drinking for relaxation."

Mr. Foote said Memphis has failed to develop an artistic heritage. "It looks like the people of Memphis swapped their artistic heritage for a way to get their garbage picked up on time."

But he said it is not unusual for cities of Memphis' size to fail to produce major artistic figures. He is hopeful there will be artistic advancement here.

The author chose Memphis as his home because "I'm from the Mississippi Delta. Memphis is the capital of the Delta and that's why I'm here."

Memphis to him is "an interesting cross" between a Western and Southern city. "People in Memphis have a Western quality of accepting you on sight. Then, if they don't like you, a Southern freeze goes on."

Mr. Foote feels there is a change developing toward less reading in this country and he views the trend as "really serious."

"Television has turned people away from reading more than a lot of people think."

The full effect will not be known, he said, until a couple of generations pass. "Maybe they will come back to books."

Mr. Foote regards Mark Twain, Henry James and William Faulkner as the leading talents among American writers "not because of their originality, but because of the body of their work, the solidity of their work."

Personal and political views have nothing to do with an artist's skill and style, he said.

"It's not important to be right or wrong . . . It's a man's style that makes him communicate . . . You can like John F. Kennedy or hate John F. Kennedy. It doesn't make any difference . . . Most people think you (a writer or artist) have to be on the side of the angels. This is not necessarily so. These people don't know writers."

Dostoyevsky was conservative and Charles Dickens was liberal, but both were equally fine writers, Mr. Foote said.

Such artists as Beethoven and Shakespeare through their works were able continuously to open new avenues, he said, but many writers "get locked up in their style."

"It happened to Hemingway . . . He got to the point where he was frozen."

Pleasing the public cannot be a writer's foremost goal, Mr. Foote said.

"It's ridiculous for you to try to figure out what they (the public) want. They don't know themselves. How are you supposed to know? . . . It's the Beatles this year and God knows what next year."

To Mr. Foote, writing is a seven-day-a-week job with working hours from 8 a.m. to 5 or 5:30 p.m.

"I've found over the years if I quit for one day, it takes me two to get back. If I quit for one month, it takes two months to get back.

"A lot of people think we (writers) wake up in the middle of the night with something called inspiration. But what you'd better do is get a good night's sleep. You've got a hard day ahead."

He writes in longhand and turns out 500 to 600 words a day. Once a day's work is completed, no major changes or revisions are made. At the end of a day, he types up what he has done. Careful research and outlining precede the writing.

Each of his Civil War volumes is about 500,000 words long and each is taking about five years to write. When he concludes the third volume, Mr. Foote plans to return to writing what he likes best, novels.

His novels, for which he also has won wide acclaim, include *Shiloh, Tournament, Jordan County* and *Follow Me Down*.

During 1963-64, Mr. Foote spent a year in Washington where, under a Ford Foundation grant, he studied and observed the Arena Stage, professional theater.

The year on the Alabama coast followed that, and the family moved back to Memphis about a year ago and lived in Raleigh before moving into the spacious 36-year-old brick home on East Parkway early last month.

"I've moved four times in the last three years, more than in all the rest of my life . . . I don't plan to move again."

Writer Critical of 'Tokenism' in South

Bob Mottley/1968

From *Roanoke World-News*, 18 April 1968, 56. Reprinted by permission.

An interview with a Southern author usually means good whisky, having one's coat held at the door and listening to soft-spoken laments for the late Confederacy.

Shelby Foote, Hollins College's current writer-in-residence, wasted no breath on antebellum days. He provided the requisite whisky, good manners and an uncommonly thoughtful view of the modern scene.

"The main problem facing the white, upper-class South" he said in the drawl of a Mississippi native, "is to decide whether or not the Negro is a man. If he is a man, as of course he is, then the Negro is entitled to the respect an honorable man will automatically feel to an equal."

"It is stupid," he continued, "to make token gestures toward the Negro, such as permitting him to use a water fountain in one community and perhaps go to the main white theater in another. White people in a position to do so should make every effort, in the small ways that count as much as in the large ways that get headlines, to erase 200 years of persecution."

"The Klu Klux Klan could not make any headway if it weren't for the responsible white folks who sit back in silent approval during the burnings and atrocities—ministers, businessmen, even newspaper publishers who prefer to let the redneck white trash do their work," he explained.

Foote, who is 52, warmed to his viewpoint with a story "from the time I lived in south Alabama." There, a few years ago, "I would be in a service station and a mechanic would start cussing Negroes. I'd say, man, you're wrong as hell, and there'd be trouble. Now the white mechanic in Alabama is worth any ten New Yorkers—he'll give you food, a bed, all the courtesy his sense of values will permit. But that doesn't keep him for being wrong in his prejudice."

In Alabama, he continued, "they thought I was a nut. But they knew deep inside what was right. Just admitting it is the white Southerner's biggest hangup."

As a writer, Foote is his own man.

"My resources as an author, what few I have, are fenced off from other people. I work alone, without a secretary, the only way I've ever been able to write. I live in Memphis with my wife and children, among people who don't expect me to put on a minstrel show. In New York, I would be conned into doing the 'Southern writer bit,' and I would find my resources trampled on."

"Rattler," Foote's bull terrier, began barking outside the writer's leased house on Hollins' faculty row.

"He doesn't like being tied up," Foote said. "I don't either, which is why I stayed away from Hollywood. Movie pay is funny money to a writer—it never turns out to be as much as you're promised. Faulkner told me something about Hollywood— 'take the money and leave quietly. While you're there, take the people seriously and the work lightly.' Me, I would take the work seriously and the people lightly, and God knows what would happen."

Foote has written a screenplay for director Stanley Kubrick, but only on the condition that he could do so in the South.

Tournament, Foote's first novel, was published in 1948. His next four novels were *Follow Me Down* (1949), *Love in a Dry Season* (1950), *Shiloh* (1951) and *Jordan County* (1952). Foote has since been working on a three-volume history of the Civil War. Volumes one and two were published by Random House in 1958 and 1963, the last is shortly to be finished.

"Then," he said, "I hope to write five more novels, if I live long enough. The first will probably be called *Two Gates to the City,* about a struggle for values in the modern South."

Historians, jealous of a novelist's intrusion, have occasionally resented the author's narrative about the Civil War. "But, I'm accurate," Foote noted wryly, "and that stops them cold."

"When I write about a battle, I go first to the battlefield in the season of the year when the conflict occurred. I look at the foliage, smell the land, watch the sky. Then I go home and write it up. The revelation comes in going back to the battlefield afterwards, in knowing who died or won at a particular spot," he explained.

"Young writers today," he continued, "seem to shirk any opportunity to experience life. They are moralists, not activists, and their work may suffer from it. I went into the Army when Hitler went into Poland. There was no question that I should enlist. War brings out the worst and best in men, and combat can be a valuable experience for a writer."

"Of course," he sighed, "a man can be killed, a young career ended tragically. But you can't go through life with a ball of cotton wrapped around your head."

When the sun was low, Foote held the interviewer's coat and saw him to the road.

"You might find this amusing," he said with a twinkle in his eye. "Most deep Southerners revere Virginia. Their reverence even survives a visit here. Any folks of quality, black or white, always insist their ancestors landed here. I suppose being from Virginia means that you're not a Snopes—Faulkner's family name for white trash."

It's Worth a Grown Man's Time: An Interview with Shelby Foote

John Carr/1970

From *Contempora,* (July-August, 1970), 2-16. Reprinted by permission.

This interview, one of several by John Carr conducted for an anthology of interviews with Southern writers compiled by him, was conducted in Shelby Foote's home in Memphis, Tennessee, in April 1969. Foote, who has written the novels *Shiloh, Follow Me Down, Jordan County, Love in a Dry Season* and *Tournament* is currently hard at work completing the third and final volume of his distinguished work *The Civil War: A Narrative History.*

Carr: I just reread *Follow Me Down* and before we get into other questions, I wanted to know if that was influenced by Mann's *Doctor Faustus.*

Foote: No, I think *Dr. Faustus* came out after that. I think, I'm not real sure. *Follow Me Down* was an attempt to examine a crime of passion with religious overtones by the technique of penetrating into a story and then coming out again. If you'll remember, the first person, the first speaker is involved because it's his small town job to be involved. The second person involved is a person who's involved because of his profession, but involved only on the fringes. The reporter. The third person involved, if I remember, is the lawyer. And he is professionally involved, deeply. That's the first section. In the middle section are Eustis and the girl, so that you are coming out again. And the third section reverses the first section. For instance, now it is the dummy who winds up involved personally. So you had slight professional interest as you went into it, then as you come out of it, the people are less and less involved. So that you had these people describing what happened and they get closer and closer to the bone, and then they get further and further away from it, and the girl's monologue on her life, which is a four or five page paragraph, is the capstone of the arch. It is your deepest, most intimate involvement.

Carr: Eustis is a perfect Old Testament character.

Foote: Well . . . he had a flaw in him that I think you will find throughout my work, if it is a flaw. People who have tried to dramatize various short stories, novels, things of mine find that they have great difficulty because the central characters are fairly inarticulate. And that's tough.

Carr: But that is the strength of your work, the inarticulateness and yet the power of your . . . protagonists I guess we can call them.

Foote: Well, lately we have found that the theatre can give you a situation in which the tragedy is that two people cannot communicate. But that's very recent. People didn't use to think you could write a play about the fact that people cannot communicate.

Carr: Now that you're almost out of the Civil War narrative history, do you plan to go back to Jordan County and pick up on those people again?

Foote: That's right.

Carr: Is there more planned out now in your mind?

Foote: There's a great deal I've got planned out in my mind. All sorts of minor characters in these books are important characters in later books.

Carr: This is next in the works after *The Narrative History?*

Foote: I'll probably write a short novel to get my hand back in and then I'll go on.

Carr: Let's talk about your working habits. Do you generally go very slowly in the average work day, the average work week?

Foote: Five hundred words is a good day.

Carr: Is that right?

Foote: Yeah, it's a good day. I've done as many as 1500 but I've also done as few as 200. Five hundred words is a good day with me, and I manage to do about that.

Carr: You're probably the foremost practitioner of history as novel. What goes into a novel that is rooted firmly in the past we can examine . . .

Foote: Well, the historical novel is about bankrupt and perhaps it was bankrupt when it started, in spite of *War and Peace* and *Red Badge of Courage.* But a novel should, I think, be rooted in the place where it happened and in the time in which it happened. And I think you owe that place and that time accuracy. I think that it's a great sin to put words in the mouth of a person who really lived, unless you know what those words really were. I don't think you have the right to do that. I don't believe it's right to have Billy the Kid come walking into a novel and have him say a few things and then walk out again—let alone write a novel about Billy the Kid, which is absurd. You could call him Joey the Fact or something, but not Billy the Kid. Billy has got his validity and that you shouldn't fuck with. And so the historical novel as it's been practiced is a bad form . . . unsatisfactory. I thought that Styron's novel on Nat Turner was a serious mistake, a very serious mistake. It's a beautifully written book; it's a hard thought-out book; it's got a great deal of validity to it; but the sum total is a mistake. It's not Nat Turner, it can't be Nat Turner. It's a distortion of truth, even though he's trying for a higher truth. It is not a higher truth, it's a distortion of the truth. So I think the historical novel is about bankrupt. That is not to say that I think a novel shouldn't be accurately sited. I think it should.

Carr: Do you think a new horizon would be to write about the man in the street during the Civil War?

Foote: Yes, I think that has validity, but it puts a cramp on you that I think you shouldn't have. I like to be limited by forces, but that somehow seems to me to be too great. It's best to write about what you know about so that you're free to have the truth available in your head, rather than out of documents.

Carr: So your approach to the historical novel is not really to recreate actual people, but to recreate the time and place.

Foote: Keep in mind at the same time that I would not write a historical novel, but if I did, that is what I would do, and any novel I wrote I'd hope would do that. I really have no plans for anything that could be called a historical novel.

Carr: And so the next *Jordan County* efforts will be more or less contemporaneous, such as *Follow Me Down.*

Foote: Yes. Now this doesn't mean I won't write about people in the 1870's and 80's and 90's, but they won't be historical novels.

Carr: Do you think the whole genre has suffered because so many patently B and C writers dabble in it?

Foote: I don't think that cheap writers do good writing any harm.

The novel is right there, ready to come alive again. This doesn't mean it won't die. I presume it will, sometime, just as the verse play died. But I see no signs of it. I don't mean that anybody today is writing novels as good as Hemingway's or Faulkner's or Fitzgerald's. They're not. But I'm very encouraged now and then by a novel like Updike's *Couples*. I think *Couples* is a good job. Because it's concerned with the things a novelist should be concerned about. It appears on its face to be concerned with nothing but sex, but it's not just about sex. It's very much concerned with people.

Carr: What kind of corners have novelists been forced into by the movies and other visual things that—

Foote: I don't think any of these influences have hurt novels. I think the novel is as viable, as jumpy, as alive, as it ever was. Hell, any art form that's got room for *Don Quixote* and *Madame Bovary* and *Light in August* is a big form.

Carr: Do you really think modern readers want to mess around with novels anymore? We sell a lot, but I don't know to whom.

Foote: I've always known that something like 75 percent of the fiction-buying public are women. But they buy mostly bad books. I mean, most of the bad books are sold to women. I've always had an idea it was men who bought Hemingway, Fitzgerald and Faulkner and Dos Passos, those authors. And that women went way up on the percentage thing on Faith Baldwin.

All good novels are kin to each other because they're concerned about the relationships between people. I've often thought and straightened it out in my mind that a good writer starts . . . his conception of a story is: "how about a man *who* in a situation does so and so?" A bad writer starts: "how about a situation in which a man does so and so?" The people come first, as they do with George Eliot, as they do with James Joyce, as they do with Ernest Hemingway . . . the people. Not the trick situation that put *these* people into that situation, but the people made the problem. See, the Greeks knew that better than anybody. A man's own character is his demon. Not what society is trying to do to him. Not this, not the other. His own character, his inner workings are what made his tragedy. And all the good novels I know, the writers knew that. And that was what made the novel.

Carr: That's what made Proust fascinating.

Foote: Proust I put right with Shakespeare, right with him. Proust is the greatest writer of modern times because of this thing that I'm talking about . . . a superb craftsman who had all the talents. He had 'em all. They all came his way.

Carr: A tormented life though.

Foote: That doesn't make any difference at all. And it didn't make any difference what Proust wrote about. He was tremendously concerned with homosexuality, being a homosexual. But Proust could have written about labor trouble if he'd been a working man, and it would have had the same validity. He was a very, very great writer. One of the giants.

Carr: You know, a lot of people nowadays are getting off into what's branded as the topical novel . . . you know, the novel about integration trouble and . . .

Foote: It's okay. It's not my bag, but it's okay. Dostoievksy's *Possessed* is such a novel. So is *Crime and Punishment.* So is *The Brothers Karamazov* . . . great, great, great monumental works. So I have no objection to topical stuff. It's the writer. It's the man pushing the pen across the page. He's got to have a combination of talent, knowledge, intelligence, and luck. He's got to have those things.

Carr: Luck is the cherry on top of the pie.

Foote: Yeah. Luck is nice to have. I'm not talking about the kind of luck that gets his book published and sold. I'm talking about the kind of luck that makes it possible for him to *understand.*

Carr: Do you think that the present American concern with . . . I don't know I think that America's trying to become a nation instead of sections and races, even though all the surface proof is somewhere else. Do you think there will continue to be a Southern novel, a Jewish novel, a Midwestern novel?

Foote: It appears so, and it's somewhat regrettable, because I think the Southern novel has run its string. Maybe Faulkner used it up. Certainly Carson McCullers is the last little kick left in it . . . and it often read to me like parody when she worked it. But I think there'll always be regional fiction, and I think that's good. I found out a thing that you never have to worry about people not understanding conversations your characters have because they use phrases and things that would be unfamiliar in another part of the country. They understand perfectly well and in some ways even get more from it than the people who understand it best, because it has a strangeness to them that's very attractive. I never worry about whether somebody from out of my region will understand a regional thing as I write about it. I think it will help the book far more than it would hurt it. So I never worry about being regional or provincial.

Carr: What problems exist for someone writing a narrative history of the Civil War?

Foote: They're all technical, and therefore enjoyable. I'm fascinated with doing it because everything I learned in writing those five novels has been of enormous use to me in this. It has sharpened my talent. It has made me more aware of certain technical problems that I didn't even know existed. It's been very good for me.

Carr: Is history more of an aesthetic than a guide? Is the study of it more of an aesthetic thing than say, "look what happened in 1860?"

Foote: Oh, it's both those things at the same time if it's either. You just want to know what happened. That's what a historian ought to be doing, he ought to be able to tell you how it was, what it was like. What was Lincoln like when he walked across a room? You read a lot of descriptions of Lincoln crossing a room until you know how Lincoln crossed a room. And you write it. And there he is, crossing a room. And it's *very* important . . . how he sat down, what his knees looked like when he sat down. They were very strange. They rose much higher than his waist. Lincoln's height was all in his legs. When he sat down to talk with you, he was no taller than you. When he stood up, he went six feet four, and it was all these legs of his. He was split high. It's important to know these things. If he were in a novel I was writing, I would want to know all about him. He was a vivid character. And so when I'm writing history, I want to know all about him.

Carr: There's been a lot of discussion of what history is. Can we know? Do you think we can know what went on in the minds and hearts . . . ?

Foote: No, but that doesn't keep us from trying to find out and it doesn't keep us from being responsible to find out. History at its best is an approximation. But that's no reason for not trying. And I think we can approach the truth even if we can't present it. And of course, my truth would be different from yours. And mine would be read as mine, and yours would be read as yours. And it would be absorbed by someone who would absorb both of them and put them together and come up with a third truth.

Carr: So that you get third, fourth, fifth distances away.

Foote: The best historical reading is the source material . . . the writing by people who saw it.

Carr: Do you allow for their particular intellectual and social hangups?

Foote: You allow in a tremendous way. You find out that some men lie, and others tell the truth. This David Dixon Porter; he's not capable of telling the truth, so I have to take everything he says with tons of salt. But he's very useful to me now that I know he's a liar. And another thing about history; I don't make judgments against men, or at least I don't let those judgments determine how I handle them. Edwin Stanton, Lincoln's Secretary of War, was a scoundrel. The word really describes him. But I delight in him. He's very valuable to me. I'm crazy about him. I don't approve him, but my approval should be no factor in this thing. I delight in the life Stanton lends a page. When he heard the *Merrimac* was coming up the Potomac (and of course it wasn't) his legs shook under him. And that's delightful. I think it's marvelous, that his legs shook under him. And I don't have any contempt for Stanton being a coward. That's all right. He was a bully and a coward, and that's good . . . for my purposes, anyway. I wouldn't want to be Stanton, but I'm very glad to have him around in a book.

Carr: There was an extraordinary set of characters in that war.

Foote: Oh yeah, sure. But the war would have made any set of characters extraordinary. It would have made any president extraordinary.

Carr: Do you think that's the reason Lincoln is revered?

Foote: No. Lincoln put something in there. Lincoln was a genius.

Carr: Who are some of the forgotten people that you've more or less become delighted with in writing?

Foote: There's a general that I've become extremely fond of named Pat Cleburne. He was an Arkansas general who was a division commander in the Army of Tennessee. He was a very great soldier, and I've become very fond of him. There are others I like.

Carr: How about the Copperhead movement?

Foote: It's very interesting. The Copperhead movement was founded on something that came in very close during the Vietnam War. I see Fulbright all over the horizon in the Civil War. He's very close to Joe Brown and Zeb Vance and various such people. He's a man who's personally sour. He's gone sour as hell because he can't control defense, which he feels he should be controlling as Chairman of Foreign Affairs . . . He feels that he ought to be able to say no to things, but there's nobody that'll listen to him, so he's sarcastic in his references to his opponents. He's a bitter and unhappy man . . . for instance Joe Brown made an important speech in the spring of '64 in which he said, "This war has to be stopped. Generals can never stop a war; statesmen stop wars." He didn't propose that Georgia leave the Confederacy. He proposed that the Confederacy go the way Georgia wanted to go. He wanted the war stopped and the country reunited on what he called the Constitutional Principle of 1776, and Lincoln had big problems with his top aides. They were the people who were losing the war.

Carr: About the Copperheads, do you think that they were a peace party such as we have today or dissidents against the whole structure of the North?

Foote: They were somewhat pro-Southern because they admired the Southern ideals. They were for the most part disappointed Democrats who saw the country going Republican. They did not want that to happen. They were people who feared what they thought they saw the country was going to become in a mechanistic way. Many of them were agrarians. They were afraid of a government such as Alexander Hamilton wanted and Thomas Jefferson did not want. They were afraid of what they thought was going to happen to this country. And they had good cause to fear it.

Carr: Do you see that as an ever-continuing strain in American politics?

Foote: Yes, there's that conflict all the time. As I get older, I think it is less and less important. But yeah, it goes on all the time.

Carr: What are some of the blank spots that you've found in your research?

Foote: It's very hard to get straight in your mind how different people in the South felt about the war. It's hard to get hold of, balancing their pride against the strain, balancing their losses against their hopes, balancing their early hopes against their later realizations, the bitterness of the thing. They had a terrible adjustment to make. They thought they were going to be successful at the start. There was no doubt about it. They thought there wouldn't be anything or if there was any fighting, it would all be over real quick because Southerners could whip Yankees. They had to adjust to it. And then when it was over, they had the hardest time of all. They had to admit that they had been whipped, and that was hard. They explained away being whipped by saying the other side had all the money and men. Then they had to say that they would have been whipped no matter what happened, because the North won the war fighting with one hand, and if it had had to use both hands, it would have done it.

Carr: I hate to draw parallels, but I think the Normans were able to completely subjugate the Anglo-Saxon culture, because the *culture* just wasn't able to carry on.

Foote: Yeah. I think the Southern culture was not able to support the strain that was put on it. People were not able to unite and lay aside differences. They were not able to give up things. Southerners have a curious way—they would send their sons, but they wouldn't lend their slaves. They would make all kinds of sacrifices, but they would not make certain sacrifices. Their conservative principles were more important to them than their new country was. They would pass resolutions saying, "Better that we be tumped off the end of the continent into the Gulf of Mexico than that we should compromise our principles."

Carr: Sounds like two bunches of very limited people fighting a tremendously bloody war.

Foote: You don't want to overlook something that they did have and that was tremendous courage. I've studied and studied hard the charge at Gettysburg, the charge at Franklin, the charge at Gaines Mill, or the Northern side charging at Fredericksburg wave after wave, and I do not know of any force on God's earth that would have gotten me in any one of those charges. It absolutely called for you to go out there and face certain death, practically. Now I will do any kind of thing like that under the influence of elation and the adrenalin popping; it's just inconceivable to us nowadays that men would try tactics that were fifty years behind the weapons. They thought that to mass your fire, you had to mass your men, so they suffered casualties. Some battles ran as high as 30 per cent. Now that's just unbelievable, because 4 or 5 per cent is very heavy casualties nowadays. You go into a battle and suffer 30 per cent . . . at Pickett's charge, they suffer 60 per cent and it's inconceivable to us . . . the stupidity of it, again. The stupid courage is inconceivable. Originally, the South had a big advantage. They were used to the castes of society and did not take it as an affront that a man had certain privileges. They didn't think that it made him any better than they were. But those privileges came his way, and they were perfectly willing for him to have them as long as he didn't think he was any better than they were. But the Northern soldiers, they weren't putting up with any privileges. A Massachusetts outfit spent its first night in the field and damn near had a revolution because the officers wanted to put their bedrolls out of the line. Well, Southerners never had that problem. It seemed to them sensible that the officers should be over here, and the men there.

Carr: We talked about blank spots in the Civil War, and one of them is home front. Are there any campaigns that are not as clearly documented as you would like?

Foote: Plenty of them. All the Western fighting is underdocumented. When I have to do the Virginia thing, the research is quite simple, and I get in five or six good authorities, and there it is. But when I start writing about the battle of Smyrna Gap, I got to dig.

Carr: What are your sources for this front?

Foote: Well, sources come in different categories. There are the memoirs by the men who were there, there are the reports and *Official Records of the War of the Rebellion* which were written at the time. That's my main source. Then there are good studies. The work of Bruce Catton has been of great help to me. Douglas Southall Freeman's books, Stanley Horn's books, Robert S. Henry, a lot of good treatments, and they serve as a guide through the labyrinth of this material, to keep you from missing any of it and really show you the salient features of the source material.

Carr: Is there any state whose soldiers did not keep enough memoirs? Do you run across that, not enough regimental history and so forth?

Foote: Well, regimental histories are not much count. They're always interesting to read. You pick up good little features out of them. But they were written after the war, and the war took on a sheen when it was over.

Carr: Did the Southern fighting man keep diaries and write as much as the Northern fighting man kept diaries?

Foote: Yeah.

Carr: What impresses you most about the accounts written during the heat of the conflict—letters home, I mean.

Foote: One simple thing impresses me and it's very interesting: the good hand they wrote, as compared to now. It's funny—they wrote a lot better hand than we do. Penmanship was much better. Their spelling wasn't as good, but the penmanship was superb. That seems like a simple little thing, but it tells you a good deal about the soldiers. Soldiers' letters are mostly concerned with food and clothes. They're begging their folks to "send me that pair of bluejeans that I had. I need 'em. Send 'em on."

Carr: Northerners as well as Southerners?

Foote: Yeah. Well, Southerners did it more because they had a harder time getting ahold of clothes. And I find a great deal of similarity between soldiers of that time and soldiers of our day. They felt the same way about the rain. They felt the same way about "hurry up and wait." They felt the same way about the stupidity oppressing them from above, and it was the same kind—it never changes, not really. Of course 99.9 per cent of that war was fought by home folks. The fighting men were of very high quality, too. You see, those units were together for four years, many of them, and they became superb machines. You take an outfit like the 23rd Virginia: after four years and large numbers of casualties in great battles, it becomes a very skillful military instrument. You tangle with the 23rd Virginia and you've got a problem. They can melt into the ground, and they can hit you with the damndest blast of lead that ever came your way. They were superbly skillful in handling their weapons. And after all this experience, they really knew how to kill. They didn't shoot their guns up into the air and everything else. They were superb machines, and everybody knew it.

Carr: A citizen army must be a fearful thing to behold.

Foote: It is after it's been in existence a while. They never went home. Very few furloughs were given—some during the winter months to a few people. The Civil War was an interesting time. It was very important to make what was called "a good death." When you are dying, the doctor says you're dying, he tells you you'll die about 9 o'clock tonight. You assemble your family around you and sing hymns and you are brave and stalwart and tell the little woman that she has been good to you and not to cry. And you tell the children to be good and mind their mother, Daddy's fixing to go away. That was called making a good death, and it was very important. It was of tremendous importance.

Carr: I don't see how we could get that far into the acceptance of our role, which is to die.

Foote: The doctor now won't even tell you you're going to die. It would be too cruel. The best thing to do is to let you think you're going to be all right instead of leaving you to suffer in anguish. But back then, it was thought very important to give a man a chance to make a good death.

Carr: Let's veer away a little bit. What is the advantage of a narrative history over a monograph or a considered work about one campaign?

Foote: The authors are after different things. I want to know how it was, and the writer of a monograph is generally concentrating on explaining some action, the consequences of it, how it began, what it did, and what came of it. You could say that what I'm writing compares to a monograph the way that, say Flaubert compares to Victor Hugo. That's not right, really, but I'm talking about the way Flaubert realized perfectly well that how Bovary ate the arsenic, the motions of her hand while she ate it, are enough explanation. He doesn't have to say, "poor sinful woman, there you are, getting your due." He just describes her eating the arsenic. The monograph man would want to say that she had gotten her due. And I'm not concerned with that. Now what the superiority of Flaubert's novel is over the other novel, I'm not prepared to say. I'm not even prepared to say it *is* superior. It just seems so to me.

Carr: When I was investigating the war in the west, I found out that there were some white Mississippi outfits fighting in the Union armies, for instance, the Tippah Rangers and Tishomingo Rifles, who were attached to Union Tennessee units. What did you find out about dissident Southerners?

Foote: I found a whole belt of dissident Southerners right along the lower reaches of the Appalachians. It comes down through the end of Tennessee down into northern Alabama and peters out in northern Mississippi. There were a lot of Union-loyal Alabamians, for instance, along that range of hills, and they rode with Streight on his raid through there. They were mountain people who did not have any use for slavery or slave owners. They were not abolitionists, they just didn't *like* them.

Carr: There was a social chasm between them and those who were Confederates, wasn't there?

Foote: Yeah, there has always been a chasm between those Piedmont or mountain people and the plains people, and the sea coast people. The Red Strings, those were the Southern Copperheads, were more active in North Carolina than anywhere else. The Red Strings wore little red strings in their buttonholes, just like the Copperheads wore a penny in theirs.

Carr: Have you ever read Tatum's study of—well, she calls them disloyal Confederates, still laboring under the delusion that they were disloyal to the Confederacy instead of loyal to the Union. Anyway, it was a wonder to me that the South was able to carry on with all the people down here who, for one reason or another, didn't much like the war and didn't much like the ruling class.

Foote: What the union-loyal Southerners had, more than anything else, was not a love of the Union as much as it was a fierce independence. They were not going to let the state of Mississippi carry them into something that they had no interest in.

Carr: Do you think Wallace finds strong support in these old Piedmont counties which were strongly Unionist?

Foote: Yeah.

Carr: And Huey Long was born in a parish in Louisiana which had voted Socialist at one time. Do you think that the same kind of people who were in the Populists and who were loyal to the Union, or rather, people who feel as they did, are behind the third stream in the South?

Foote: No, I don't, but I think certain advantages have been taken of those movements. For instance, there is a vestige of the Populist movement left, and these people are cashing in on it, like George Wallace. George Wallace is no Populist by a long shot, nor is Wallace anything faintly resembling a Confederate. Wallace and his followers are about as different from the whole conception of the Confederacy as you can be. I have told Mississippians that anytime that I have spoken in Mississippi. The Confederacy asked for nothing more than to get its case before the Supreme Court, and the tragedy was that they couldn't get it there. Davis, after the secession of Mississippi, stayed in Washington, hoping to get arrested as a secessionist, because then he could get to the Supreme Court, and the Supreme Court would almost certainly have declared secession legal. Almost certainly. The Civil War was fought in the wrong decade, so far as the South was concerned. It was fought at a time when no one in Europe could interfere. If it had been in the 1850s, England would probably have come in. If it had been in the 1870s, France would probably have come in. It was fought at the wrong time. Don't misunderstand me, though. I don't really regret having lost the war, but from the South's view it was fought at the wrong time.

Carr: The thing that always interested me about the Confederacy was that as a nation, it was stillborn. There was Joe Brown of Georgia, for instance, who never could understand that he was hampering the Confederacy with his constant refusals to let troops fight outside Georgia, and the other things he did to trip up Davis and his cabinet.

Foote: You see, they were trying to do an extremely difficult thing: they were trying to mount a conservative revolution, and it is an extremely difficult thing to do if your people are not radicals and won't hang together. Anytime, you ask one of them to give up something for the sake of the whole, he says, "Not me, that's not why *I* got into this thing, to give up *anything.*" Alexander Stephens said if he had to have a despot ruling him, he would prefer it to be a Northern despot. He said about the suspension of the writ of *habeas corpus* in certain areas, the use of conscription, various other things—all utterly necessary if they were going to survive—that he would rather go down in defeat than enact any of those things.

The Confederacy's position got idealized because it was never put to the test. The Northern position got run down something awful because it was put to the test and failed. They won the war and had their war, and led us through one of the worst eras in this country's history. The South never had a chance to do anything, so it can't be blamed—practically. The monument at home says: "To the memory of the Confederacy, the only nation which lived and died without a sin on its record."

Carr: Do you think the Administration inserted the moral issue of slavery into the war as a kind of public relations gesture?

Foote: The question was handled by Lincoln in a political, and, above all, a diplomatic way. It was Lincoln's Emancipation Proclamation which absolutely insured that the one thing the North had most to fear was not going to happen: that England might come into the war. The British people, once the war was defined for them by Lincoln as a war against slavery, were not going to let their leaders get in on the slave side of that war. And if England couldn't move, neither could France. And Russia was already pro-Union. They had freed their serfs in '61. So Lincoln used the slavery issue as a tarbrush against the South and used it with complete success. And this is *not* to say that Lincoln didn't believe in freedom and emancipation, but it was, frankly, a war-time measure.

Carr: In *Jordan County,* what interested me were the Indians.

Foote: Yeah, I see them as very primitive, cruel, blood-thirsty people with all kinds of redeeming virtues. They are, if they are anything symbolic whatsoever, they're the force that's in the land itself which will continue to influence the people that live on it. *Jordan County,* if it is a novel, is a novel which has place for its hero and time for its plot. *It* is the main character in the novel—the land itself. And you go backwards through time to find out what made it what it is.

Carr: I remember the man who kills himself after a very unsuccessful marriage. Is he punished because of what the whole plantation system has done to the land and the people?

Foote: Yes, I think that it was his mother's pseudo-planter outlook on life that forced him into the negation that he arrived at. That story was also an attempt to write a modern Gothic novel, which has always interested me, with ghosts and spooks, creaking doors.

Carr: There are an awful lot of what people would call "white trash" women in your novels.

Foote: Yeah.

Carr: Are they fascinating to you?

Foote: Yes, I like them. I like simple women, I always have.

Carr: Jordan County is actually Washington County, Mississippi, isn't it and Ithaca is the town of Greenville?

Foote: Yeah, the geography is exactly the same.

Carr: Greenville has influenced a lot of people. Well, Jessie Rosenberg, William Alexander Percy, you can see this is not in any order, Hodding Carter and Hodding Carter III, the woman who writes under the pen name of Ellen Douglas, Charles Bell, Walker Percy, and you, all of whom lived or are still living in Greenville. You know them. Now Faulkner was brought up in the hills. Would one get a different interpretation of the South if he was raised in the Delta?

Foote: Yes. And of course, we in the Delta have been strongly influenced by Faulkner and so we were raised where we were and also reading Faulkner, which is a tremendously persuasive thing to encounter. It had an influence on us similar to the influence of the Delta itself. So that you got both of them. So that writers since Faulkner have tended to make Delta people sort of like hill people under the Faulkner influence, but they are very different people.

Carr: What about this whole blackbelt mentality?

Foote: Well, the first thing you have to understand about the Delta is that all this business about moonlight, magnolias and Anglo-Saxon bloodlines has to go out the window. The Delta is a great melting pot. It is totally different from the hills, where the bloodlines are clean. The Delta is a . . . a conglomeration. When I was a boy, the population of Greenville was 15 to 18 thousand. There were in those days fifty Chinese stores in the town. The Assyrians were a big part of the population. It was a great melting pot. The people came down the river and stopped in the Delta because of the richness of the soil and the ease with which you could make a living. The Chinese influence is considerable. When I was a boy, the Chinese had their own schools in Greenville.

Carr: I think it was in 1948 that they were finally admitted to the white schools.

Foote: That's right. And four years later, they had a Chinese valedictorian in the graduating class.

Carr: Do you think this has made the Delta more liberal than the hills?

Foote: The Delta has been more liberal than the hills because of this, this co-mingling, at least for one thing, so they are more sophisticated or whatever you want to call it. At least they are aware of an outside world and ties with the Old World. My grandfather, for instance, came from Vienna. My mother's father. I was perfectly aware that there was a world outside because my grandfather came from the world outside.

Carr: How much are we to make of the French influence on the Delta?

Foote: Practically nothing. I don't think the French had much influence on the Delta. Not really in any sense. New Orleans was always down there, but my end of the Delta, which is the northern half, was oriented entirely towards Memphis, which had no French influence. Some German influence. But no French.

Carr: What kind of position did the Jews enjoy in the Delta?

Foote: It varies from town to town. In Greenville, they are part of the founding force that made the town. There was no anti-Semitism insofar as country clubs or anything like that went, but you can move up the road a bit to a little town like Greenwood and find it completely anti-Semitic so far as the country club goes. But we not only were not anti-Semitic in Greenville, but a great many of the most prominent people in Greenville and most admired people, and most liked, were Jews, so that it would have been ridiculous to be anti-Semitic. And the KKK could not get anywhere in Greenville. They were put down just as quickly as they arose.

Carr: Why did the Klan go under pretty quickly in Greenville? Was it because of the Percy influence?

Foote: It was primarily because of the Percy influence, but he was only the figurehead of the influence. The whole community was outraged at the notion of holding people's religion against them—Catholics and Jews.

Carr: Was it as much disgust at the anti-Semitic and anti-Catholic outlook as it was disgust at the anti-Negro invective?

Foote: Well, the Klan of the '20s was mostly anti-Catholic, incidentally anti-Semitic and really was not much concerned about the Negro.

Carr: Are you sure?

Foote: They did not have to be. The Negro had nothing they could take away from him.

Carr: I have been kind of wondering what you would have to say about the Snopes family? Are they typical rednecks, do you think, or something larger? Many readers think they have no value in the myth except as rednecks.

Foote: They have typical characteristics, but the Snopes are very private monsters all their own. They are not representative of anything, I mean the Snopeses.

Carr: You don't think Faulkner meant this to be a slam against the peasantry of north Mississippi?

Foote: He did, especially when he first started out. He was trying to draw a cunning poor white, but they very quickly developed their own characteristics, which were so special as to take away their representative qualities.

Carr: How about the poor whites in your work? Do you try to get closer to the bone of what it is to be poor? You handle the Eustis family very well.

Foote: You see, the Delta is not only a melting pot where different races assemble, but the Delta is a place where the credit is easy and the crashes are hard, and I do not know personally of anybody in Greenville, Mississippi, who didn't have a grandfather or a great-grandfather who amounted to something considerable. Things are so up and down in the Delta. Both of my grandfathers were approximate millionaires at one time in their lives. And both of them had scarcely the money to dig the hole to bury them in. And that is normal for the Delta, so that's why most of the very poor families could look back to a time of affluence. That is, if they had been there, and when I was a boy they had *all* been there. There were no newcomers. Now they have put in things like rug factories or whatever, and some people have come in, but the people who were there when I was young had lived there always. They might have come from Belzoni at the farthest. But they were all native Mississippians.

Carr: Do you think this takes people's mind off materialism? If you know, for instance, that you are likely to go down as far as your grandfather went down, does this put your emphasis on something else?

Foote: No, because it is a very acquisitive society in the Delta. The opportunity to make money breeds a great desire for money. No, you see, the villain of the Delta, and maybe of the whole South, is the planter. He's the son of a bitch who fed false information into the society. He's the one who said, "Do as I say do, because someday you will be in my position and you will be allowed to do as I do. So don't rock the boat. I have your best interests at heart. And you must understand that." And they used to pretend to subscribe to the whole *noblesse oblige* notion. Well, that was pretty quickly shown not to be true. The planter is less conscious of that. What he is likely to say is, "I got mine," not "I owe the society something which it has made possible for me to get. I owe it to society and must put back into it." He doesn't say this at all. He has no respect for art in any form. He leaves that up to his women, and they have no respect for it either.

Carr: Right on. A thousand times right on.

Foote: The planter is the real villain of the piece and he should have been brought down by the Populist movement, but the Populist movement got all caught up in the anti-Negro thing, which was started by the Bourbons, not by the Populists. So the Populist movement never got anywhere in the Delta. Bilbo was the tail end of the Populist movement. And everybody in the Delta hated Bilbo. When I was a boy, you perfectly understood that Bilbo had a pair of horns under his hat. And that the man on the white horse was Leroy Percy, a decent, honorable man—which indeed he was. But later study has shown me that Bilbo, who would steal, literally steal, money, really did have the people's concern in his mind at all times, if for no other reason but to get their vote. Whereas, Leroy Percy, that honorable man, had his own concerns to look after. I don't mean that in an ugly way, I mean that he would do what he thought was best for the people whether they wanted it or not.

Carr: Right.

Foote: Well, Bilbo would do what the people wanted. And I incline, after looking back over the whole thing, to think that Bilbo, in spite of his thievery, is a better man to run a region than Leroy Percy, who was completely honest . . . It's a spooky business.

Carr: Why do you think the Populists faltered?

Foote: I think the movement faltered because the poor whites and the Negroes were not able to coalesce.

Carr: Did you hold out any hope for a black-white movement when, for a time, nonviolent tactics and integration seemed to be winning?

Foote: I think it still is, you see. I don't think that has gone by the board. I don't think that the Black Panthers, the Negro radicals, are in control of anything, really. I think they have already served their purpose. I think that violence is going to decrease, not increase now. I think integration is the answer and I think everybody thinks so—white and black—except a few nuts.

Carr: What did it mean to you to be raised in Mississippi? Now you were educated in the Upper South at a fine institution, Chapel Hill campus of the University of North Carolina; it was the *only* UNC at that time, and it has a tradition of liberalism. What did it mean to you to go from Mississippi to the Upper South to be educated—if you can remember what it felt like back then.

Foote: It did not appear greatly different. It was different enough for me to be thoroughly conscious that I was in a different atmosphere, but it was not like going to New York City. Chapel Hill was still a country town.

Carr: What does it mean to you as a novelist to be from Mississippi?

Foote: It means a great deal to me. It means that I have been in touch with the grass roots of American life. I really know what they feel like. And that is very important to me.

Carr: Why is it so many good writers come from Mississippi?

Foote: There are a lot of jokes about it. One being that there's nothing else to do down here. But I *know* why there are so many writers from Greenville, instead of from Greenwood or Clarksdale. It was the presence of Will Percy. There was no literary coterie, no exchange of manuscripts, no deep discussions about novel plots or anything like that, but he was an example of a man who had written and published books, and you not only believed it could be done, you *saw* it could be done. And I think if Will Percy had been from Greenwood, it's entirely possible that Greenwood would have been the place the writers came from. There is more to it than that. Will Percy also had a fine library, so that good books were available in Greenville, which perhaps they were not in some other places.

Carr: When you were growing up, you were around the Percy family. Did Will Percy influence you personally?

Foote: He influenced me by example, but his writing did not influence my writing. But, yes, he was a big influence on me because

Will Percy had a culture that was alien to me and to that country, and it was a good thing to come into contact with.

Carr: Then you don't think Greenville has any special sociological makeup that makes it produce these people?

Foote: It has that, too, but there again, it was done by Will Percy and by other men around there. Greenville never had but one lynching, for instance, and that was a horrible mistake, where they lynched the wrong man. It's a crazy story. There was a telephone operator raped in the alley next to the telephone building and she raised the outcry somehow and some men came running down and there was a Negro standing there and he said, "I seen him running that way." So they followed, running, and went into a Negro house in Lickskillet and found a young Negro man in bed with his shoes and clothes on, pretending to be sick. So they dragged him out and took him downtown and hung him from a telephone pole line in front of the telephone office. And it was, oh, some years later when the man standing outside the alley, who had told them he had seen the man running, confessed that he had raped the woman and told this young Negro that was passing, "Boy, you better run, there is going to be trouble around here." That was the only lynching Greenville ever had and that is enough to cure anybody of lynching anything.

Carr: Let's get back to the Civil War narrative a minute. What are your working methods for this? Is there a steady regimen that you follow?

Foote: It is a steady regimen of work from a fairly complete outline and much taking of notes. I can show you over here how I do it. I organize it into blocks of time and geography. For instance, I am going to be eighty or one hundred twenty pages in Virginia. And I have a calendar showing everything that happened in that area at that time and I am going over to Georgia and cover the same amount of time that was happening over there. And my calendar is drawn up so that I can see that these things were happening simultaneously. And I tie the two together. What I try to do in that, except for the obvious breaks, which are made on purpose too, is to lead from one to the other. For instance, if Lee and Burnside are fighting up in Fredericksburg, I draw back and go to Davis and get his opinion on the battle and what he has in mind to do next and then it is a very simple step to get from Davis to Lincoln and then back down to Burnside. It's a question of plotting, and it's a fascinating business.

Carr: Do you think Lee had a psychological hang-up about the war?

Foote: No.

Carr: Do you think he really wanted to win?

Foote: Oh yes. The trouble with trying to deal with Lee is his amazing simplicity. It is almost impossible that anyone could be as simple as Lee is. "Simple" I say as a high compliment. That is the unbelievable thing about him. Freeman discusses that at some length. He says there are not any problems, there are no questions.

Carr: It is almost like a put-on.

Foote: It is, it is. Now Lee *is* a very complex man, but he had *achieved* simplicity. He had trained himself to resist all kinds of urges that were in him. So by the time the war comes along and he is past fifty years old, he is not even having to resist them anymore.

Carr: Wasn't there something in his family that is partially brought out in biographies, about his father being—

Foote: Many scandals. His father was involved in horrible scandals and his half-brother was involved in an incestuous scandal. All those forces were rampant in Lee. And you only see little glimpses of them occasionally. Such as when he said of one of his daughters: "She is like her father, always wanting something." And when after the war—wherever he went after the war, crowds would always gather around and hold up babies for him to kiss and everything—some woman handed him a baby to hold and he held it. And as he handed it back to the woman, she said "Is there anything that you can tell me that I can repeat to the boy?" And Lee said, "Yes, teach him to deny himself." And Lee had done that all his life, so he had more or less burnt this wildness out of himself. He is a gentle man, and that is a paradox, because he would literally rip the living guts out of a man. He is a great killer, but a very gentle man. Capable of enormous anger, but always in control of himself.

Carr: Didn't he get really livid when he was about to go into battle?

Foote: Longstreet used to say that when his blood was up, there wasn't anything you could do about it. You just had to hope he would calm down.

Carr: He was a strange type, to be a so-called cavalier, then?

Foote: He is right in that tradition. He is very much in the cavalier tradition and thought of himself so too. He had some vanity, and had other things, but it was always balanced by modesty. He is the only man I know of who cut his own hair. He went to the barbershop in Richmond once, but the people made such a ruckus about picking up the hairs that he never went again. He cut his own hair, which is no easy thing to do.

Carr: What about Forrest, to look at another leader, even if he's thought of as a lesser light? And speaking of that, don't you think that the people in the eastern theater were under some kind of delusion that he was this ole boy who was an illiterate, if somewhat lucky, tactician.

Foote: Sure. Someone once said to Mrs. Davis, after the war, that it was most regrettable that Forrest had not been given a higher position sooner and she said, in not as snobbish way as it sounds, but said, "Well, I admire General Forrest enormously, but if we were really going to have people like that in charge of our revolution, we would have lost the revolution while we were winning the war." Davis was here in Memphis for Forrest's funeral, in 1877, and riding to the funeral in a carriage someone with him regretted enormously that Forrest had not played a bigger part earlier in the war, and Davis said he absolutely agreed, but, he said, "We in Richmond did not appreciate him. We thought he was a partisan and ranger type and it was not until late that we saw his qualities."

Carr: Do you think that is the sort of thing that would have torn the Confederacy up eventually—the class difference?

Foote: No, I don't. The thing you have to understand about the Confederacy and the people who made it up is the fierce independence of the Confederate yeoman. He was not only convinced he was good as you were, but if you questioned it, he would shoot you off your horse. Literally. If he had to hide in the bush to do it he would—which is not unfair. After all, you have many advantages over him, so if he shoots you from ambush, that's all right, because God knows what you could do to him without ambush. You own the big house and he's got nothing but an old shotgun or something. No, the sort of fierce independence of the Southerner did not make him worry too much about somebody thinking that they were better than he was. He knew they weren't.

Carr: People who write about the South say that the white Southern yeoman was willing to go along with the whole bag as long as there was a model of white supremacy around, i.e. the Southern planter. But how long do you think the system would have held up? The economics of it would have destroyed slavery eventually, don't you think?

Foote: I never have been really sure how long it would have taken economics to destroy slavery. It seems economically feasible to me today. Economically. Slavery was perfect for cotton farming. It was a marvelous thing to have a couple of hundred slaves running the plantation, and you could make a lot of money doing it, a lot of money was made doing it. How long it would have taken slavery to die—and, of course, it would have done so sooner or later and probably sooner—I don't know. The condition of the Negro when I was a boy was not very much above slavery. He couldn't move. It certainly amounted to peonage.

My grandfather, that is, my mother's father, was involved in serious peonage charges. He and two other men, Leroy Percy was one of them and a man named O. B. Crittenden, brought southern Italians and Sicilians over to a plantation they owned just across the river in Arkansas, named Sunnyside. And they brought them over by the boat loads and they were marvelous workers. They'd get down on their hands and knees and pull the grass. It was truly beautiful. But my grandfather and the others were wide open to the charge of peonage. These people were working out their passage on the boat.

It was fortunate that my grandfather, O. B. Crittenden, and Leroy Percy had known Theodore Roosevelt, because my other grandfather had Theodore Roosevelt down here on a bear hunt and asked Leroy Percy along, so he (Percy) was able through his friendship with Theodore Roosevelt to get the indictment quashed. But to get it quashed, they had to turn these people loose.

Carr: Chinese labor was brought in at one time.

Foote: They worked on the levees and railroads and so did the Irish.

Carr: Really?

Foote: You see, at one time, you could get a good hard-working Irishman for fifteen cents building those levees.

Carr: God, fifteen cents a day; even with the difference between our time and their time, that was nothing.

Foote: That's right, but it was very dangerous work, and you weren't going to waste any seven or eight-hundred dollar Negro doing such work.

Carr: They were buried right in the levees sometimes, weren't they?

Foote: Yeah. If he had an accident, throw him in the hole.

Carr: No wonder they knew they had to disenfranchise both blacks *and* whites in the 1890 Constitution.

Foote: They sat down and wrote, as Bilbo said, a state constitution that "damn few white people and no niggers at all" would understand. They made damn sure of it. And so the Mississippi Constitution is the wildest reading you ever saw. Paragraphs in there scarcely make any sense at all. If you want to eliminate somebody from voting, you ask him to read and explain that paragraph. It can't be done.

I believe things are pretty squared away now, though. I think what is going to happen can be seen clearly enough. I believe integration is at hand, and that everybody believes in it, as I say, except a few nuts. And it just depends on the *will* in which people enact it—it is the only answer.

What you can do for instance . . . women, and the majority of voters are women, you can just tell women: "Suppose you have a child and when he gets to be 3 years old, you have to tell him, 'No, you don't go drinking in that fountain, that's for white people, you do not drink that.' Put yourself in that position, telling your children that they are not good enough to do things that they see other children doing. Would you do that?" And they say "No."

Most of the fear of Negroes, which is a very real thing, is based on what you would do if you were in his place, and that will scare you to death. You think you would kill people all over the horizon. Well, you wouldn't. But you think you would. So you're afraid of him. I've seen people just frozen with fear when some Negro who had too much to drink got out of line. They think he's fixing to blow them up, because they're thinking that if they were in his place, they would blow everybody up.

Carr: What do you think about the black separatist movement? Is black capitalism economically viable, for instance?

Foote: Not for an instant. There will be some black leaders making some money off it and that is how far it will go. What the Negro should do and do now is exactly what whole minority groups before them have done. The Jews did it superbly. They were offered a challenge in which the odds were absolutely staggering. And they said, "My God, that is not fair, look at the odds." The man said to take it or leave it and they said "Okay, we'll take it. What means the most to you—money? I will make more than you. Whom do you respect? Doctors and lawyers? I will raise my kids to be doctors and lawyers." And they take these people on, on their terms, and beat them. Now I don't expect the Negro to be able to do that because the odds against him are too great, to begin with, having a different color skin, but I would like to see a hell of a lot more of it in their approach to the problem.

I think this black separatist movement is a bunch of junk. I don't think it amounts to anything. Not anything. The only thing it does is to restore some pride to the Negro. "Black is beautiful" is the good part of the movement. But as for this separatist thing, like going to school and demanding black dorms and everything, that's nothing.

I think nonviolence is the only answer for the people in the minority that they are in. I think their achievements under nonviolence have been huge, and will continue to be. Violence is the easiest way I know of for them to lose the rights they have gained, and not gain further rights that they certainly have coming to them. Not that certain violent acts don't serve a real purpose: they do call attention to a situation that people don't like to look at, and they have a value, and if I were a Negro, I might be a violent Negro.

Carr: Let's go one step further: what about saying "I will not fight in this war."

Foote: Yes, I can see a Negro making his protest that way, saying "No, you can't do to me what you have done to me and then ask me to fight your war." I can see saying that. Once again, I don't believe in that. I believe the best thing a Negro can do is go and make a better soldier than anyone else. That is the best way.

Carr: What do you think about whites who say the same thing?

Foote: I think they ought to be dealt with as harshly as everybody wants to deal with them. The thing that disturbs me about the young people is that they think they can do things and not pay for it. They really think you can walk up to a Chicago policeman and spit in his eye and not get your head split open. I am not opposed to going up and spitting in a policeman's eyes, but I do expect to get my head cracked open when I do it. And they are absolutely outraged: "The cop came out swinging; what is that, he's supposed to be a public servant? What is he doing hitting me? All I did was spit in his eye." And they expect to be able to do all sorts of things without consequences. And they do frequently do things without consequences. And if, when I was a rampant young radical, I had thought I could get away with some of that stuff, I am sure I would have done it.

Carr: What do you think about young radicals, looking at them from the outside?

Foote: I don't think young people today are any more radical than I was, but after all, I was in an extremely radical time. We had communists all over the campus, and everything else. We really *were* radicals. I think the biggest difference is not in the young, but in the middle-aged, who are permissive and frightened. Take people my age: I was born during the First World War, spent my adolescence in the Great Depression, and I came of age in the Second World War. Now that is a hell of a thing. And it tends to make me skittish, to make me perfectly aware of the tragedies that can happen from not humoring the young, and so on and so forth. We have humored the hell out of the young and spoiled them badly. I like young people. One of the best things about going to Hollins as writer-in-residence was that I had been greatly disenchanted by young people, and when I got to Hollins, I had a class of about forty-two seniors and graduate students, and although they were not any smarter than I expected—they were about as smart as I thought they would be—they were a hell of a lot more likable. They were a very nice, likable bunch of people. So that was good for me, to find those qualities there. Now that is a little bit unfair, they obviously weren't drop-outs. They were fixing to graduate from college. Now as for the hippies and that bunch, I have not lost any of my prejudice against them.

Carr: The thing about hip communities that appeals to me and that I think is valid is that they want people to examine the things, all the things, people your age have taken for granted and then decide whether they shouldn't become part of an alternate community, live an alternate life-style.

Foote: Well, I've been for the negative aspects of all these things. I thought the beats had a good thing and the hippies have that, too. And the hippie's protest against suburbia and the rest of it is valid. But it's not enough to know what you're against. Young people seldom know what they're for, but they don't go so far as dropping out of society. I think that is a mistake. I think you ought to stay and bounce off things. You ought to get where they don't touch you. You ought to be in there, bouncing off of it. I would never fail to tell my kid there was a Santa Claus, because that would deprive him of the enormously valuable experience of discovering there is not a Santa Claus. I would never dream of keeping my boy out of Sunday School because I am agnostic. I think he would go to Sunday School and bounce off it, maybe be an agnostic. I hope so.

Carr: Some of us think we don't have to go any further into the middle class thing to renounce it. What do you think?

Foote: I think they *should* experience it, so they can renounce it with validity. The thing I have the hardest time understanding is relating it to myself and the generation that came before me. That is Hemingway, Faulkner, and all those people. A war comes along and you know how crooked the war is, and that there are a lot of people who are totally innocent who are going to be killed in it, and you know how wrong it is . . .

Carr: Right.

Foote: But you would not miss it for anything. It is your war. It doesn't make any difference if it is a good war or a bad war or whether you are right or wrong. You can't even make those judgments. But this is your war. Now here are these kids today, twenty-two, twenty-three, twenty-four, twenty-five, or twenty-six years old, saying "Hell no, I won't go." Well, they could not keep me out. They couldn't keep Hemingway out, or Faulkner, or any of them out. They would run off at the age of eighteen and join the Air Force or something. Anything to get there. Something that big going on in the world and be nineteen years old and miss it? It's unbelievable.

Carr: Let's talk about your work. Who influenced your writing?

Foote: I was influenced, like most people, most strongly by people in two categories. One, I was influenced by the writers I liked most. That's a simple kind of thing to say, but it's true. For instance, Robert Browning had a great influence on me because I liked his work. And William Faulkner influenced me for that reason, plus another one, and that was his proximity to me. He was writing about people that I knew, and I took it that that was how you wrote about people you know. So that his influence was greater on me. But Faulkner and I were very different writers. I'm not talking about Faulkner as a *greater* writer, which of course he is, but we have a totally different approach to the work. I am more interested in sociology than Faulkner was. Faulkner was more interested in the human heart than perhaps I am—or he certainly liked to think he was.

Carr: Your work is very lyrical, while at the same time it is very terse.

Foote: Well, I am crazy about words and I am crazy about compression. You talk about the writer that influenced me more than any other writer, well the same writer that influenced me more than any other writer that influences everybody more than other writer, is William Shakespeare, because he is the greatest writer, it is just that simple. And the lyricism, such as I have, is an outgrowth of my awe of Shakespeare . . . tremendous admiration. It's a miracle that anybody was able to do the things that he did.

Carr: Who do you think is a good writer now?

Foote: I think John Updike is a good writer, and this boy, Cormac McCarthy.

Carr: Are they among those who have proven themselves, or are they still in the company of those who are struggling?

Foote: Well, it is very difficult to talk about writers because of vogues which have nothing to do with who is a good and who is not a good writer. I think there is something utterly ridiculous about the fact that John O'Hara is living and writing and that none of these coteries seem to know that he is alive. Well, it doesn't make any sense. (Editor's Note: This interview with Mr. Foote was taped more than a year before the death of John O'Hara this spring.)

Carr: I agree.

Foote: O'Hara is a good writer. Now he may not satisfy their desires in various directions, such as symbolism and so on, but O'Hara is a very great American writer. I don't mean he is

Hemingway's calibre, let alone Faulkner's, but how they can pretend O'Hara is not there, I don't know.

Carr: Killing him off.

Foote: Well, a lot of people have been killing him off all this time, but he is not dead. It's absurd. It's like ignoring Thackeray, who is not a very great writer either, but it's silly to ignore him. So I don't know what to make of it. I do know that a lot of people that are being taken as good writers are very, very bad writers by any standards that I know.

Carr: Aren't you rather alarmed by fads in the literary world?

Foote: No, not at all. I think that those fads have always been with us and that they will be with us. You see, I remember a time when all criticism was Marxist. *All* of it.

Carr: Yeah.

Foote: Faulkner, Hemingway, Fitzgerald, even Proust, were considered to be of no weight whatsoever because they had not come up with this big thing that made the world go around. And some of the writers got worried about it. Fitzgerald was very worried about it. So was Hemingway. So Fitzgerald wrote *The Last Tycoon* under very strong Marxist influence, trying to make up to these people who said he amounted to nothing because he didn't understand. He was trying to prove that he understood. Faulkner never fell into that trap. So I am never inclined to take very seriously the judgments of literary coteries. I think they can be depended upon to miss the point.

Carr: Right.

Foote: They will discover O'Hara safely after he is dead. They are not going to discover him while he is living. They are not going to have anything to do with him because he wrote for *The Saturday Evening Post.* Now you get him good and dead and they will look at him. And I think it is entirely possible that O'Hara will be considered a serious writer after he is dead.

Carr: He's influenced me, I know that.

Foote: He is a superb technician.

Carr: There is the same careful attention to the way people act, how they dress, and what they drink and smoke in both you and O'Hara.

Foote: That is one of the things I like about O'Hara. It has a sociological weight, or whatever you want to call it. O'Hara has got some flaws that are fairly clear. He poses and does not succeed at all in this pretended profundity of research, but he is a good serious writer. And how they can ignore him is more than I can understand. It is not O'Hara who suffers, it is they who suffer.

Carr: Do you prize felicity of expression?

Foote: Very highly. Yes, I don't want it to be precious, I want it to be felicitous, just as you say. My favorite of my books is *Love In A Dry Season.*

Carr: Why?

Foote: Not because it's any better than any of the rest of them, but because I had a very happy time writing it. I had a facility of work that I remember with great affection.

Carr: Are some of your novels hard work, and some like *Love in*—

Foote: They are all hard work, but it was work I enjoyed. You know, "labor we delight in physicks pain" and so on. They were *all* hard work. I have always worked very hard, very long hours, like eight or ten hours a day, seven days a week, because I never believed writing was something you could do in your spare time. It had to be everything with me. First thing I ever sold was to *The Saturday Evening Post* and I got $750 for it, and the day the check came, I quit my job, went downtown and bought a shotgun, a leather jacket, and a desk light. And I have not worked for anybody since then and I am not thinking about doing it ever.

Carr: What would be your advice to a young man or woman who wanted to be a writer, yet had to live at the same time?

Foote: Go get a hard job, like driving a taxi or digging ditches, or anything else, and write when you are not working, and work when you are working, don't even think about writing.

Carr: You wouldn't advise the life of the academy?

Foote: I would advise against it as strongly as I could.

Carr: Some of us have this problem.

Foote: Well, it is a problem now that I didn't have then. You get a good life, an enjoyable life, good money—decent money, anyhow—and complete protection from the shocks and throes and convulsions of the world. Well, that is very tempting indeed. But when I was coming along, I don't know whether I would have succumbed to temptation or not, but there wasn't any temptation. Nobody wanted me to come to a college campus. They had no use for me, thank God. But that was not one of the things I might have done. No college campus would have me on it as anything but a student.

Carr: You more or less have to forget about making a great deal of money?

Foote: The only way to make a lot of money is to forget it. Work at your craft, and if you are lucky, you will make a lot of money. There *is* a lot of money to be made, so that your expectations are not unreasonable.

Carr: What do you think about this thing, and I think it's just the foundations and the government trying to appease people in a pitiful little way—I mean the whole thing about writers getting grants and living from grant to grant. Of course, you have it pretty good right now.

Foote: Well, it is my craft, and anything which makes it easier for the people who practice it I should be for, but I am not. I think grants are a bad thing for young, beginning writers. I think after a writer has established himself, and begun to get soft in the belly, and perhaps in the head, a little money is good to have and it is not going to hurt him. I think it is very important that you make your living, pitifully poor and small though it may be, with your pen. It gives you a sense of accomplishment which you can't get from a grant, and which a grant will interfere with.

Carr: I know a guy who drank up two Rockefellers and doesn't have a word to show for it.

Foote: Sure. It is a bad business. You see, when my first novel came out, I had just finished my second one. When my second one came out, I had just finished my third one, and when my third one came out, I was hard at work on my fourth one. And that's the way it should be. Now I don't mean for everybody. There were writers like Flaubert and Joyce who turned a book out every six or eight years. And I guess that's all right. But I think a young writer should be a very hard working person and learn how to write by writing . . . I don't believe that you should be in a hurry to get into print. I think the best thing to do is to sit down and do your very best writing for two novels, and then, no matter how good they are, put them away. Then write your third one and let it be your first novel. Go back later and get them, if you want. I didn't say burn them up. Because anything that's in the closet, you'll make more money off of later than you will now, anyway. There are a hell of a lot of writers who wish they *had* put those first two away.

Carr: Did you get any static off your first novel? Are you a little ashamed of it now? A little embarrassed?

Foote: I had an excitement about language that flawed the book, but did me a lot of good. I got some static around home about it: I was in the barbershop, getting a haircut, and the beauty parlor was in back of it, and you know how women talk loud when they have driers on their head, and so I could hear one woman screaming, "They say it is about his grandfather, but I knew his grandfather and he was a nice man!"

Carr: Writing is very hard on people who are married, isn't it?

Foote: Oh, you see, what you have to give up is *enormous*, but it always has been. Some guy was telling me, "What do you expect me to do? I have two kids." And I said, "You ought not to have two kids." You shouldn't. And if *you* are willing to go hungry, you ought to be willing to let *them* go a little hungry. You will wind up a lot better in the end. What you are going to wind up with now is a busted-up marriage and everything else, probably. It is tough. I am not denying that for an instant. But it is supposed to be tough. It is a tough and a sad *métier,* as Hemingway said. It is a *métier triste.* And that's why it's worth a grown man's time.

Carr: It's a grown man's game.

Foote: Damn right. And if you are not getting out of it what you are putting into it, or if you are not putting into it what you are getting out of it, you're cheating on the game—it's no good to you or anyone else.

Carr: Do you think writers ought to work every day?

Foote: Yeah. Except for deliberate take offs, which are good too, but yeah, I think you ought to hit it. The only way you can do is sweat, sweat, work very, very hard and then after a certain amount of that, you ease up and you fly.

Carr: Some people feel that the next one is going to be the really great thing they've done.

Foote: No.

Carr: Stay with it, stand pat?

Foote: That is right. Just go as you go. I wrote so as not to have to revise. I work very slowly so when I finish I don't have to go back and revise. I don't have to go back and revise anything, because I have done my revision as I go along. And I don't worry about making the next one better than that one. It is a different set of problems, so you cannot compare the next one to the one you've just finished.

Carr: What's been the worst thing about writing history, as opposed to your natural inclination?

Foote: There is no worst about it. I enjoy it very much, I find that it does something that interests me. Now the thing that disturbs me about it is that I am spending fifteen years out of what I hope is the middle of my life, maybe the end of it. I'm a little less than halfway through the third volume. It will probably be another two years.

Carr: You said a while ago you would write a short novel when you finished this project. Will it be a novel about this time, more or less?

Foote: Yeah, I plan to do a short novel, probably about crime and violence. I've been thinking about a kidnapping.

Carr: Crime against the person rather appeals to you, doesn't it?

Foote: Yeah, it was really a crime against the person to burn down that old man's mansion in *Jordan County.*

Carr: What is it about crime that draws our attention?

Foote: Whit Burnett or some other popular writer said that crime is a left-handed form of human endeavor. It is simply, an example of watching people work under extreme pressure. Crime is just a manifestation of feelings, but it's compressed into rapid action to give you a chance to see it better. Proust always claimed that outrageous characters were simply a way of getting a magnified look at normal characters, and I think it's true. There's no element of a monster that's not present in a perfectly normal person. It just goes out of control and gets enlarged.

Carr: Southern writers, and you are often accused of being rhetoricians.

Foote: Because they are. That's one of the reasons for their goodness. They take an excellent delight in language for language's sake. And I think that's good. You've got to be careful that you're not saying nothing. But you say it in a form that goes back to Southern oratory, which is the only art we've ever had, and I think that's good.

Carr: Do you see any theme running through the novels of this decade?

Foote: No, the novelist's theme has always been the same. It's to tell the truth—to distill the truth out of a story. And no, I don't . . . I see things like Kerouac and all that, but I think it has much to do with the novel. It's always a delight to come across a novel that *is* a novel. It can be as experimental as *Ulysses. Ulysses* is a real novel. It gets to the heart of the situation. T. S. Eliot said the truth. He said in one of the *Quartets* that you're only interested in doing what you have not done, and once you've learned to do it by doing it, you're not interested in it anymore. You have to go on to something else that you don't know how to do. And that's the tragedy of art, he called it a "mess of imprecision" and it's true. But that's its glory. You always feel you're trying to do more than you can do. But you want to get it, and it's the elusiveness of getting it that makes moving ahead worth it. Beethoven is a superb example of an artist functioning just exactly the way an artist ought to function—always moving ahead, always trying to do something new, something beyond. Not *better,* but beyond.

Talking with Shelby Foote

John Graham/1970

From *The Mississippi Quarterly* 24 (Fall 1971) 405-27. Reprinted by permission of *The Mississippi Quarterly*.

The text of the following brief, conversational interviews is transcribed from the tape recordings for "The Scholar's Bookshelf," a fifteen-minute radio program conducted by Professor John Graham of The University of Virginia. The text has been only very slightly edited to facilitate reading.

The four broadcasts with Shelby Foote were taped on June 19, 1970, in a quiet room of the library at Hollins College. The occasion was the Hollins Conference on Creative Writing and Cinema, June 15-June 28, 1970, during which Graham managed to tape more than a hundred programs with some thirty-five of the writers present.

A gathering, a selection based upon the best transcripts of all these programs, will be published in book form by William Morrow and Co.

The particular situation, the context of the interviews, is important. In a brief and intensive period, a time when a great many writers were working with the more than two hundred writing students who had come from all over the country, it was to be expected that there would be much talk about the fundamentals of reading and writing. It was a gathering of writers of all ages, at all stages of their careers. For the most part the talk was direct and straight, in classrooms, seminars, lecture halls, in the college dining room, in dorm rooms and apartments. The transition to the taping sessions was accomplished with a minimum loss of the workshop atmosphere. Moreover, Graham knew most of these writers, personally and socially. He was actively participating in the Conference, and he was known and respected in his own right as a writer, critic and scholar. Even though most of the taped programs would go on the air completely unchanged, the sessions were, in fact, tapings, not live broadcasts, and therefore fairly relaxed. All this, together with the strict time limit for each program, helped to engage the easy, open attention of the individual writers.

For broadcasting, then, Graham's primary aim was to get the writers talking, using their voices in their own characteristic speaking styles, and doing so, building, unself-consciously, from one program to the next. What was demanded of Graham was the exercise of a very special craft, an adroit, often-concealed craftiness (without any loss of integrity), a kind of shifty spontaneity, assuming now one role or mask, now another, never so much the interviewer as the moderator of a dialogue on which others would later be eavesdropping. The perfection of that craft lies in the capacity to bring forward at least the most typical characteristics of the "subject," and, sometimes, the very best qualities.

Presenting these four programs in print (for which the tapes were not originally intended), to be faithful to the structure and to demonstrate both the means and the ends, we offer them in chronological sequence, as they were made.[1]

GEORGE P. GARRETT
University of South Carolina

I

Graham: My guest today is Shelby Foote, noted American historian and novelist. We're at the Hollins Conference on Creative Writing and Cinema, and Mr. Foote has agreed to talk today a little bit about his novels . . . . All of the novels that you've done are rather on the short side, are they not, sort of a novella . . . ?

Foote: About one hundred thousand words, except for *Shiloh*, which is about half that.

G: That's a distance I'm particularly fond of. It does seem to me that I read too many novels and, for that matter, too many short stories where maybe a full third could be pulled. I'm not talking about *War and Peace* now, I know that needs its breadth. But I am very keen on—I don't want to damn with the wrong kind of praise,

[1]A selection of the transcripts of all these programs was published in the book, *The Writer's Voice*, edited by George Garrett, William Morrow and Company, Inc., New York, 1973.

Shelby—but a kind of poetic compression that it seems to me you are after.

F: I like for the middle of a novel to occur in the middle of a book. I like this distribution of space to keep the balance. I think it has its effects. I think you ought to come out of a story just as you came into a story. I think all these things balance.

G: The particular novel that I'm interested in right now is *Follow Me Down,* which may be a rather distant item in your memory, but one that I've almost finished and am enjoying immensely. I am very keen on the multiple points of view where you have an incident, a major incident, a murder, and a small packet of people, but nevertheless a varied packet—all looking at the same incident. It seems to me that I can hear the voices of the murdered girl, of the murderer, of the "dummy" who observes, and, I'm afraid, I can hear the voice of that cheap-shot reporter with a clarity that I'd rather not pick up. He's got that murder in front of him and what he's interested in is whether he can make a thousand words out of it or not, and, really, whether he can make a few bucks, a very few bucks. He's not even a very highly temptable person.

F: That's right.

G: How do you feel about point of view? Does it frighten you when you write a novel like that when you have to make leaps into very different types of characters?

F: It didn't then. Whether it would now, if I did it, I don't know. But this novel was an experiment on my part: to examine a crime of passion by moving into it and then out of it, which is what I mentioned a moment ago about the middle being in the center. This is in three parts. The second part, the middle of the novel, is devoted to monologues by the murderer and the "murderee." The first part has three speakers who are increasingly involved. The first one to speak is a minor official connected with it because he happens to be the turnkey of the jail. The next one is the reporter who is professionally involved, so he has to find out the facts to write them for his paper. The third one is not professionally involved, and he is interested, indeed, because he's the "dummy," and he is involved in the crime itself. He was at the scene of the crime so he's an eyewitness. Then, having gone from a person slightly professionally involved, heavily professionally involved, and then as a minor character who was present at the crime, we are into the crime. Then, we deal with the crime, told by the man who committed it and the girl who was killed. And then, we come out of it again, by having a minor character who was slightly involved, an eyewitness, the murderer's wife. We move from there to the lawyer, who is deeply professionally involved in somewhat the way the reporter was, and, then, finally we're out again with the turnkey . . . the person I call the "turnkey" . . . it was really the circuit clerk, but it's the same kind of involvement. We get deeper and deeper involved by people who are more and more aware of what happened, where the very heart of it was, the girl who was murdered. And then, as you come out of it, you get less and less involved until you're back out in "the world" again.

G: The interesting thing for me about this was that even with the characters that are not attractive—and again, I find the reporter a rather repellent insensitive man, he has no sense of characters or life, all he can see is that it's an incident that will make copy . . .

F: And he has a mean nature. He plays bad tricks on people I think.

G: That's right, cheap little shots of typographical errors. You get a funny sense that he might cheat a little bit at poker if he stays sober enough to do it.

F: Right.

G: But the thing I like about the use of this multiple point of view, the people speaking in their own voices, is first of all, the change of pace to hear these voices come through. You give not only credibility to the characters through the change of voices, but they can kind of justify themselves. And your—I find that I'm rather willing to accept their justifications—I'm talking about *sympathy,* I think.

F: I think it's only fair to accept a man when he . . . you should give him a hearing when he talks. It's true. And, then, discount him after he's through. Give him a sympathetic hearing while he's talking. The whole problem of writing, whether you're going to write in the first or third person, is an interesting choice, anyhow, because you make very large sacrifices in both directions. I'm inclined to think that your largest sacrifice is when you write in the first person because your point of view is so restricted that you cannot walk around a subject and look at it the way you can in the third person. But it does lend immediacy to the thing.

G: While you were talking, it suddenly struck me the narrator of *All the King's Men,* Jack Burden, who is a kind of coarse man in a way . . .

F: Yes, Burden is interesting . . .

G: The novel is very exciting, but there are these limitations of sensibility, I'm tempted to say, because of the nature of the narrator.

F: Warren, it seems to me, was thoroughly aware of this problem we're talking about, so he injects it into the novel and drops into it somebody's Master's Thesis, if you remember.

G: Oh, that's right. It had that superb shift.

F: He had to relieve this thing. And that was his way of doing it.

G: I never thought of that as part of the purpose. I remember the section very clearly with the stylistic change. And it took things back into the history and it was splendidly done.

F: He claimed that he had to do something at that point to stop the novel, do something, and then start it again. And you would start again, refreshed by this change of pace.

G: Is there a danger—I can remember again, Graham Greene in *The End of the Affair*—it seems to me that's told from a number of points of view—is there a danger of a novel becoming a non-novel, turning into a collection of short stories? Is this something that could happen?

F: No, I don't think so. If you have these people concerned about the same thing, the different points of view on that same thing, I think it will carry the validity, the drive of a single unity on through even though there are different speakers. Browning, of course, did it first in *The Ring and the Book*—one of my favorite things and always has been.

G: This is an item like Wordsworth's *The Prelude.* These are great books that for some curious reason—and *The Dynasts* by Hardy—these are things that must be brought back into the main stream.

F: They go largely unread nowadays because people are unwilling to get down and bite on a nail with regard to reading anymore. If they would bite on a nail, they'd find it tasted pretty good, but they won't do that anymore. They won't really read *The Ring and the*

Book. It's not true they won't read it; there are probably a lot more people reading it than we know about. But generally speaking, it's not too easy to find a person now who likes *The Ring and the Book* and has read it two or three times. I've read it three or four.

G: I hadn't thought of Browning. I was thinking of this multiple point of view as a discovery of you twentieth-century novelists. And yet, there Browning was doing it.

F: Browning did it—Browning, incidentally, is one of my very favorite poets, lyric as well as dramatic—was a master of technique anyhow. He's got a great deal to teach any writer, and not just poets either. He's got a lot to teach any writer. However, the influence on me in this book is by no means limited to Browning. There was Faulkner, for instance, *The Sound and the Fury* and *As I lay Dying,* both of which used this technique. I think it's a valid one. There's a trick to it. It's very easy to do, easy to fill many pages, anyhow. If you want to, you can stop and have your character muse awhile. You can do almost anything you want to and that, of course, is very dangerous. I don't think that any person should undertake to tell a story this way unless he is prepared to bring to it the discipline that Faulkner brought to it. I think it requires more discipline than the third person, because of the dangers of just letting your pencil wander.

G: This is a minor point now, Shelby, but with *Follow Me Down* what kind of a judgment were you making when you used as your witness a deaf mute and, as an extension of that, the rather strange mother that he has? Her tale of real woe does do things to one of your major characters, Eustis, the murderer, and yet I don't think I understand the necessity, shall we say, even dramatic . . .

F: I think I was, in the course of that book, which deals with a violent and messy crime—drowning a girl, tying weights to her so she would sink in the Mississippi River, and then later she comes floating up having been eaten on by shrimp and gars—I think I was trying to show that this is indeed a sad world in which people live under nearly unbearable pressures. So many of the people in that book are people who have lived very unhappy lives, way beyond the ordinary. But, my point was that when you get looking at the ordinary, it's probably more unbearable than anybody knows. So that, it's the terrible sadness of life, the tragedy of it, that I was trying to get in touch with in that novel. And I hope that I did because it interested me enormously at the time. I began to find tragedies everywhere I looked.

G: Then a very minor figure—you may even have forgotten him, he's so minor—but there's a poor, florid photographer on the newspaper.

F: Right.

G: And the poor devil has to go out assisting the coroner.

F: And take these dreadful pictures.

G: And take these photographs that make him physically ill.

F: He nearly throws up in the camera, that's right.

G: Shatters the poor man. And that particular scene I admired enormously because the horror there was real, but the horror was transformed because you focused your camera on the photographer's disturbance, and everyone else started reacting to the photographer. I thought they treated him very kindly and considerately.

F: They did, that's right.

G: So the scene developed by reactions rather than some . . . grossly detailed . . .

F: That's what I wanted.

G: Focus on this poor, dead girl . . .

F: That's right. That's very much what I wanted. Somewhere in Hemingway's *The Sun Also Rises*, one of the characters says, "What they are big for back home now (meaning back in the States) is irony and pity. You got to have a little irony and pity." That is what I was after in this book, irony and pity, the irony of these grotesques, trying to lead beautiful lives. The man who murdered the girl took her off to an island to live an idyll. And it turns out to be this horrible crime. That's the irony.

II

Graham: I'd like to ask you about a novel of yours that I've *not* read, about this black trumpet player, since I've been hearing about this novel for so long. *Ride Out* is the title. What does this term mean?

Foote: "Ride out" is a jazz term. When a song has a "rideout" finish, it means they ride it hard at the end. In the story, the main character, whose name is Duff Conway, dies in the electric chair, and the executioner says he's going to ride him right out of this earth. The term "ride out" is a jazz term and also applies to the end of his life.

G: One thing that troubles me, and it's one of the big problems now that I'm going to spring on you—I can remember so clearly the writing of *The Red Badge of Courage* by a very young man who had not, in fact, experienced the Civil War. And yet we usually say that that is our best Civil War novel. It may be our best war novel, an act of the imagination. But he did, I understand, talk a great deal with the veterans of the battles. Now my real question here is, believing, in memory, believing that a writer must work out of his own experience, how could you, as a white man, as a non-trumpet player—at least in low dives—how did you strike on this particular story? How did your imagination serve you here? How did your experience serve you?

F: It came directly out of my background, out of the country I grew up in. Negro musicians were very much part of the scene where I grew up. There was a section of town very much like the section of town described in this story. There was a place called the Mansion House where musicians did play. It was a house of prostitution with orchestras coming and going. The music itself was my first fascination for all this . . . all my life I've heard this music and loved it very much. Most of it was guitar music, but sometimes there were trumpets, clarinets, and always pianos in these places. So that, the music drew me first, and then, as I got older, I was interested by the people who make the music. What kind of life was it that drew a person into the world of music with all its limitations?

G: It's an upside down world, I mean, you're working while other people are playing.

F: That's right. The thing that interested me and I didn't understand it until I'd written about it . . . . Incidentally, a lot of people think that writers are wise men who have some answers to questions to give people. Nothing could be further from the truth. They are looking for answers while they write, and when they find them, they are no longer interested in writing about that problem. But jazz music means a great deal to me.

G: We really are of the generation that grabbed the New Orleans, Chicago and New York styles . . .

F: That's right, and what I knew about jazz was that it was an attempt to communicate with the listener. The trouble was, and it was a large trouble, the jazz musician himself was not equipped technically to do this communicating. Often even his instrument wasn't. He was playing an instrument, say a trumpet, with valves that would stick on it. He could not read music. His technique was marvelous, but it was by nature an inferior technique. He could not play that instrument the way a man in a symphony orchestra can play it. He knew nothing about music the way a musicologist knows music. But he was doing his best to communicate with you in an absolutely direct way, loaded with feeling. All his feelings he was putting directly into that music. Now that's what characterized good jazz. You can see why cheap bad jazz is so bad. If a man, if he's not giving it all, it's bad music . . . very bad music; but when he's giving it all he's got, his technique becomes relatively unimportant because there's something about the very basic best of jazz, something about the blues, that communicates from one person to another. Bessie Smith, to my mind, is as great a singer as ever lived. Nobody could sing better than Bessie does, because she does this thing. She has a tremendous hurdle to get over from not knowing music, in the sense that a musicologist knows it. But, her humanity is so large and the song in her soul is so strong that she leaps all these hurdles and she communicates to you directly as well as Flagstad or anyone you care to name could ever communicate to you.

G: I'm fascinated by your saying this because as a reader of your work, I see you as something of a precisionist.

F: I would never say this in a story or a novel. I don't believe in talking to people in books.

G: Well, I mean your own style is one of a very careful craftsman. You're not a flamboyant, bursting writer.

F: No, no!

G: And yet, you have this obvious, deep warmth and love for Bessie Smith's art.

F: I hope that it would come through in the story *Ride Out,* for example. I would never launch into telling you how soulful this music is in the course of writing a story about it. It would have to speak for itself. But my feelings in back of it are strong indeed and my love for that music is very great.

G: Can we find any live jazz now, if you can bring us up to date on it?

F: I've been looking into it. Every now and then, I hear somebody who I think has got it again. I thought Elvis Presley had it at the start, before he ever made a record or was heard of. I heard him in Memphis and I thought he had it. I thought he was going to be one of the great Blues Shouters, anyhow. Before him, there was a man, Johnny Ray, that I thought was going to be good. He was not good, he was terrible. But, just the beginning of it sounded good. I think maybe the record people get ahold of folks and keep them from developing. They don't stay hungry long enough. Somebody said, what you need to write the blues is "no money in the bank and nobody loving you." Then you can write the blues. Elvis had a great deal of money in the bank and a lot of little girls loving him almost from the day he stepped out.

G: I guess part of this problem of development is that you do get trapped in the commercial world which wants you to repeat the winning formula that you scored with.

F: I used to not think that that really mattered, if a man had it. But I was talking about writers. I think that if you're in the entertainment business they do get hold of you and turn you upside down. For instance, the most admired blues singer of our time, now that Jimmy Rushing doesn't sing anymore, is B. B. King. Well, B. B. King plays an electric guitar, and when I contrast him with, say, Leadbelly, or Jimmy Rushing, he just doesn't sound anything like as good as them. He's as earnest as they were, maybe more earnest. But, something has gotten in the way. Maybe it's the electrical guitar, I don't know. But something has happened, and it may be something simpler than that. It may be prosperity, I don't know.

G: In writing *Ride Out,* it clearly was generated then by your experience with the music. Now let me switch you just a litle bit and put you in the guise of an historian, or a novelist in the act of both researching and imagining. Did you talk with a lot of musicians? Did you step into their world?

F: Yes, I did, and some of my inspiration, if you want to call it that, was literary in a sense. For instance, I was familiar with the story of Louis Armstrong's life. I'm sure that's why the jazz musician in my story spent some time in a reform school. I knew that Louis learned to play the trumpet in the reform school. So my man learned to play the cornet in a reform school, and I'm sure that that's where that came from. But, what came of it, the way he speaks, and the life he lives, is out of having listened to many people like him speak and having studied at first hand the life he lived. His relationship with his mother is one of the most important things in the story and I had plenty of opportunity to see that, from growing up down in the Mississippi Delta where this music was important and these people were the way he was.

G: I can't remember whether I've heard this about a half dozen jazz musicians or just one, but they started off as very young boys. Didn't one, a great leader, or a great singer, trumpeter, lead a blind trumpeter, and then he learned his . . .

F: Yes, that was Josh White with Blind Lemon Jefferson. That's right, that's what he did, and Leadbelly himself was with Lemon. He was with him down in Texas in Blind Lemon's earlier days. He was blind then. Yes, there was nearly always that. All the singers and guitar players served an apprenticeship. They worked with an older man and he often was blind . . . from syphilis, usually.

G: And this then, is nearly always a part of society, isn't it? It's not some institutionalized thing. The apprenticeship is a nice idea really.

F: He served an apprenticeship and he chose his master. He went looking for him, hoping he would take him, because he had heard of him, and finally heard him and attached himself to him like a pilot fish.

G: So it's something for a young boy to do, not just to accidentally come into.

F: I heard Sugar Ray Robinson one time on the radio or television, telling how when he was a boy he used to beg Joe Louis to let him carry his trunks for him from the hotel to the boxing ring. And, he used to carry his trunks. It struck an immediate response in me. Isn't that amazing that Sugar Robinson as a boy should have carried Joe Louis's trunks? But, it's not amazing at all. It happens in the music world from start to finish. Josh White led Blind Lemon Jefferson around by the hand.

G: Is there this indigenous sense of an apprenticeship still in the deep South?

F: It's all gone because the Negroes are gone. There's no sharecropper life anymore, there's no Saturday night anymore. Saturday night is gone. Saturday night's no different than any other night down home now. We got the forty-hour week, which is a good thing, but the price you pay for it is higher than a lot of people know about.

G: So our total sociology now is, in effect, making your story *Ride Out* no longer possible, really. The traditions are being lost.

F: That's right, it's impossible, and I am talking from a point of view that's not with it. I don't like electric guitars. That doesn't mean there's anything wrong with electric guitars, it's just I like unelectric guitars.

III

Graham: I heard Mr. Foote give a lecture not too long ago in which, Shelby, you pretty much decided that you really can't make a fiction writer or poet. Would you like to hazard what goes into the making of an historian? It would seem to me, a little bit of fiction, a little bit of poetry, and a lot of other things.

Foote: I think that, ideally, those things go into the making of him. The truth of the matter is that they seldom do. There's not enough poet in most historians, not as much as there should be. But I ought to make myself clear. I do not want to give historians any license to distort the truth—nothing but harm could come from that, but I do think that historians need to learn many of the writing techniques which poets and novelists know they need to be familiar with before they can function.

G: I don't want to get, right now, into that muddy ground of the historical novel, but surely any historian, unless he's going to be nothing more than a statistician and a date keeper, certainly has to give us some sense of place, some sense of person, to go to the schoolboy terms that you and I learned, of "plot, character, action, and place." And it would seem that he would have to exercise himself on novelists. Point of fact, many historians do turn to the novel of the period they are writing on, do they not, to get tone and attitudes?

F: If they don't they should. I have difficulty in speaking about historians. I am not a professional historian. I am writing what I hope is authentic history, but I do not know any professional historians. I have never had much conversation with professional historians.

G: And yet, not to be vulgar now, but this three-volume history of the Civil War you are doing is recognized by professional historians as an important work, is it not?

F: I hope so. I hope my dedication to the truth is as sound as any historian's could be. But, I think of myself as a novelist. What you said a moment ago seems to me to apply eminently well to what we're talking about. An historian would do very well indeed to go to the novels of the period to learn about the period. I have said—and said in the lecture awhile back—that I thought historical fiction was not really of much account. That's bad historical fiction. I consider George Eliot's *Middlemarch* an historical novel, an examination of England on the eve of the Reform Bill. If someone wants to know what England was like on the eve of the Reform Bill, I do not know of anyplace he could go to find it out better than *Middlemarch*. I think she's done a superb job in *Middlemarch* as an historic novel. Now there are no historical characters in it. William Pitt doesn't walk through her pages. But, it's a very fine historical novel because of its accuracy as to place and mood.

G: Your basic strong feeling is that when a novelist turns to William Pitt, but instead of going to the documents, going to the contemporary reports, he dreams up a "William Pitt" with his idiosyncracies, his vocabulary, strictly out of the novelist's mind . . .

F: I don't give him the license to do that. Almost since Shakespeare's time, the license to take a historical character as Styron did Nat Turner—I disagree with that. I think it's always a mistake.

G: Can you get enough distance, really, on Nat Turner? But suppose it had been *The Confessions of Bill Weaver,* a fictional revolutionary?

F: Then I would have been all for it. That's the trouble.

G: You're talking then about the purity of history, are you not?

F: I am, indeed. I'm talking about the purity of the need for accuracy with regard to dealing with men who once did actually live.

G: And our data on Nat Turner is extraordinarily limited.

F: If I write a story about a very tough little western badman, that is very different from pretending to write a story that I made up out of my head and call him "Billy the Kid." I have no right to do that to Billy. No one has.

G: The stream is muddy enough when we're trying hard without throwing more dirt into the water. In what ways could you hazard that your experience as a very finely crafting novelist—how do you feel that experience has both helped or hindered—maybe hindered is a bad word—maybe set you up with problems as an historian?

F: I consider that it was all a gain, no hindrance. I don't know of anything I learned about the writing of novels in the course of practicing my craft that's not applicable to the writing of history. And, I quite literally mean that. The historian gets his facts out of documents. The novelist get his facts out of his head. But they both are, or certainly should be, true to those facts. The novelist is true to his facts. He does not distort them for the sake of selling books or something, the good one doesn't. Therefore, it's not really different from an historian distorting documents; so that is not the problem. Many people think that a novelist, trying to write history, would distort the facts. He is not accustomed to distorting facts, if you understand what I mean by that. So that what we're really talking about is the technique he learned as a novelist. I claim that all his techniques are applicable. Plotting of his novel, if he did learn how to plot a novel, it is of enormous value to him. Now, he does not make up the events that happen, but the making up of the story is not the plotting of the novel, either. It's what he does with the story. In one case, he has made the story up out of his head, in the other he has gotten it out of documents. In both cases, plotting is necessary. Point of view, chronology, the release of information at a time, these things are the thing I'm talking about with regard to the technique of the novel carrying over to history.

G: I would think that tonally your experience would be fantastically helpful in the sense that you have learned enough through your novels not to let some minor character become so brilliant that he or she would obscure the major thrust of your history.

F: That's right. There's a use for flat characters as well as round characters. People have often pointed this out and it's quite true. And it works well in history. Your characters who come round become rounder because of the presence of flat characters along beside them. This, too, is a novelist's technique that carries over into history. Now, in history, for the most part, you're so glad to get bright, jumpy, colorful material, that you are very much inclined to include that material for value as color. I've found that it does have its place, but you have to be careful in persuading yourself that it's right to do something that you want to do. I have found that these spots of color, and, mind you, valid color, are of great use to the historian to bring his story alive—in other words, to bring it closer to the truth. I'm not talking about making it livelier than it was, I'm just talking about some attempt to make it as lively as it was.

G: Certainly in the fact of history your great man may be comparatively colorless while all around him in life again you have brilliant stars.

F: An example of what I'm talking about. If you're writing a story of the Civil War and one of your main characters (and he certainly will be) is Robert E. Lee, you have a certain amount of biographical information about Lee. Instead of releasing it all the first time Lee comes on the scene, you can withhold parts of it. When you get to the battle of Fredericksburg, you can have Lee look through his binoculars across the Rappahannock and see the house, that has a tree in its yard with a seat under it, where he was when he proposed to his wife. These things are very real. They are not false. They are not hoking it up—unless it's bad writing, which will hoke anything up. But if this information is released over the pages instead of in a clump . . .

G: As Lee would naturally absorb it.

F: Just so, just so . . .

G: He is experiencing as we are going through history. It's not a matter of wrapping him up and then moving on to other things.

F: That's right. And it is not a distraction at that point with the battle of Fredericksburg thundering all around you, Pelham with his two guns holding back the whole Yankee army and so forth. It is not a distraction to say that Lee could see across the river there, this house. It makes Pelham's fight realer, if you see what I mean by that. That's what I'm talking about, about a historian learning from a novelist.

G: The temptation that I would imagine that you must have to fight and stay conscious of is the one we touched on briefly at another meeting. Some characters, not the documents or the facts, must grab your imagination, but your imagination is triggered by some man and there must be some tendency here for the historian Shelby Foote to become the novelist Shelby Foote.

F: Yes, you have to fight it down if it's going to lead you to think you can take any such liberties as a novelist is free to take. I'm not giving the historian license to invent facts, or use facts really in any twisted sort of way. Neither does a novelist do that, if you follow what I mean. He gets this thing straight in his mind and wants to tell the truth; and he knows that nothing worse can happen to his novel than for him to distort these things that he recognizes as true. It is not dissimilar, as I was saying earlier, from the historian's problem.

G: You are really saying that the novelist's imagination puts certain perimeters around a character which are very sharply defined to work in the totality of the novel as well as for psychological credibility and so forth.

F: Compression is as important as expansion. It is to be used with wisdom, in both these mediums.

G: And with the compression, I would think, this is right where your work in poetry and short fiction would be of enormous value to you.

F: That's right. I don't know, personally, of any writer who didn't start out trying to be a poet, and I think this is right and exactly as it should be. I haven't known any good prose writers who didn't give up poetry. They gave it up.

G: I remember Faulkner saying that he gave it up because he wasn't good enough.

F: Called himself a failed poet . . .

IV

Graham: Not to be annoyingly facetious, but after I read your novels and your history, is there anything in particular that you're reading now that I might enjoy?

Foote: I've come back to the books I liked best when I was young. When I was about seventeen, I got crazy about books. I have a great fondness for the memory of those summers on the swing on my front porch and reading all these books. I was in a little Mississippi town that didn't have a bookstore, so I ordered them all directly from the publisher. I'd get their catalogs and order their books, and I used to wait for the mailman every morning to get me a new book. But the books I read then with the most pleasure are the books I read now with the most pleasure. The writers who influenced me most were writers that I like best now.

G: I picked up Stevenson's *Treasure Island* not very long ago when I was so busy, Shelby, I should not have looked at the newspaper headlines. And I quit about two in the morning. The story line grabbed me and I remembered an old swing and the park bench.

F: Well, you're having a Proustian experience, there. You're not only reading *Treasure Island,* you're the boy who read *Treasure Island,* and it is a fascinating business. And, incidentally, you see a great many things that you didn't see as a boy. One summer—it's a big summer in my life—someone told me, I think Will Percy told me, that the three big novels of our century were *Remembrance of Things Past, Ulysses,* and *The Magic Mountain.*

G: That's a summer's reading right there.

F: So I ordered those three books and sat down and read them, you see. In the summertime, it's sixteen hours reading I guess. And I went through them like a colt in clover. They were an absolute delight to me all the way. And I have reread those three books, especially Proust, the rest of my life, I've reread them and reread them and reread them. I've read Proust six or seven times.

G: I cannot imagine any firmer stones in twentieth-century literature.

F: That's right. They were the best books. I had another experience, and you have to understand that this is operating out of an unliterary family in an unliterary region, in a little town in the middle of that region. So I had to have some kind of help for this thing. I was enjoying it enormously, reading, but I wanted to read what I *ought* to read. So I got a book, I found it in a junk shop or somewhere, by a man whose name I couldn't even pronounce . . . his name was John Cowper Powys or something like that.

G: That's right.

F: I can't even remember.

G: There were brothers, on the edge of the arts.

F: That's right. I didn't even know how to pronounce his name—and I thought "Proust" was "Prowst," I never heard anybody say it. This book was called *The Hundred Best Books.* And, it began with the *Bible* and the *Iliad* and the *Odyssey* and went all the way up to, I think Arnold Bennett, or somebody like that. So, I read those hundred best books, which is kind of a strange thing for a kid to do.

G: How old were you then, Shelby?

F: Seventeen.

G: Glorious! I read an awful lot of junk at that age, you know? It was a shame.

F: I read a lot of junk before that—Tom Swift. I was a great Tom Swift fan, and Tarzan and all that. I had read those things, but this I enjoyed reading so much. The first book I had ever read—I know the first piece of music I ever heard that hit me between the eyes was *Eine Kleine Nachtmusik,* which is a splendid piece of music, to introduce you to classical music—but the first book I ever read that made me understand that reading was going to be worth a grown man's time was *David Copperfield,* which looked to me like the longest book ever written in the world and it is a long book, but my delight with *David Copperfield* was from the first page to the last. And that was when I was about twelve years old, you see, so then I went on reading a lot of junk. And then finally the pleasure I was getting out of good books made me realize that that was the best way in the world and the most exciting way to spend your time and so I read good books.

G: What happened to you when you hit college? Did you just keep bobbing your head at reading lists, indicating that you'd read all of them before?

F: Yes, I had read them. I had a funny experience in college, though. I ran across a lot of things I did not like that were supposed to be good. Walter Scott was one of them.

G: I cannot get through him.

F: I took a course from a man named MacMillan at Chapel Hill who was a very good teacher. And he had ten novels for us to read and one of them was *Quentin Durward.* When we got to *Quentin Durward,* I started it, and I went to him and said, "Dr. MacMillan, I'm having real trouble with this book. I honestly don't like it and don't want to read it. Do you take that into consideration at all?" And he said, "Well, if I were you, I wouldn't read it." And I said, "That's mighty nice of you." And he said, "No, if that's the way you feel about it, do that." So, I said, "Fine." We were having a book a week, and when it came time for the test on *Quentin Durward* I wrote on my paper, "I have not read this book and it was with your permission I didn't read it, if you remember." And I turned the paper in. When the papers were handed back to us, the following Monday, I had an F on the paper. So, I went back to Dr. MacMillan and said, "What have you done to me? You told me I didn't have to read it." And he said, "That's right, you didn't have to read it."

G: But a simple matter of cause and effect . . .

F: He said, "I admired your attitude and I think you were right not to read it, but, of course, as you know, I had to fail you. You couldn't get a passing grade without reading the book." He was a nice man.

G: You've been talking about a lot of novels, would you introduce me to some historians, perhaps?

F: My favorite historian and the one I read to get the flavor of history, to get a real notion of what history is all about—I have to read in translation because my Latin is nearly nonexistent and my Greek is totally nonexistent—but Tacitus is my favorite historian. The whole notion of this terrific compression that Tacitus brings off—and the way he deals with scoundrels is very interesting. It teaches me how to write about Edwin Stanton and all kinds of people who are pretty scoundrelish. So that Tacitus is my favorite historian. There are others I like. I like Gibbon a lot. The Gibbon periods roll out and give me a lot of pleasure.

G: I was about to say the styles there are so radically different.

F: That's right. Style is what matters. Tacitus's silver Latin, or at least the translations I read; and the Latin I try to stumble through is stupid. I do nothing but translate when I try to read it, so I might as well read a good translator. But the tone of Tacitus comes through in a good translation.

G: Offhand, do you have a favorite translation of Tacitus you can think of? Didn't Penguin have a good translation of it?

F: Penguin has a good translation of it. I'm ashamed to say that I can't remember the man's name. A good translation, very good. Brodribb is good. Somebody really ought to translate—I wish Robert Graves would translate Tacitus. It would be a great service, I wish he would do it.

G: I read a C. Day Lewis *Iliad* or *Odyssey* that was knocking me down. I had no idea someone could pull that off so well.

F: I so much like the Shaw *Odyssey*. The T. E. Lawrence *Odyssey* is one of my very favorite books in that translation. And the Richmond Lattimore translation of the *Iliad* is good. I have not read Lattimore's translation of the *Odyssey* which came out two years ago, but I don't need it because I think so highly of the Shaw.

G: Well, you go to Tacitus and Gibbon. Any contemporary historians? Do you enjoy Churchill's histories?

F: I'm a little too conscious of Churchill being a sort of imitator of Gibbon that it bothers me some. I like Bruce Catton's work, I like it very much. I like Douglas Southall Freeman's work. He's a good chance for me to tell you about what I meant about good writing. Freeman is about as far from a good writer as you can get. He likes a sort of jog trot prose—here I am in Virginia talking badly about their leading man—but it fits, perfectly, his subject matter. I like the way Freeman writes. I would not like it out of context. But when he's writing about Robert E. Lee, or Lee's Lieutenants, or the American Revolution, this sort of jog trot prose fits very well, gives the book a good tone. I like it. It's dry, unskillful, and there's something I like about that in connection with his subject.

G: Is it because of the quick-paced movement of things?

F: No, they don't really move that fast. It's the awkwardness of the sentences themselves. It's hard to say exactly how that can be good, but it fits. The style fits. Style is not the way somebody puts in flourishes. Style is the way a man is able to communicate to you the quality of his mind. And this does communicate to me the quality of Freeman's mind when he turns it on Robert E. Lee and it's a very satisfactory kind of thing to be in touch with.

G: Maybe an analogy, someone like Theodore Dreiser who, as a stylist, will drive you up the wall, and yet, given his rather grimy subject matter, this heavy-handed style functions.

F: There's a certain ponderousness that has validity about it. I don't read Dreiser with much pleasure. I don't read some good writers because I don't like their writing. I find Stendhal to be pretty hard reading; although it's always interesting, I find it pretty hard reading. Balzac . . . I'm crazy about Balzac, but I . . .

G: I'm just the reverse.

F: I have a pretty hard time with some of his writing. Nobody could not like Flaubert, I don't see how they couldn't like Flaubert, but some of the great writers make pretty rough reading for me since I have no respect for them as stylists.

G: What about the Second World War? You were an artillery captain, were you not? Have you any book on the Second World War that seems to . . . ?

F: No, and they never will write one. I'd just as soon be done with that. I don't want any part of it. In fact, I don't want any part of any other war. When I finish the Civil War, that's it.

G: Do you read any poetry at all? Any contemporary writers that you are interested in?

F: I read a great deal of poetry. It's very interesting to me. There are rhythms to reading. Now that I'm older, I'm able to see that there are whole decades of no poetry reading, and then I'll go in for three years of reading a great deal of poetry. I've been reading a lot of Browning lately and I've gone back to Shakespeare, with enormous pleasure, great pleasure because my appreciation of their technical facility is coming forward to me in a way it didn't before.

G: One thing I've barked at students about, when they say some work is terribly difficult, such as a play of Shakespeare's—I've gotten a little snappish, almost, trying to point out that he didn't write for boys. You've got to grow up to Shakespeare, you've got to grow up to Mann, Proust, Joyce. They were not setting themselves up to present a college textbook for nineteen-year olds.

F: Shakespeare must be a very great writer if for no other reason than that he survives being taught the way he is taught in high schools today.

G: You know, one thing suddenly occurred to me when you were in mid-stream. How do you feel about Stephen Vincent Benét's *John Brown's Body?*

F: I find it overblown. It's too much striving to be really American with the bark on "really." I don't know what it is with me. I don't like it, though.

G: He reaches awfully hard for the metaphor, and even when he finds it there, stretching is distracting, wouldn't you say?

F: I do, I feel that about him.

Interview with Shelby Foote

Evans Harrington/1971

From *The Mississippi Quarterly* 24 (Fall 1971) 349-77. Reprinted by permission of *The Mississippi Quarterly*.

Shelby Foote's home in Memphis is Tudor style, landscaped into a low, terraced, well-kept lawn. Outside Foote's den is a heavily wooded area in which, on the June afternoon I visited him, birds sang so loudly that they threatened the integrity of my tape-recorder. Our appointment was for two o'clock, and I arrived almost on time. A Negro man was hosing off the pebbled-concrete drive to the two-car garage. He directed me to the proper entrance and helped me rouse Foote, who had gone to the kitchen for coffee.

Foote wore slacks and a plaid sport shirt, in which he looked slender, almost youthful, despite a strand or two of gray in his hair. His manner, from the first moment of the interview to the last, was unassuming and friendly—with, however, no suggestion of familiarity. He took me straight to the kitchen and poured me a cup of coffee. We drank standing in the kitchen, chatting about mutual acquaintances, but I was never under the impression that I had come upon a plain old homespun boy. Later Foote said of William Faulkner's celebrated difficultness, "It's true, perhaps, that he drew lines and rebuffed people who crossed them; but they were lines no gentleman would cross anyway." The comment is strongly suggestive of Foote's delicately balanced manner.

The interview was recorded in Foote's book-lined den. He spoke readily, decisively, animatedly, gesturing elaborately and often. His voice has a pleasant light-baritone quality, and his diction is that of a cultured Southerner (Turner, for instance, is rendered "Tuhnuh.") Though he frequently displayed the irony which is prevalent in his work—and occasionally relaxed into humor—he seemed a deeply serious man, absorbed by all aspects of literature. His face is rather long, wide-lipped, with vertical creases between the brows and beside the mouth; the eyes are large, green and thoughtful. Altogether, it is a grave, forceful face, rarely breaking into an unqualified smile.

Q: The first thing I was interested in was how you came to be a writer—not in the sense of "what makes you write" (I hope we'll answer that in connection with some other things), but was it a choice or an accident or a combination of those two?

A: It wasn't a choice so much. It was, in a sense, an accident, as I guess it always is. I began at the age of sixteen or seventeen the way most writers begin, by writing poetry. And I was editor of the high school paper. And then when I went on to college I worked not for the paper but for the literary magazine—wrote stories. And then when Hitler went into Poland, I protested by going into the Mississippi National Guard. We were at home for a year before we mobilized and left, and in the course of that year I wrote my first novel and sent it off to Alfred A. Knopf. And there was an editor there—and he's still there—Strauss was his name. He wrote back that several of them around the office had read it and liked it and were interested in it, but that it was so experimental in nature that he was sure it wouldn't sell. And his advice to me was to put it away, go on and write the next one—which they were certain they would be glad to print—and then come back to it later on and see if I didn't agree with him. He said if they published it then [in its original form] the booksellers would get a very low opinion of me and it couldn't do me anything but harm outside of the pleasure of seeing myself in print. Well, all that made sense to me, so I did what he said. I put it away in a closet. And about that time we were mobilized into federal service and left for Camp Blanding. Then when I came back five years later, in late forty-five, I took it out of the closet and looked at it and saw more than ever that they were right about it; but I thought there were things in it that were good. So I decided to keep on writing. And I did.

Q: Before you started writing, in high school, had you read very much? Was your home literary, would you say?

A: No. No, my principal connection with a literary home was through my friendship with the Percys [William Alexander Percy, author of *Lanterns on the Levee,* and his three nephews, among them Walker Percy, winner of the National Book Award (1960) for his novel *The Moviegoer*]. There were literally thousands of books in the Percy house. My house had the Harvard Classics and Stoddard's Lectures, the Book of Knowledge and current novels, I suppose—Rex Beach, Viña Delmar, Percy Marks, and lots of others, mercifully forgotten. No, I do not have a literary background; my family doesn't. That was what I meant by accidental. It's probable that if those Percy boys hadn't moved to Greenville, I might never have become interested in literary things.

Q: So you would say that the Percys were the most important individuals in your early literary development.

A: That's right. Will Percy, and then my friend Walker, who was going through the same sort of thing at the same time.

Q: Often we talk about Southern literature as a distinct type, and of the influence of the South on its writers. Would you say that the section you lived in was a factor in your writing?

A: It certainly had a great deal to do with the way I write, what I write about—

Q: I mean, in becoming a writer.

A: I think it did that too. I think that Southerners—how true this is of other sections I don't know—but I think there's a tradition of story-telling and story-listening in the South that has a good deal to do with our turning to writing as a natural means of expressing whatever it is we've got bubbling around inside us.

Q: I noticed in your writing an extensive knowledge of literature. You came by this in your reading from the time you were about seventeen mostly on your own, or did you get it through—?

A: These things are accidental. I read intensively from the time I was sixteen until I was twenty-one or -two and went into the Army where I had a four- or five-year gap of not reading again. But during that period of time, I read quite literally almost everything that I had any reason to think was solid and worthwhile that I could get my hands on. I remember in my seventeenth year I heard somewhere that the three great modern novels were *Remembrance of Things Past, Ulysses,* and *The Magic Mountain.* So I read those three in about one six-week period. And I moved like that—filled in my gaps of classical literature, Greek and Roman, moved on to all the

Frenchmen and the Englishmen and the Russians. So for about five or six years I was like a sheep in clover with all those books.

Q: How much did formal schooling have to do with all this?

A: I think almost nothing, practically nothing. Another accident that was a great help to me in this reading was that we had a very poor library [in Greenville] so far as the number of books it had and *what* books it had, but the women of Greenville had something I think called the Tuesday Study Club, and there was a little room in the library where they kept their books separate from the other books—theirs didn't belong to the library. And I found I could get in that little room, and I found many books that I had never heard of, that I perhaps wouldn't have been able to get hold of otherwise. I remember one of them was *The Brothers Karamazov.* Many such things were in there, and I used to steal them and read them and take them back again when I went for others. I would buy them for myself if I especially liked them. I think I still have almost every book I ever bought because I have a long-standing, unbreakable policy of never lending a book to anybody under any circumstances.

Q: Probing just a bit more into education, at the University of North Carolina again you didn't find that the formal schooling had a great deal to do with your literary background?

A: No, I hadn't been on the campus more than two or three months before I knew that I did not want to get a degree. I also had serious doubts about how long I wanted to stay there, but I did enjoy what I was getting. I was absolutely amazed at the Carolina library. I had never seen anything like those eleven stories of stacks and everything, and that excited me a lot. And, oh, halfway through my first quarter I dropped all the subjects I didn't like and sneaked into classes—including graduate classes—that I did like. And for the two years I was at Chapel Hill I took whatever I wanted and did not take anything I didn't, such as math. I did not take creative writing or anything like that. I took courses in medieval history, philosophy, various English courses, like the English novel and so forth. But no, my schooling wasn't formal. It had almost nothing to do with either my education or my writing, although I did, as I say, try to read everything I had any notion was a classic, ancient or modern. That was where my schooling was.

Q: I noticed in one news story that you mentioned Crane,

Stendhal, and Tolstoy as influences on you. Were they particularly strong influences?

A: That had reference to the influences that went into *Shiloh*. Those three wrote of war. Stendhal wrote of war the way he did. Tolstoy learned from Stendhal and added to it. Crane learned from Tolstoy. And all I meant was that this book *Shiloh* is, I hope, in that line. The major influences on me as a writer, among modern writers, are certainly Proust and Faulkner. I once told Faulkner that I had every reason to be a better writer than he was, because he was primarily influenced, as I thought, by Conrad and Anderson, and I was influenced by Proust and Faulkner. And both of them were better writers. [Laughter.] He was very polite about it. He didn't point out that the person himself [being influenced] might have something to do with the result.

Q: I notice in your work a rather unusual interest in the 1890s and the 1900s. Did any of the writers of that period particularly interest you?

A: I was interested in that whole period, all the writers. But when I got to James he practically smothered all other interests in that era. James, to me, was such a big talent that he just sort of blotted out all the others. He didn't blot out Crane, but he did engage my interest for that whole period so much that I had very little left for the others.

Q: Proust and Faulkner you've cited several times as very strong influences on you. Which would you say has influenced you most?

A: Surely Faulkner.

Q: And yet while I've seen (and if I were you this would be a very touchy point with me)—people, including Faulkner, saying you write like Faulkner—

A: Yes.

Q: —yet in reading your work I was very much impressed with a kind of continental quality.

A: I think the Proust influence is deeper but I think the Faulkner influence is more apparent. I agree that Proust has had a deeper influence on me than Faulkner. Proust, I suppose, is a—well, he certainly is a greater writer than Faulkner, whatever that means. And his influence is therefore more apt to be deep. But my debt to Faulkner is huge. He taught me to look at the world within the close atmosphere of the novel. He taught me what an exciting thing the goings-on within a novel can be. My idea of excitement came from Faulkner. My understanding of human beings was far more from Proust. But as for the mechanics of the novel and the mechanics of style, which Proust called "a quality of vision," Faulkner did give me that. He was the first good writer to touch a responsive personal chord in me. How much of that was due to our having a common heritage I don't know. Probably a great deal. But Faulkner is the man who first made me understand the possibilities within what I call the close atmosphere of the novel, and that reality within a novel can be realer than reality outside a novel.

Q: It seems to me James would have also had an effect like this.

A: He did have, but that was later. I didn't read James until after the war. I found him unreadable before the war. I found him quite unreadable. It's interesting. I began *The Wings of the Dove* I think four times and got no further than thirty or forty pages, and now I think there's good cause for saying it's the greatest American novel. But I had a terrible time reading *The Wings of the Dove*! In fact, I never did read it until I had gone back and read *The Portrait of a Lady* and some of the earlier things. Then I was tuned in to it.

Q: Obviously you thought Proust and Faulkner very great writers at first. Have you had any occasion to revise your opinion about either of them?

A: There certainly have been writers that I thought more highly of in the past than I do now, but I've had no occasion to revise my opinion about Faulkner and Proust. I think they're as great today as I ever thought they were; in fact, I think they are greater because I now understand more about writing. There have been writers, though, like Dos Passos and Wolfe, and several others, that I don't think nearly as highly of as I did in the enthusiasm of my early reading of them.

Q: Did Hemingway have much influence on you?

A: Yes, Hemingway did something for me that I prize highly. He taught me that a writer should rough it up some to keep it alive. But what Hemingway taught me better than anything else is the terrific ambiguity of life and especially the terrific ambiguity of life in a novel. I began to see that Hemingway's very clear eye was so good, so valid, that it put in information that went against his opinions. *The Sun Also Rises* is a novel in which it seems to me, without any doubt, he has a good deal of contempt for the character of Robert Cohn.

But his eye for Cohn is so good and his eye—his critical eye—turns on the people that he likes with such accuracy that I think there's solid ground for saying that the only decent person in that book is Robert Cohn. And this is the ambiguity that comes in through the clarity of his vision. Hemingway has been under a cloud for ten or fifteen years; it's very fashionable among intellectuals to run him down. I think that that should be reversed, and I can say that Hemingway's position is as high as a writer's can be. His contribution will never be doubted truly, and his enormous skill, especially this eye of his and his particular search for the right word without being precious about it—Hemingway gave us that, and it was a tremendous thing to have given.

Q: I wonder if you're saying, in reference to the "eye," something that parallels what Hemingway once said to somebody—Hotchner, I believe—that as a man you've got to be judging all the time but as an artist you've got to understand.

A: I got so I thought of Hemingway a little bit the way some people think of my favorite painter, Vermeer. There are those who say he was nothing but an eyeball; there was no brain back of that eye at all. And I sometimes think—ridiculously, of course—that there was no brain behind Hemingway's eye. The eye was so good and the judgment so faulty, but the faulty judgment did not affect the clarity of the vision. That interests me enormously, and it adds this ambiguity we're talking about.

I began to understand something with Hemingway, specifically, when I read the story "Big Two-Hearted River." On the face of it that's a story in which nothing happens. But when you read it, think about it, and read it again, think about it, and read it again, you begin to see that a great deal is happening in that story. And the only way you have of knowing what is happening is this clear eye; there're no hints, really. It's all there. And then you begin to see that this man is just on the point of exploding, of cracking, of breaking clean across. And yet the evidence in the story is by no means clear. I remember a strike he got from a trout while he was fishing, and he got so excited he had to sit down and rest. Well, that is not a clue. Anybody who's ever had a trout hit his hook and get away has had to sit down and rest. It's not in those things that you're shown the man is under terrific tension. It's the way he eats his spaghetti which he heats in a skillet, or it's the way he crawls into his tent to sleep for the night. And that's what I'm talking about. My debt and surely I think every modern writer's debt to Hemingway is enormous.

A: Aside from your histories for a moment, you've worked mostly as a novelist and a writer of long short stories. You said that you started by writing poetry. Have you continued to write poetry?

A: No, I haven't written any poetry since I started writing fiction. I have not written a poem in twenty years.

Q: I know Faulkner regarded poetry as the highest form of literature, and a novelist as a spoiled poet. Would you agree with this?

A: No, I think the novelist is superior to the poet and to anybody else, as D. H. Lawrence said—the top dog. I agree with that, in our time.

Q: About the short story, you don't like it as well as the novel?

A: I don't. It's a form that's unsatisfactory to me unless it's tied in with other things. Then I can get some interest. But to create a perfect little thing doesn't interest me at all. If somehow it were part of a whole—all the short stories I've ever written are tied in; in that book *Jordan County* [Foote pronounces *Jordan* as if it had a German umlauted *o*] they are related to each other, and when I get that I'm happy working in the form. But unless I have that, I'm not.

Q: You started as a fictionist and had a spurt of creativity from 1948-52, and then moved into history. I wonder if this development is connected with the current theory about the death of fiction. Do you feel that fiction is on the way out?

A: No, I don't. And people have always been wrong who thought so. I don't at all. As for me, though, those five books made a unit, a definite stage. I didn't see any point in adding a sixth to that group of novels. But apparently I was not ready to move on to another style of novel at that point. So I turned to history, which, in my handling of it, is another style of novel—that is, not with any fiction in it but an exercise very similar to the writing of novels, to me. So that was my style of novel that I moved on to. I'm not making claims like Truman Capote that I've invented a new form, as he says he did in *In Cold Blood,* but to me it was the same kind of activity. And when I finish my history, as I hope to do in two or three more years, I will go back to the novel, and I hope into still a third form of work.

Q: You don't then agree—one hears all the time talk about the vitality of the essay, for instance, and the weakness of the short story and the novel. Do you feel that this really exists?

A: No, I don't think so. I think that we have good novelists working. I just read a short book called *True Grit* by a fellow over here in Arkansas, a newspaper reporter. It's a good story, and well written. I think that Updike's novel *Couples* is a good novel. I think it has a kinship with George Eliot's novel *Middlemarch,* which is perhaps my favorite of all English novels. And I think such things are encouraging, and I don't at all agree about even the decline of the novel, let alone the death of it.

Q: What kinship do you see between *Middlemarch* and *Couples*?

A: They both seem to be concerned about a group of people within a society, in a way of life, in a time of change. *Middlemarch,* of course, is concerned with the Great Reform Bill of 1832 in England and what society was like on the eve of it. And I think that *Couples* is concerned with a critical time in this nation's history, and I think the approach is very much the same, although George Eliot, of course, doesn't have people jumping in and out of bed with each other—at least not ostensibly.

Q: About the current fashions of writers. For instance, what about Capote's "non-fiction novel"? What is your opinion on that? Is that a good book, or is it just a mistake he's making?

A: I have no high opinion of the book. I think it's a bringing of movie technique to the writing—the skillful writing—of the sort of thing you find written badly in cheap detective magazines. It's a case history pumped up with a lot of skill and a lot of cinemagraphic technique. I'm not opposed to it, but I have no very high opinion of it, and it's certainly not a new form.

Q: And it doesn't say anything one way or another about the art of fiction?

A: No, it doesn't move me even. I may be interested to find out what will happen to the people, but the book itself didn't move me, whereas some much less skillful jobs have moved me greatly. There's something about mixing fact and fiction that goes against my grain. Mr. Capote denies that there's any fiction in that book. It would be a sad thing if there weren't, and I'm sure that there's plenty of fiction in that book. But there's something about it that goes against my grain.

This is true of Styron's *Confessions of Nat Turner.* There's something about that that goes badly against my grain. Nat Turner, we don't know much about him, but from what little we do know, surely Nat Turner was a burning flame of a man. And for Styron to presume to call him Nat Turner, catch him on paper, especially as he's strained through the mind of James Baldwin, seems absurd to me, and I have some resentment for this. Perhaps if he hadn't called him Nat Turner all my objections would disappear, but the very fact that he called him—

Q: You mean the close friendship between Styron and Baldwin has affected—?

A: Baldwin is supposed to have influenced strongly Styron's notions of the race question in his *Confessions of Nat Turner.* I think that I am closer to Nat Turner than James Baldwin is. I'm talking about, I am personally more like Nat Turner than James Baldwin is, even though they are both Negroes. I consider somebody out of Harlem to be very different from someone out of Tidewater Virginia, especially with the other differences that are very much there; in Baldwin, I mean.

Q: What about Styron as a novelist before this book?

A: I like Styron's work very much. I think he's an interesting writer, too—and I don't say that about a lot of them that I really like. But Styron is a truly interesting writer. He has the thing that I prize highly in Southern writers, a true interest in people. He has that. Any time he writes he has what Faulkner has superbly. He's very excited about having something to tell you, and you feel his excitement; it's contagious. And you read the books with great pleasure as a result of the drive that's inherent in his conception of people. I like Styron's work.

Q: The books that we might call surrealistic—black humor—*Catch-22* was one of the early ones. What is your opinion of those?

A: I like *Catch-22* a lot better than I do most of them, but I have no high opinion of those books in general.

Q: You think this is just a fashion, something superficially different that people are—

A: Yes. Yes. I don't believe they are all that different, though.

Q: What about the French phenomenologists? Do you think they are introducing anything new?

A: You mean Sartre, Camus?

Q: Well, Robbe-Grillet.

A: I haven't read the latest Frenchmen, so I don't know enough to comment.

Q: You've mentioned several current writers that you think are good. Are there others?

A: I like Calder Willingham's work very much, but I wish he'd come to grips with himself instead of continuing sort of writing fairy tales. I wish he'd really come to grips with himself. He's got all the equipment. I wish he'd work harder, and more. But I like Willingham very much.

Q: Is the so-called Southern Renaissance dead?

A: Yes, I think so. I do think so.

Q: What do you think is the reason?

A: Faulkner killed it with superiority. I think it was Flannery O'Connor who said that when the Dixie Special is coming down the track everybody's got to get off. I think that did it. I think Faulkner worked it about to its limit. And others, too—Erskine Caldwell, perhaps deservedly neglected; I think he's an interesting writer.

Q: What about Wolfe?

A: Wolfe is a writer for young people, I think. It's when you're satisfied with wondering and don't care about the depths that Wolfe is fine. But if you're looking for depths, you can't find it in Wolfe, either by example or by statement. So he won't do in the long run, which is the only run that counts.

Q: What do you suppose caused the Southern Renaissance in the first place?

A: It would be a great big question as to all the factors that came together to cause it, but it's the Southern branch of a general renaissance. It took its Southern character from the land and the people who live on it. But there was a renaissance in many parts of the country at the same time. I think the Southern one was perhaps the most successful of the renaissances, aside from the expatriates like Hemingway and Fitzgerald, who are very large exceptions indeed. But I think there was a general reaction to the First World War that coalesced at that point to produce all this talent.

Q: What about the effect of Naturalism as a kind of spearhead or forerunner which cleared the way for artistic utilization of its point of view?

A: I think you're right. I think that Naturalism performed the service that prepared for better work. Most of the Naturalists, so-called now, were unfortunately bad writers, like Dreiser and Norris and the rest of them, so that they are hard reading. But there's no doubt that they prepared the way to have Naturalism at their disposal, among the other tools, and—

Q: Use art with it.

A: That's right.

Q: It's frequently stated that the Southern dominance in American literature is past and a Jewish intellectual movement now dominates. Do you agree with this, in the first place?

A: I agree that it dominates, yes.

Q: Well, what do you think of it?

A: I think it's by default. I think we've come to a sort of pausing, resting, taking-account phase, in which the Jewish intellectual novel has moved to the front by default. I think it will subside back into where it came from. I like Bellow. Who doesn't? But he's not to me a sizeable talent, not out front; he's just something that's biding us through this quiet time, I think. It'll make a contribution and a good one. But I do not see it as an example of the best we can do by a long shot.

Q: What about Mailer in this?

A: Mailer has sort of opted for journalism, opted out, at least through these last few years. His next-to-last book, a novel called *Why Are We in Vietnam?*, I liked better than anything he has written. He did a curious thing. He crossed God knows what, including the comic books, with Browning's dramatic monologue, which is very good, because it's many-faceted: it flashes this direction, flashes that direction, and really gets hold of the thing. I like that book very much, along with his follow-up journalism on the march on the Pentagon. I think he's hit on a style which is truly interesting and many-faceted and serves him well. I hope he comes out of it with some real accomplishment. I really think, however, that he's probably blunted, snarled, wrecked the instrument he works with badly enough that he'll never do really great work. I don't know that, but I feel that.

Q: Do you think those two are the leading figures in the Jewish intellectual group today?

A: I don't really put Mailer in the group with Bellow. I don't include them as writers of a kind. I see Mailer as a much bigger writer than Bellow. He's a failure in a sense, but I think that his equipment is much superior to Bellow's.

Q: Do you rank Mailer with Styron, as is often done?

A: Yes, I would rank him with Styron, and Jones. I'm not saying that they're all three equally good writers, but they are my idea of novelists. They are concerned about people and their relationship with each other. Bellow is, too, but Bellow is more interested in ideas, or it seems to me he is. I don't read him with much pleasure. I've never read abstract things with much pleasure.

Q: This is a debatable question. Which, would you say, Styron, Mailer—which writers, or which pair of writers, are today our leading writers of the so-called younger generation?

A: I honestly don't know. Mailer, Styron, Jones—all three have serious flaws which seem to me to deny any one of them a position as a leading writer. Their talents are considerable, and they are my notion of novelists. But each of them is badly flawed. Styron has been working for twenty years, and he has produced something like three-and-a-half novels. Not enough. Jones has produced, say, four. Mailer—I don't know how you'd go about counting what are novels and what aren't. But they haven't worked hard enough, it seems to me. My idea of a novelist is Henry James, or Charles Dickens. And when we get to talking about great novelists of our times, I want them to have a resemblance to those men. Now, there are certainly exceptions to that. Joyce and Flaubert produced three or four books over large spans of time, but it's easy to understand why a book like *Bovary* or *Ulysses* would take a number of years to write. It is not understandable to me why the books of Styron, Jones, or Mailer should take tremendously long times to write. They're not that kind of book, I think.

Q: This, then, leads to the question, are we in a period of lapse or decline in the novel? I believe you said earlier we were.

A: Yes. I tell you, Dos Passos used to say a thing that seemed absolutely foolish. He used to say that it was harder to be a good writer in America than anywhere on the earth because the temptations are large, that when you achieve success and begin to hit your stride, you immediately were tempted by offers from *Ladies Home Journal* and Hollywood. I think that was foolishness. I don't think

Hollywood or *Ladies Home Journal* can offer you anything as rewarding to yourself as what you get from doing good work. So I discount that. But it does seem that these three men and many others on the present scene are distracted not by the money offered by somebody and not by the possible short-term fame offered by somebody else; but we live in a time that's pulling you against yourself, and you get pulled on the bias, you get ripped cross-ways. There does seem to me something about our time that makes it difficult to do hard, sustained work. It may be that we haven't learned to deal with our confusion yet. But there does seem to be, not Dos Passos' kind of difficulty, but something kin to it—not the specific enticement, but a sort of being caught up in things. It's very hard on young writers to be on the cover of *Time* apparently. It creates its own ethos.

Q: Would you think that Podhoretz's statement in *Making It* is relevant here; that is, that the very philosophy of "making it" in America is hard on an artist's development?

A: I wouldn't, really. No, I don't think these writers are very much concerned with the things that concern him most. So I don't think that's a clue. But there is something about our life that is tearing, and we don't know how to handle it yet. But it's not temptation. It's the encroachment. It's the temptation to be writer-in-residence somewhere, which you will gain from. So you think. And it isn't true. I happen to believe that the worst place on God's earth for a creative writer is a college campus. I think that the kind of exchanges you engage in sap your creativity, not stimulate it. That may be wrong; it's my personal opinion. I just did a semester at Hollins as writer-in-residence and enjoyed it enormously, but I do not want to do it again. Too many people have gone academic. Too many have been given energy-sapping grants. Too many have engaged in all-night bull-sessions, and joined coteries and this, that, and the other. And I think that's very bad. Most of our good writers preserved their privacy, did not discuss their work while it was in progress. I think these current people are breaking some very sound rules, and that may be part of the reason for the let-down, the tearing.

Q: On the other hand, am I not right that the French, for example, had Paris always?

A: Yes, that is true. I think it was a question of time. A nineteenth-century man could maybe do these things, with nineteenth-century standards. It was very different from the twentieth century. I would call your attention to the fact that France, which has continued to pursue this Paris thing, hasn't had a writer since Proust who can compare with any number of American writers—certainly can't compare with Faulkner, Hemingway, Fitzgerald.

Q: Shifting now rather specifically to your work, history obviously played an important role in your work from the beginning, even in your novels. Any special reason?

A: Yes. What I want to find in a novel is truth, and part of the truth always seems to me to be an examination of the milieu. To neglect that always seemed to me a mistake, so that, if a thing was set in the present, I tried to look hard at the present and see not only what the man was doing but what was going on around him; or if it was in the past, even more so. I wanted historical accuracy because I believe that truth is superior to any guesswork or distortion. And in the present I wanted to thicken the texture by bringing out the background.

Q: It's so marked in your work that I wondered if even as a boy, before your literary period, history appealed to you.

A: It did, It did. I always enjoyed reading it, if I could find historians who were good writers. Even back in the days before I started really reading, I enjoyed reading history. I remember reading *The Conquest of Mexico* way before I was a reader, and I read it with great pleasure because it was well written. But skilled writing is not easy to come across in history. Most of our greatest historians have been nonprofessionals, all the way from Gibbon. They're not professional historians, so that it's hard to find a good writer who's willing to devote his time to writing history. They're not satisfied with history.

Q: History—specifically the Civil War, of course—has filled a great part of your work. And I noticed that you have Major Barcroft, in *Love in a Dry Season,* play Civil War games. I was wondering—where did you get this? Did you as a boy—is there any similar incident in your own background?

A: Not exactly. All that came as a result of reading various Civil War materials around my house. I knew, for instance, the mechanics of the battle of Fredericksburg, so I was pleased to be able to set them forth as Major Barcroft showed them to his little boy with the tin soldiers. But that was the result of some of that historical reading I enjoyed doing—

Q: That you did later. In your own boyhood the Civil War was not focused particularly.

A: Not particularly. I remember a couple of old veterans—I think they were probably drummer boys at the most, but I remember a couple of old men around town who were said to be Civil War veterans. They were probably ninety-five years old, and their connection with the war had probably been small.

Q: I noticed in *Tournament,* "Child by Fever," and parts of *Love in a Dry Season* the 1890s and the turn-of-the-century, up to the First World War, seemed particularly interesting to you. You have a great deal of information about the period. That seems a little odd. Any particular reason for that?

A: I think so, I'm fascinated by the year 1910, which I think is a sort of watershed year—how accurate that is is something else. In any case, I see it as a time when all the old America was still there and all the new America was coming on fast—men started flying in airplanes, women started smoking cigarettes, big things and little things; a Negro won the championship of the world—many things. I see it as a time when men stood and looked in both directions. And it was a curious time. Small town America in 1910 is still my notion of the happiest time on earth. And yet I have those people troubled at night in their sleep by the future that's moving against them so fast. It's a fascinating time, I think.

Q: Several characters in your work are observers. Sometimes you carry it to the extreme of voyeurism. Is this a device . . . it seems that it recurs as a kind of pattern. I wonder if there is any reason.

A: It does. Yes, I think that it does. It all ties in with my notion of what a novel is and what's at the middle of a novel. Many people many times have attempted to dramatize novels and stories of mine. They think they would make very good plays or movies. And they start trying to dramatize them and they discover that the main character doesn't *do* anything—which won't do, for their purpose. Nor does he express what he's thinking in conversations with people. In the story "Ride Out"—which many people have tried to dramatize, the movies are very anxious to make it until they start trying—the boy, the jazz musician in there, is very close to his mother. But they never communicate. His inability to communicate with her is part of the story, and if you do a play in which he communicates with her, you've destroyed the story. So I write novels; I don't write plays or movies. And I think this is a characteristic of novels.

Q: In what way?

A: I don't think you can take a really good novel and put it on the screen. They've put several of Faulkner's novels on the screen quite wretchedly—which proves my point. You can't put *Gatsby* on the screen; it won't go on the screen, unless you turn it into something different from *The Great Gatsby.*

Q: Because it is an observed—?

A: Yes, I think so. The silences are sometimes more important than the action. And I think that's what it *should* be in a novel. So I'm not surprised that you see this in my work; I do intend for it to be there. That's what my novels are about.

Q: To say this is another way—what you said in an article about history—that history (and movies) concentrates on action, the novel on reaction.

A: That's right. Yes. There've been many attempts to do things which seem obviously fated for the screen. Then they try to write them. *Tender is the Night* is full of action. It's perfect; it would make a marvellous movie, so they think. Actually, it can't make a movie at all. You have to turn it into something it's not to make a movie out of it. They did: it's a terrible movie.

Q: I have a novel called *The Prisoners,* about a penitentiary. Nothing could be better for the movies, they said. Till they got right down to it. Then they bought another book on the same subject, which they explained was more melodramatic.

A: That's right. They will do it every time. And they're right. They're exactly right. Those people know what they're doing, for all their shenanigans. There is, however, hope in that. The modern theater of the absurd can handle this—you can write a play nowadays about the fact that people can't communicate.
They can sit up there on that stage for an hour and a half and fail to communicate. And it's a play. But it would have to be something like the theater of the absurd, and then I'm not sure what would come across.

Q: You've said that you're not an "autobiographical" novelist, and yet that you want to write the truth and you never know the truth until you touch it. You say you've never consciously used a character from life without changing him. Yet some are so vivid, it's hard to believe that you didn't know something about them—for instance, Hugh Bart in *Tournament*. How did you come upon him?

A: He is based on my notion of my grandfather, who died about two years before I was born. And it's not even by hearsay; it's a notion not even prompted by hearsay. But I have seen men more or less like him, and I used things from people I've seen all over the place, of course. That's the only way you do get hold of reality. Reality doesn't come out of your head. It comes out of observation.

Q: This is a notion you put together from some things you heard about him but also much that you observed in other men who were like him?

A: That's right. That's right. The conception is one that's sort of a private notion of a man who died before I was born. What would he have been like if I had known him? That's the trigger mechanism. But what I made him was many men I have observed over the years.

Q: In Hugh Bart and Harley Drew and many other characters you draw impressively rounded figures. How do you go about characterization? How do you get such rounded figures?

A: If I do—and I hope I do—it's because I do what I approve of in a writer. I separate writers into two large categories. One of them says, "I would like to write a book about a situation in which a man does so-and-so." That's one type. The other type is, "I want to write a book about a man who—" and then you go into the situation. The man has to come first, for a good writer. It seems to me his concern is not with the idea for a novel, not the confrontation, but the two people confronting each other. And I hope that the people always come first with me. I think it's very important that they do. And I have never conceived a story as a situation. It has always been a man's character creating the situation.

Q: Do you get just the basic idea for the character first and then elaborate him? How do you go about elaborating him? Or is this the way it happens?

A: He elaborates himself, to a large degree. You put a man like Harley Drew in a town like Bristol and things are going to happen; they're going to naturally come about. He's going to be attracted to certain women, he's going to be attracted to certain financial finaglings, he's going to come into contact with people who oppose him because they have a nature different from his, he's very apt to pursue some woman whose father disapproves—because what father wouldn't disapprove? And the story really works itself out. Once you set him in the milieu, things start happening. And I don't mean they happen just in the course of your writing about it; I mean the minute you conceive it things start happening.

Q: But I mean even—this fascinates me in your characters, like Bart or Harley Drew—even down to the kind of fingernails they have. How do you get this?

A: I think all that is well worth while, and where you get it is that you say, "What kind of fingernails would Harley Drew have?"

Q: You do consciously ask yourself questions like this?

A: Not too consciously, but partly consciously; they just present themselves.

Q: It's your interest in people.

A: That's right.

Q: In other words it comes naturally to you to think up these details?

A: That's right. And I think the details nail them down in a way nothing else can. You take an invalid. Florence, in *Dry Season,* is an invalid. Well, I've seen invalids. I know how they smell; I know the particular waxy quality of their skin; I know the way their hair looks lank. I put all those things in Florence, and I hope she's the realer because of the things I put in there.

Q: Well, do you, as John P. Marquand is said to have done, write out dossiers, character sketches?

A: No, I write a careful outline of any work I'm going to do, but I never take notes of that kind. And I always write straight through a book, and I don't re-write, except in the tickiest kind of way—commas and such. But I write from start to finish. I don't think of a future scene and get it down on paper so I can pick it up when I get to it. I've never worked that way.

Q: You get it right before you turn it loose.

A: That's the notion. That's because, for me, revision would be a particular form of heartbreak. I just couldn't do it, this large-scale revision.

Q: What would you say is your average output in the middle of a novel?

A: Oh, 750 words is a good day; 1500 words is phenomenal.

Q: You say that you write a careful outline of your work. I was impressed with the detail, what James calls "solidity of specification." Again, do you achieve this from your careful outline? How do you get so many right details—the Rev. Clinkscales' ankle is broken, for instance, and it's always mentioned. Is this done with great care?

A: I tell you one peculiarity about me—I suppose it's a peculiarity. I have a very small visual quality. When I read a book I do not see a scene. When I write a scene I do not see people moving around. It's verbal with me. I read words and they go in my mind as words, not pictures—I don't mean I'm totally blank so far as pictures go, but I mostly read words and commas and semicolons. And when I write it's words and commas and semicolons. And I think that paradoxically this results in a particular attention to details, where you might think the pictures, the visual things would. But with me, it's words, and I want these words to tie in with these people. During the writing of *The Civil War* one of my projects—which I dropped—was for every major battle in that war to have a particular color or combination of colors. I remember Gettysburg was going to be gold and dusty blue. Sharpsburg was going to be copper and silver, Fredericksburg was going to be white and red. I let it go. I didn't work the symbolism on it. But this is an example of what I'm talking about. And forever after in the book, looking back at Gettysburg, there would be some touch in there, some way, about the shimmer of the golden wheat, or the copper-colored little stream running through Sharpsburg—Antietam Creek . . . all these things were going to give a touch of solidity to the book. And I'm sorry sometimes that I didn't keep on with it. These are tricks, or whatever you want to call them, that are very interesting to the writer. They don't have much to do with the reader.

Q: Well, I think they do with the reader. They help—

A: Well, the kind of reader I am.

Q: This would also account for the uncanny dialogue you write. You do what Mark Twain claimed to do in *Huck Finn*. You distinguish more than five kinds of dialect very carefully.

A: Well, I hope to have a good ear, because I make up in that for what I lack in the visual thing, I hope. I think it is important to hear the differences in people's speech. I think that Harley Drew speaks a syntax that identifies Harley Drew. I think Amanda talks the way she should. I think the Negroes talk the way they should. All these things are very important, as Mark Twain said. If it doesn't have that, it doesn't have anything; and that's where it gets it from, these small identifying characteristics.

Q: You've spoken of style as the produce of a private vision of life and of hard work in putting words together. Perhaps you don't want to comment on your private vision of life directly, but would you comment on your putting words together? How did you develop your style, would you say?

A: I don't really know. I think that early I learned from Hemingway that roughness should be a part of the smoothness. You could be a writer like Robert Nathan, I think he's called, or Thornton Wilder in *The Bridge of San Luis Rey,* and it won't do. With Hemingway it was new. You rough it up, mispunctuate, stick prepositions where they ought not to be, repeat words where a smooth writer would never repeat a word. It's these things that Hemingway learned, that I learned from him, I think, more than anyone—

Q: Faulkner also uses those.

A: Right. And always, always the writer has to have his rhythms. Prose rhythms are to me infinitely more interesting than poetical rhythms, which is why—a while ago you asked me if I didn't think the poet was superior: no, I don't think he's superior; I do not think he needs as much skill as the prose writer. Everything I write I test by reading aloud or reading to myself, and there have to be speech rhythms in what I write. My style is based on speech, always. I don't mean it necessarily makes beautiful listening, but it is based on speech rhythms rather than grammatical rhythms, or what is called syntactical. And I've been criticized for it, particularly by some New Englanders, for colloquialisms and this, that, and the other.

Q: The blend of speech rhythms and sometimes even colloquialisms with yet what seems a carefully preserved dignity of style impresses me in your work. Do you think about this much?

A: Yes, a great deal. And I think I know the basis for it. It's unquestionably the Bible. The Bible is the best written book I know, the solidity of that style. And it caused all sorts of things in my work. I remember in *Tournament*—something interested me enormously. I was writing and discovering while I was writing—I was describing a dream that a man named Jameson had. He had a dream in which he saw the pioneers come on the land and cut down the trees and then the farmers come along and plow the furrows. Then he re-dreamed it. Then it said, "The dream returned, comma, and the plowmen." This is an enormously interesting device to me: "The dream returned, and the plowmen." There's no question it's Biblical. And yet it had that quality of speech that I'm talking about. I can remember the day I wrote that, how excited I was over the discovery of this device—which had been discovered two thousand years before me. But it interested me very much. The way the Bible, for instance, uses the phrase "he said." You can repeat "he said" at certain points, in a monologue or an exchange of dialogue, and it puts a rhythm into the page and it puts a rhythm into the speech itself. All of these things—they're enormously interesting. They sound like foolishness, but they are really what make writing worth a grown man's time.

Q: They're part of the total vision of life, too.

A: That's right. There's a serious misconception about writers held by most laymen—I'll call them that; Jimmy Durante calls them civilians. Anyway, most people seem to think that a writer is a man who has acquired wisdom and wishes to impart it to a reader. He knows the answers, so he writes books to you. So far as I am concerned, this is totally false. I, for one, write books looking for answers, and after I've found them, if I'm lucky enough to find them, I'm not the least bit interested in doing it all over again. If I knew the answer I would not be interested in writing the book. It's a search for the answer. The question I ask is how does the man act in this situation, not what is the answer to our problems. I don't have any answers, except by hindsight—and by then I have moved on to other questions.

Q: Which of your works do you think is most successful?

A: *Successful* is a word, and so would *favorite* be a word, and so on. It would depend on the definition, whatever the word meant. But *Love in a Dry Season* is a great favorite of mine, not *the* favorite all the time, but it is a favorite of mine because of a sort of happy facility I had during the writing of it. So that I remember the writing of it with great affection. That doesn't mean anything. It has nothing to do with the worth of the book, either. But I do remember that I had great facility in writing the book and it was a pleasure to discover the facility—to get something down on paper just that way. It made me happy. And I also thought that it was a funny book, which helped a lot to make me feel pleasure about it.

Q: What about *Tournament*?

A: *Tournament* was a sort of thrashing around in the English language, a discovering that maybe I could write. I worked very hard on it, but it's all a blur now, let me say. I was thrashing around in the wilds in the English language, as I remember it, and looking at my homeland in a way I had never done before. And it was all very exciting to me, but it was so exciting that it's blotted itself out, more or less.

Q: Not for a reader—not for one reader.

A: Well, I did two drafts of it. *Tournament* was that book I wrote before the war and put in the closet. And when I got it out again, I saw that it wouldn't do. It was terrifically influenced by Joyce and Thomas Wolfe and various people. So I got it out and re-wrote it.

Q: That is why you didn't include it in *Three Novels,* as one of the three?

A: That's right.

Q: Then you tend to relegate it—to consider it an early mistake?

A: I would say I'm happy enough with it, as a first novel; but that's certainly what it is, a first novel. If I were to read it now I would need a dictionary to look up some of the words.

[At this point Foote brought out copies of his novels written as a final draft in his beautiful script and bound in beautiful old bindings.]

Q: You always work in longhand?

A: Yes. And then do a final draft in longhand, from which I make a typescript.

Q: One critic has seen the mode of Southern fiction, and much modern fiction, in fact, as what he called symbolic realism—adding something to Naturalism by letting whatever the Naturalism or realism portrays stand for something other than itself. I find little of the more elaborate symbolism in your work. Yet Hugh Bart, for instance, is suggestive of his era; he could be a kind of symbol of the society of that time and place, perhaps. And in *Love in a Dry Season* the various people—Drew coming in, the outsider coming in, Amanda representing the older way of society, and Jeff. Is this conscious on your part?

A: I suppose in a broader sense it's conscious. Symbolism is something I feel that, except in these very large conceptions of somebody representing rich people or poor people or liars or Ku Klux Klansmen—except in this larger sense, symbolism is something I think a writer had better let come unconsciously, or certainly naturally. There's a scene in "Ride Out" in which Duff Conway goes to a Negro reform school. And there's a band there, and in the band there's a boy with tuberculosis who plays a horn. The boy dies, and the warden of the school gives Duff the horn. Duff is going to die, as you might say, of tuberculosis and the electric chair; and he takes the horn in both hands and holds it against his chest, walking back to learn how to play it. Now the symbolism of taking this horn, filled with tuberculosis germs, and holding it against his chest, where the tuberculosis is going to take seat and kill him, is fairly obvious; but I was not at all aware of it when I wrote it. He hugged the horn to his chest because he considered it a precious thing; it seemed natural for someone who had hold of something he considered precious to hold it to his chest. It was only later on, when some critic pointed out the symbolism of it, that I perceived it. And that is, if I may say so, how symbolism should occur, not being supplied by the writer, but being discovered by the writer.

Q: In your conception of *Love in a Dry Season* these people were interesting people in themselves and not representatives—or were they both?

A: They were both. I do take Amy to be representative of a sort of a flapper crossed with the spoiled rich girl crossed with a touch of nymphomania crossed with this, that, and the other—crossed with selfishness.

Q: And rather typical of the morals of our time.

A: Yes, especially more sophisticated than the people she's living among. She was, in fact, much more sophisticated than the people she was living among; whereas Jeff, her husband, was not a sophisticated man at all, in any sense. He was a victim in almost every situation he figured in.

Q: What was the significance of his love of jazz, if any?

A: None, really, that I know of. It just seemed the kind of thing a blind man would do.

Q: In your work men are lonely and frustrated. In fact, at the beginning of *Tournament,* you speak of your central character as a man whom "facts shook and condition altered" and you have your narrator express the conviction "that each man, even when pressed closest by other men in their scramble for the things they offer one another with so little grace, is profoundly alone." This strikes me as close to the theme of your work.

A: It is. The basic loneliness of man is a thing that fascinates me. It even leads into paradox. I find the most isolated man on earth is a man in the moment of orgasm. A strange paradox, this little island of silence at the heart of the closest embrace. He's truly alone. I find him alone in orgasm, alone in nausea, utterly alone—not to mention at his death. And it absolutely fascinates me. At the time when you're closest to God, dying, you're the most alone. This whole thing interests me. And I think wisdom, if there is any, is going to have to proceed from a recognition of the basic loneliness of man. And all you can do is combat it. You can never be not alone. Never. But you can, working from a basis of recognizing the basic loneliness, achieve contact. But you can't achieve contact and be surprised at the loneliness that goes along with the contact, or the contact will be shattered.

Q: And the frustration—it's almost Hardyesque in your work.

A: Yes, a lot of that fate business. That's right. I would like for people to become so wise, in the way that a novelist is wise—which is not what people mean by wise—but I would like for him to be familiar with the workings of man's nature so that, under strain, he would be comforted by his knowledge. Henry James at his death is supposed to have said, "Ah, so this is it: the distinguished thing." That is wisdom, and it's a comforting thing to be able to face this last enemy with eagerness to recognize him. Because you know you're going to meet him, and going to meet him just as you thought you were going to meet him. That to me seems a wisdom infinitely beyond the wisdom that can be gotten reading philosophy. That's what I mean by a novelist's wisdom, which seems to me the finest kind of all. Which is why I respect the novel so much.

Q: Religion doesn't play a significant—

A: Almost none. Almost none. I have religious fanatics in my work, and so forth; I hope the Bible's all through there and the comfort they get from it, or the lack of comfort they get from it. But no, I'm not a religious man myself. Art is my religion if I have one.

Q: What, then, about the current fascination in literature with existentialism of various brands, Christian existentialism, atheistic existentialism?

A: I think there are a lot of things going into novels today that might better be put into essays, is all I can say to that. I think that by their direct striving to learn the nature of man they're way off the scent in learning the nature of man. Not that psychological observation is so much superior to philosophical observation. But there's a greater validity to it. You do know you've got hold of something when someone makes a psychological observation, such as that a man in fear has his hand shake. If his brain quivers I don't know it, but I know his hand shakes. I have no objection to anybody putting anything in a novel. But it does seem to me with the existentialists, for instance, it detracts from the novel, detracts from the narrative drive that has to be there. Now effective thinkers can have it. In fact, I sometimes think Dostoyevsky has more narrative drive than any writer who ever lived. And yet he was certainly a philosophical writer. But it's not his philosophical quality that gives his work that drive. It's his intense concern with people, and the very reality of the people to Dostoyevsky the writer.

Q: You have concerned yourself with history, with man's condition since the Civil War at least; and you've shown in your work a definite reaction to modernism, changes that have taken place. What do you suggest in man's future? Do you have any definite ideas on that?

A: I've got one definite idea. I think we're going to blow each other up. I don't think there's any doubt about it, not even a shadow of a doubt. We're just going to blast the face of the earth clean of man. I don't think there's any doubt about that.

Q: Would you predict any time?

A: No. No. But I think it's bound to happen, and to tell you the truth I don't really mind. If that's the way it's going to be, then that's the way it's going to be. I find it a downright companionable thought that we'll all go together, like scrambled eggs.

Shelby Foote's Love Affair with Civil War Began in '54

William Thomas/1973

From *The Commercial Appeal* [Memphis], 15 July 1973. Reprinted by permission of *The Commercial Appeal.*

One day almost 20 years ago, Memphis novelist Shelby Foote dipped an old-fashioned pen into an ink well and began writing *The Civil War: A Narrative.* This is how it went:

"It was a Monday in Washington, January 21; Jefferson Davis rose from his seat in the Senate. South Carolina had left the Union a month before, followed by Mississippi, Florida and Alabama . . . The occasion was momentous and expected; the galleries were crowded, hoop-skirted ladies and men in broadcloth come to hear him say farewell. He was going home."

That scene, which begins the prologue to Foote's vast, three-volume history of the Civil War, was written in 1954. It was an incredibly long time ago. Foote was then living on the bluff near the Memphis-Arkansas Bridge. It was the year the French got kicked out of Vietnam after Dien Bien Phu; the year Sen. Joseph McCarthy was condemned by the Senate; the year the Supreme Court outlawed segregation in public schools. It was all a very long time ago.

"Back then, if somebody had told me it would take 20 years to write the history of the Civil War," says Foote, now, "I would have said, 'Sorry, but I'm a novelist and I have other things to do.'

"Originally, I thought it was going to take a year or two at the most. I didn't find out what a job it was going to be until after I got into it. By then, I not only had no choice—I didn't want any choice. I was completely fascinated. The Civil War is truly one of the great subjects of the world—the last romantic war and the first modern war combined. Even after I saw it was going to take three volumes to hold it, I wanted to go ahead with it."

And that's precisely what Foote has been doing all this time. Every morning, between 8:30 and 8:45, he walks into the writing room in the rear of his home, 542 East Parkway South, where he feels like a recluse, and sits down at a desk laid with pens, paper and plenty of ink. "Someday, I'm going to figure out how many quarts of ink I've used on the war," he says.

"I work office hours. I stay at it until about 4:30 p.m. every day. I haven't known many writers who did this. Somerset Maugham said it was a mistake to work more than two or three hours a day. Faulkner once told me the only rule he knew was not to work when you are tired. But I work so slowly that I have to put in long hours to get anything done."

By "slowly," Foote means that he turns out between 600 and 1,000 words a day. It's not a lot, especially if whatever you're working on is going to run 1½ million words in its final form. However, it's enough for Shelby Foote, who is not the hurrying kind. (He once told an interviewer that he thought exercise could kill you.)

"I'm working with a very large canvas," says he, "but at the same time, I'm trying to do each paragraph the way you'd write a sonnet. I'm trying for precision on a large scale. It's a fascinating exercise."

Sometimes, it's also a frustrating one. "I do very little rewriting, so I have to work out everything as I go along. If I'm in the middle of a sentence and a quote comes to mind that I want to use, and I can't find it, everything stops. I'll remember that it's in a green book on a left-hand page on a lower shelf, somewhere. Half the time, I can't find it. But eventually, it turns up. It just takes a while."

The first volume, which carries the war from Fort Sumter to Perryville, took about five years. It runs 810 pages. The second volume, which goes from Fredericksburg to Meridian, took another five. It is 966 pages. (Both books were published by Random House.) The last volume, which ends with the funeral of Jefferson Davis, is still being written. However, it is almost done. Foote says, "I'm on page 1,300-and-something . . . I can finish by spring."

If everything goes according to plan, Foote will wind it up in time for publication in November 1974. That being the case, he will have spent 10 years on the last volume, 20 years on the trilogy.

With the end in sight, most people probably would be pushing to get the thing done. Not Shelby Foote. That is not his style. He continues to write with dipped pen and ink, taking his time, typing it up later on big yellow sheets that hold the same number of words as a page in the book.

Why the pen and ink? "I don't want anything mechanical between me and the paper," he says, not even a fountain pen. It's a wonder I don't write with a quill."

Partly, the pace is set by Foote's fine, meticulous, careful prose. Partly, it's due to a natural reluctance to wind up something on which he has spent 20 years of his life.

"Now that I'm drawing near the close of it," he said, "I have very mixed feelings. It's almost as if I don't know what I'll do with myself after I've written the last line. It's very strange to spend 20 years on a thing and then be through with it. Like someone you love dying.

"I remember a thing (Edward) Gibbon wrote about the night he finished *Decline and Fall*. His first feeling was one of elation. Then, a great sadness. I feel a certain kinship with Gibbon. My *Civil War* and his *Decline and Fall* are about the same length (1½-million words). They are taking about the same amount of time to write."

At a glance, Shelby Foote seems the obvious person to write up the war. Born in Greenville, Mississippi, in 1916, he not only fell under the influence of William Alexander Percy, planter-poet-essayist, but he grew up in a land where the Civil War is a natural part of the regional consciousness.

"Actually, we talked little in Greenville about the war," he said. "I heard it mentioned often when I would go North. Whenever Northerners met somebody from Mississippi, I guess they don't know what else to talk about.

"Even so, I do remember little things in Greenville that had to do with the war. There were three or four old men around who had been drummer boys. Also, I still have in my memory some obscene doggerel about Abraham Lincoln." (He recited the doggerel. It was too bad to put in the newspaper.) A "damned lie."

"Another thing I remember is that we didn't have a Fourth of July. I mean it. There weren't any fireworks and the stores didn't close, except for the post office, which was federal. I remember a man coming to live in Greenville from Ohio or someplace north.

"One Fourth of July, he loaded his wife and children in the car and they went up on the levee to have a picnic. He forgot to put on the brake, and the car rolled down the levee and went into the river. There was considerable delight in town about that. People said it served him right for celebrating the Fourth."

As for Civil War history, Foote is convinced that most of what he heard as a boy in Mississippi was misconception. "It was how a noble nation, the South, founded on the highest ideals, perished because of the oppression of a stronger power. The story was that in the course of its four-year existence the Confederacy was never guilty of the slightest stain or smudge.

"Honor was the principle and it was never violated. On both sides, I think there was a feeling that superior people were fighting a superior war. One historian makes the point that if we were as superior as we thought we were we would have avoided that war."

Although he read Civil War books like other people read detective stories, Foote never considered doing a history until long after he was established as a fiction writer. He sold the first story he ever wrote to the *Saturday Evening Post.* "The story was 24 typewritten pages long," he recalls. "They said if I would cut it to 22 pages, they'd accept it. I re-typed it with two more lines on each page and sent it back on 22 pages."

Foote's first novel, *Tournament,* was published in 1948. He wrote a novel a year for five years. One of them, *Follow Me Down,* was attacked in 1959 by a small band of American Legionaries who thought it was a dirty book. They took it and D. H. Lawrence's *Lady Chatterley's Lover* out to the Memphis city dump where they had their pictures made dumping the books. Foote's comment was, "I consider it an honor to be put in the same class with such a writer as Mr. Lawrence."

After publishing five novels, Foote received a letter from the late Bennett Cerf asking him if he'd like to do a short history of the Civil War. It was to be part of an historical series which Random House was planning to publish.

"They wanted only about 200,000 words," Foote recalls, "and it seemed like a good way to spend a year or two between the first five novels and what I planned as the second five novels. So I began to write this thing. I'd no more gotten started when I saw there wouldn't be much point in writing another short history of the Civil War. I decided to take my fling at it and let it run whatever length it had to run. Before I'd written 100 pages I knew it was going to have to be done in three volumes."

Although he never expected to spend 20 years on the Civil War—that's five times longer than it took to fight it—Foote says he realized early that the trilogy was going to take him a while. "By the time I was half-way through the first volume," he says, "I saw that it was going to take perhaps four years a volume, which is a hell of a long time, but I decided to go ahead anyway. By then, I was into it, you see."

The last volume is taking longer than the others partly because Foote has interrupted his routine a number of times. He spent a year as playwright-in-residence at the Arena Stage in Washington and another year as writer-in-residence at the University of Virginia. After that, he went to Alabama to see if he wanted to live down there, then spent a year in Raleigh waiting for his present house to become available. "I've never been able to work unless I'm settled down some place," he says.

"We moved into this house seven years ago and things have been coming along pretty good ever since. The frightening thing about it, though, is that I not only feel like a recluse here—I like the feeling. I like staying away from the sweat and scramble, especially since it's getting sweatier and scramblier out there all the time."

The house is big and masculine. It is half-hidden by greenery in front and by a high wall in back. The writer lives there with his wife, Gwyn, blonde and attractive, and his son, Huger Lee, who is of Boy Scout age. There is an older daughter, too, but Foote says she is out in the world. There is an old, black handyman named John Henry Cannon, whom Foote says he has never quite figured out.

"I've always heard Southerners say how well they know Negroes because they've lived around them all their lives. Well, I sometimes think I and most Southerners know less about Negroes than anybody else on the face of the Earth."

The writing room is near the rear of the house. The ceiling is high and beamed and there is an old-world feeling about the place. A fireplace is built into the back wall. An oriental rug is on the floor. A model airplane hangs on a string from the ceiling. Foote built it. There is a bed, and next to the bed are a bunch of pictures of Civil War personalities: soldiers, generals, presidents and the like.

Pinned to the wall above the desk are a number of notes that Foote has written to remind himself to put this or that piece of information into the story at the proper time. One note tells about a Confederate soldier who shouted across the lines to a Northern soldier, saying: 'Why don't you come over to our side? We're fighting for honor and you're fighting for money.' The Northerner supposedly shouted back, 'Well, I reckon each of us is fighting for what we need the most.'

Even with the help of the notes as well as a master schedule covering the events of the war, the job of organizing the materials is almost beyond comprehension. The primary sources are the 128-volume *War of the Rebellion,* a compilation of the official records of the Union and Confederate Armies; and the 30 volumes of official records of the Union and Confederate Navies.

These were issued by the federal government between 1880 and 1927. In addition, Foote has visited every major battlefield of the war and walked the ground in the same season the battle was fought in order to get a feeling of the time and the place.

"For me, this has been one of the great rewards to come out of the work. When you write the truth about something—about what happened on a particular piece of ground like Shiloh or the bluffs at Memphis—then that ground belongs to you forever. It's a very large reward. So one of the things I've learned from writing this history is a true love of the South and a knowledge of its geography.

"Shiloh is one of the best battlefields; Gettysburg is one of the worst. Gettysburg is all ice cream and hot dog stands. It's a real mess. Perryville, Kentucky, on the other hand, is wonderful because nobody knows where it is or anything about it. It's just like it was. Pea Ridge, Arkansas, is great, too. There used to be a funny little lady living at Pea Ridge. She had a funny mouth. Her tongue didn't fit her mouth, as I remember."

Not surprisingly, Foote is more interested in the characters who lived during the Civil War. He is especially fascinated by his two main protagonists, Lincoln and Davis.

"Both are marvelous characters, each in his own way," he says. "The funny thing is the way time has reversed their roles. Lincoln is known as the great emancipator, the man of infinite tenderness. And yet, the records show that he approved the execution of 267 men during the course of the war. Davis never approved the execution of a single man.

"Lincoln hung 32 Indians out in Minnesota one morning. It was the largest public hanging ever held in the U.S. The Indians were in headdress, singing the death song. Originally, Lincoln had been given a list of 120 to hang. He cut it to 32. I don't say he was wrong. I just say it doesn't fit his public image."

Foote lit his pipe. "Actually, Lincoln was as compassionate as everybody thought he was in spite of the executions. His eyes were red with weeping about some of the things that happened. He walked the corridors at night in great distress.

"Jeff Davis, who was called a cold, bloodless creature, never wept any tears at all. He just refused to hang people. The truth is, they were both gentle and compassionate men."

The quality that many people miss in Lincoln, says Foote, is his extraordinary intelligence. "He had a mind of steel and an ego that did not need propping up. Nothing pleased Lincoln more than to have an opponent think he was an idiot. It was like swiping somebody with a razor and then telling them to shake their head.

"What Lincoln had was an extreme intelligence. But the war wore him down. If you look at a photograph when he took office and another before he was assassinated, he looks like he aged 20 years."

In writing his history of the war, Foote has aged that much, too. The picture on the dust jacket of the first volume looks almost boyish compared to Foote's gray-bearded appearance today. "When I started the history," says Foote, who has had six beards, "I was younger than the South's Jeb Stuart. When I finish it, I will be a year older than Lincoln (who was 56) when he was assassinated."

Such historical awareness seems to come naturally for Foote. And yet, though he has been studying the war for almost 20 years, he insists that he does not consider himself a historian. "Of course, I expect to answer for any inaccuracies in the work," he says, "but I am a writer, not a professional historian. I even admit to a certain sympathy for the underdog. (The South.)

"Still, I don't have anything I want to prove in writing about the war. The reason is: I'm absolutely convinced that I could prove just about anything I wanted to. I once saw a paper some place proving that the South lost the war because it didn't have enough grease for the wagon axles. I'm sure that's true.

"As far as my *Civil War* is concerned there are serious gaps in it. I have left things out on purpose. For instance, I do not go into the financial difficulties of the Confederacy. These are enormously important if you want to really understand why the South lost.

"I think professional historians are going to be able to point out shortcomings like this in my work. It doesn't bother me. Finances are not important to MY story of the war, so I leave it out. Actually, it weighs a feather against a ton compared to the military situation—and that is what interests me and what lends itself to the narrative."

"You've got to remember that the Civil War was as big as life," he explains. "That's why no historian has ever done it justice, or ever will. But that's the glory of it. Take me: I was raised up believing Yankees were a bunch of thieves. But it's absolutely incredible that a people could fight a Civil War and have so few atrocities.

"Sherman marched with 60,000 men slap across Georgia, then straight up through the Carolinas, burning, looting, doing everything in the world—but I don't know of a single case of rape. That's amazing because hatreds run higher in civil wars.

"One side looks at the other side as either traitors or despots. In this war, however, soldiers apparently were so horribly mishandled on both sides that they felt a comradship with everybody who was being butchered."

One reason the casualties ran so high, Foote says, was because the war was fought with modern weapons and old tactics. "They had rifles that would kill you at 800 yards, and generals who wanted troops to line up shoulder-to-shoulder and march across open ground.

"There were still a lot of antique virtues around them. Jackson once told a colonel to advance his regiment across a field being riddled by bullets. When the officer protested that nobody could survive out there, Jackson told him he always took care of his wounded and buried his dead. The colonel led his troops into the field."

One of Foote's best little stories involves the capture of a ragged-looking Confederate soldier who obviously never owned a slave in his life. When they asked him what he was fighting for, the

Southerner told them, 'because you all are down here.' That, says Foote, "was a hell of a good answer."

In 1961, while he and his wife were on a trip to New York, Foote bought a very special bottle of wine. It was Mouton Rothschild, '59, which, says Foote, was a good year. "Back then, I paid about $60 for it. Now, it's worth $250 or $300. It's so damn high it's almost a shame to drink it. But the day I write the last line of the Civil War, that's what we're going to do." And after that, he's going to write some novels.

WKNO Presents a Conversation with Shelby Foote

James Newcomb/1978

He was born and reared in the Delta and now lives and writes here in Memphis. To say Shelby Foote is a novelist, of course, is to say what is obvious. Yet when a writer goes twenty years without publishing a novel, we may need to be reminded that he is a novelist, and when he spends those twenty years writing a three-volume history of the Civil War, a work that wins him worldwide fame, we may be justified in forgetting that Shelby Foote is a novelist. But now Shelby Foote has returned to writing novels, recently publishing the widely acclaimed *September September*, a work set in Memphis in 1957, and because he lives and works here among us, we should take a closer look at this man.

Born in 1916, the only child of Shelby Dade Foote and Lillian Rosenstock Foote, Shelby Foote grew to young manhood in Greenville, Mississippi. Left fatherless at the age of six, he nonetheless grew up in one of the richest literary environments in America, counting among his friends the novelists William Alexander Percy, Walker Percy, and William Faulkner. As a teenager, he worked as a reporter on Hodding Carter's newspaper, and then went off to college at the University of North Carolina at Chapel Hill. The clouds of war gathering in Europe brought him home to join the Mississippi National Guard. He saw service in the Army artillery in France, rising to the rank of Captain.

After the war he returned to the Delta and began his career as a novelist, publishing five novels between 1949 and 1954. Then he began his twenty-year odyssey on *The Civil War*, a work of over one and one-half million words. This work was written in Memphis, the final volume in Shelby Foote's present home on East Parkway.

Though he is perhaps best known for his monumental work on the Civil War, Shelby Foote began his career as a novelist and continued as a novelist. In order to learn more about him and his works, our cameras visited Shelby Foote in his home in the room where he works. Talking with him about himself and his work is James Newcomb, assistant professor of English at Memphis State University.

Newcomb: When you were at Chapel Hill, you didn't let the classwork interfere with your education and spent two years in the library?

Foote: Not literally—I went to classes, but I dropped things that I really found onerous, like math. I had no more to do with that—after about the first half of the freshman year.

Newcomb: What did you read in the library?

Foote: I read all kinds of things. I read facsimiles of Shakespearean quartos, for example. I read things that were not available anywhere else, really, that amazed me to find. I got interested in some particular things. If I were interested in Shelley at home, all I could read was Shelley. I found five or six shelves full of books about Shelley at that library. You must realize we had almost no library at home in Greenville. The public library had Viña Delmar and Rex Beach—a lot of forgotten people mostly—so that was very exciting to me to find critical writings and things like that. I had a caution I observed very early on though: at no time during those years was I ever tempted to take anything like creative writing or anything like that. I stayed assiduously away from such things as that. I took a good course on the English novel, under a man named MacMillan, whom I liked very much. I took a lot of English courses because I liked them, but no creative courses. I took a couple of philosophy courses that I liked a lot—I used to sit in on graduate classes. You see, credit meant nothing to me and grades meant nothing to me, but what they were teaching meant a lot to me. I took a block of languages because they meant a lot to me; so I have very small smatterings of German and French and Spanish and Latin. I never stayed with one of them long enough to learn it, but I learned what it was about.

Newcomb: How long did you stay in Chapel Hill?

Foote: Two years.

Newcomb: Two years? Did you go directly into the service from there?

Foote: Yes, well, indirectly into the service. When Hitler went into Poland in September of 1939, I went into the Mississippi National Guard. I felt very strongly that we should be in the war—to stop Hitler—so I joined the Mississippi National Guard, and it was a year from that time before we mobilized—we didn't mobilize until November of 1940—so I spent that year in Greenville not going to college, and, in fact, I wrote my first novel during that time.

Newcomb: Did you publish that novel?

Foote: No, I sent it off to a publisher, Alfred A. Knopf, and they wrote back that they liked it very much, but they thought it would not sell. It was too experimental in nature, and what they were really interested in was my second novel, and they advised me to put that one away and come back to it after I had written a second one. I thought that was good advice, so I put it away, but instead of starting my second one, I went on into federal service, and I was away five years before I came home again.

Newcomb: Did you ever go back to that first novel?

Foote: Yes, indeed. I came back home and wrote *Shiloh,* and then got that first one out of the closet where I had put it—and really liked it. I did see that the editors had been right in their judgment of it, so I rewrote and published it as my first novel called *Tournament.*

Newcomb: That is *Tournament* and that was the experiment? Did you take a lot of the experimentation out of it?

Foote: I took a lot of that out.

Newcomb: Did you recast it? *Shiloh* seems to me more experimental.

Foote: It wasn't recast all that much. It was mostly to stop imitating Faulkner and Thomas Wolfe, and various other people, and I saw that I had done that rather clumsily too, so I took that out, but I didn't change the story or anything like that, I just brought the language down off of a high falsetto. Some of that is still left in it. When I read *Tournament* now, I have to use my dictionary—I was so crazy about words.

Newcomb: Well, there's the dynastic element in it.

Foote: Yeah, that's all stated there, and a lot has grown out of that in my later work.

Newcomb: Did you envision pursuing this dynastic element? It appears elsewhere in your work.

Foote: Yes, I did. I saw that this first novel was something to build on, even at the time I was writing it, and I had many stories connected with it in my mind that I did not include in the novel that I knew I would pick up on later on. By no means everything I wrote, but some of what I wrote later on was picking up on those leftover things. What *Tournament* did—besides some other things—is establish a geography. Jordan County was laid down, Bristol was where it was, Ithaca was where it was, the lake was where it was. The county in general is industrial in the northern part and agricultural in the southern part, so it's a microcosmos of the upper country, in a sense. All those things were quite conscious from the start. I built on them in later books.

Newcomb: If I can—without sounding too much like a professor —ask about some things in the novels. There is one scene that is not to me just a recurrence, it's almost a repetition: the son who has not been up to snuff, who comes home . . .

Foote: It happens all of the time in my work and happens all the time in the Mississippi Delta. The whole story of the Delta is the failure of the following generation to measure up to the one that came before it. Now for all I know that's the story for all the counties in the United States, but in the Delta it recurs over and over. It's because credit is easy—that's one reason—people get into bankruptcy very easily in the Mississippi Delta. The other one is a more pernicious thing that will take some examination. Delta men are not inclined to turn loose of their authority so that you will find fifty-year-old men still working for their daddies and running to get cigarettes from the plantation store for him. They do that to the young down there, as a fairly common thing. What they do to the son-in-laws just shouldn't be told. They cripple them up something awful.

Newcomb: There is an interesthing thing—in two of your novels—the son who is in this position, and over the holidays, he finally makes a move on his own and marries. He comes home with the bride and the parents immediately think that the kid has been drinking. And in both cases, the boy speaks nonstop at locomotive spead, full throttle to tell what he has done and it is a disaster.

Foote: Well, he's a crippled person to start with, looking for some little wife to save him, and in both of those cases, I think he picked the wrong little wife. (*Laughs*)

Newcomb: It's strange, though, that taking a wife should be considered a form of salvation. Is this common?

Foote: Yes, quite common—and by no means limited to the Mississippi Delta. Girls get married for the same reason. They are liable to marry any scamp that comes along to establish their independence. But the boy in this case seems to be trying to establish his dependability, his commitment to life or something. It doesn't work very well.

Newcomb: In both cases, he is coming back to authoritarian parents, and say, "You see, I can do something well."

Foote: Well, I'll tell you one thing. You may find scenes from *Tournament* recurring in the other books rather repeatedly. It's out of print now. Nobody can get it and I consider *Tournament* a sort of grab bag into which I can reach and get anything, and recast it, and frequently do—or used to anyhow because *Tournament* is a thing out of my past.

Newcomb: To change the subject slightly, in addition to being a novelist, are you also a book designer?

Foote: I think of books as books—that's right—I know how I want them to look.

Newcomb: I wonder if you are a modern Blake.

Foote: I have never set any type or drawn any pictures.

Newcomb: Well, maybe not set the type, but you have drawn . . .

Foote: I often make up a dummy and send it to the designer at the publisher, as a suggestion that he might want to follow.

Newcomb: I have seen some things in your *Love in a Dry Season,* is it? The Δ?

Foote: Yeah, the use of the Δ for dividing things. I use that in the new book too—and I use it in *Jordan County.*

Newcomb: But also when you write, the very physical act of writing, as if you are composing a book, pre-Gutenberg.

Foote: I do that for a reason which I think I understand and that is I think of good writing being done in a very deliberate way. That's why I use a dip pen and pay attention to how the words look on the page. It's to slow myself down and to keep myself from rushing the writing. I like to write slowly.

Newcomb: Will you rush without your dip pen?

Foote: I am not going to find out.

Newcomb: At first, when I looked at the pages in your hand, I thought this was an italic hand, a very studied one.

Foote: It's not really like that.

Newcomb: If you don't mind my saying so, it looked affected, but then I realized this is not the graduate student's italic hand that he labors so hard to make sure his signatures will always look good.

Foote: I am always kind of surprised when people find it hard to read—and I guess it is—but the one characteristic that I know it has is that no letter looks like any other letter. You don't mistake an *n* for a *u* or an *e* for an *i*, and that's the basis for it. Every letter is of a completely different shape from every other letter.

Newcomb: You had your earlier novels bound in beautiful bindings. Why did you not do this when you started writing the *War*? Is this a Mississippian trait;, by the way? Is there only one war?

Foote: Yeah, that's called the War, and the rest of them are identified, the First World War, the Second World War, the Spanish-American War, but when someone says the War, it means the Civil War. Now you have to make one exception to this; it could also apply to the latest war. During the Vietnam War when you spoke of the War, you would have to say the Civil War, but now there is no war going on, if I referred to the War, it would almost certainly be the Civil War, unless I was referring to my war which is the Second World War. But I would never refer to any of the others as the War.

Newcomb: I am curious as to why you did not copy out and bind *The Civil War: A Narrative*, as you did the novels. Had you thought you were doing something that wasn't like writing a novel?

Foote: I saw a difference since the others came entirely out of my head or memory, but in any case out of my head, and this was researched out of documents, and I simply did not find the physical manuscript itself as interesting to save. I wrote it as carefully. I did the same thing of making fair copies of everything as I went along, but then I used them to build fires with. Except for the last two-thirds of the third volume—it's in those thirteen boxes there. That's just the last two-thirds of the third volume, but you can see if I had saved all of that stuff, there wouldn't be any room in this room.

Newcomb: It would have kept you warm anyway. I want to talk about the War, but first let's go back to something you said earlier about fathers in the Delta crippling the next generation by not wishing to let go. Is this true of Memphis also?

Foote: No, I don't think so. This crippling thing mainly has to do with planters, who are not willing to see the land abused by a young man who doesn't know what he is doing, and he is also scared to death that he will lose the thing. In business this is true somewhat, but not nearly as much so as with regard to the farms where it involves not only land, but—especially in the old days—dealing with labor. The secret to a good farmer down home was a man who knew how to get the most work out of some people who were willing to do as little work as possible. He was afraid of the young man on that account, too. And he had a profound mistrust of innovations, which the young man was apt to be very interested in, rotating crops and things like that. Now I suppose all of that has changed a great deal in the last twenty-odd years, with the new innovations in farming, but it was certainly that way up to then. He seemed not able to turn loose, not able to sit back and watch a young man learn how to run a plantation.

Newcomb: I guess it could be lost a great deal more quickly than it could be built up . . . In the twenty some years from the time you published one novel to the next, is there any chance that the novel has changed where you haven't?

Foote: Yes, there is a good chance of that. The novel has become a lot opener, a lot more experimental, the average novel has. There is no novel today more experimental than *Ulysses* was in 1922, but the average novel has become more highly experimental. The novel certainly has opened up with regard to censorship or the absence of it. But I don't feel that break did anything to me except sharpened my perceptions by writing history. I felt just as much at home in what I called the close atmosphere of the novel in 1976, as I did in 1956. I feel just the same way. I worried about it some. I had a big family novel that I wanted to write. Before setting to it, I thought I would write a short novel to get my hand back in, so I wrote *September September* for that purpose, but I found myself just as absorbed in the work with very much the same attitude toward it as I had when I left the novel in the early '50s.

Newcomb: None of your novels are these overly long, Thomas

Wolfe kinds of things, and I wondered if this is what prompted Random House way back to plan for a history of the Civil War?

Foote: The original contract for the Civil War narrative called for a short history of the Civil War, which was to run about two hundred thousand words, and I thought it would take me a year and one-half or so to write, and I was very interested in doing it, so I signed a contract to do it. And I had no sooner started than I saw I was not going to be interested in writing any short résumé of the Civil War, so I went on spread eagle, and the whole thing ran a million six hundred thousand words, and I saw—as far as I was concerned—I could't do it in less. It had to be three big volumes, and Random House was very decent about it. They said, "OK. Go." So I did.

Newcomb: What had Random House seen in your novels . . . ?

Foote: I don't really know. Bennett Cerf was the one who approached me to do it, and just what he had seen that made him think I could write a short history of the Civil War, I am not too sure. I guess he liked what he had read and thought that I would be able to carry that over. It was to have been the beginning of a series that Random House was going to do on history, something like the Landmark Series or whatever Doubleday calls their historical series of books and this was going to be the first one. They didn't go on with it and this would not have been the first one anyway.

Newcomb: *The Civil War: A Narrative* appears to hold together as a unified work from start to finish.

Foote: It was planned that way. It was outlined, climaxes were distributed.

Newcomb: For the entire war?

Foote: Yes, for the entire war—and in more detail for each section as I approached it. If you will notice all three volumes, each of the three is divided into three sections that balance each other. The climaxes are distributed so that you will want to know what is going to happen in the next chapter. The writing of the *War* gave me an intense pleasure because it enabled me to go all out at a job that I think is enormously interesting, and that is plotting. Plotting is a fascinating business, and this was an exercise—a gigantic exercise in the handling of plot and I enjoyed it enormously. I go from point of view to point of view. I am with Jefferson Davis, then I am with Abraham Lincoln, and I will drop back to some general in the field,

Lee, say, or Grant, and move the reader around among these things so as to produce dramatic confrontations distributed throughout the story. That's what plotting is—and it interested me very much. It interested me also to do no violation whatsoever to the truth so far as I could learn it in this process. I didn't wrench anything out of shape so as to make it fit better. The problem was, without destroying its shape, to fit it in properly. It was like a huge jigsaw puzzle, in part.

Newcomb: But obviously very successful, no question about that, commercially, and reviewed well. But I find it strange—you say you enjoy plotting—yet one novel of yours that gets mentioned less than the others, *Love in a Dry Season*, seems to me to be more carefully plotted than the other novels.

Foote: I have great affection for that novel. The other thing I like about it is that it's funny, most of it. I like that in a work. I think no good writer ever wrote a single page that didn't have something funny on it. It might be sardonic or wry, but anyway, it was funny, had some form of humor. I think without that, writing is dead on the page. Shakespeare knew that superbly. If you read *Macbeth,* the irony of *Macbeth* almost weighs down every line that is spoken, and it's funny as hell. It's raining and, as the murderer drives the dagger home, he says let it come down. Those things Shakespeare knew superbly well. He knew how to relieve tension with laughter. In *Macbeth,* the porter's speech about the knocking at the gate, that's what it's for. That's what plotting is: an increase of tension, a release of tension, an increase of tension, a release of tension makes for greater tension later on. That's what plotting is: that something happened to you and you want to tell somebody about it. The best way is to sit down and think for a minute how you are going to organize the telling and then, when you tell it, it will be interesting to you as well as to who is listening because of the technical problem.

Newcomb: And yet you did something in this history that I think seems unexpected. It's characterization, too. Of course, there are individuals, personalities in history, but in *The Civil War: A Narrative,* they are individuals, but they are characters, too.

Foote: Well, the beautiful thing in writing about the Civil War—far more than any other war I know of—although I haven't researched the Napoleonic Wars really well—but in the Civil War the material is enormous and that's the beauty of it. If you want to know what kind of nose Grant had, somebody has described it; if you want to know if he had a wart on his left cheek or not, somebody mentions it. There is an enormous wealth of material. Crazy as it sounds—I spent twenty years writing those three big volumes—I could go back now and spend the next twenty years doing that same three-volume set over again and use a completely different set of material. As long as it is, I left out as much as I used and a lot of good stuff, too.

Newcomb: Had you been a student of the Civil War before?

Foote: Yes, I read certain Civil War things when I was a boy, practically the way other people read detective stories.

Newcomb: Did it seem presumptuous at first, to move into this—I am thinking here you are a novelist . . . ?

Foote: It didn't to me then; it does now. Looking back, how, in God's name would I take on that size of a job? How could I presume to tell the rest of the world about the United States and the Civil War and sit in judgment on Robert E. Lee? It seems madness now. I would not have started the *War* if I had had any idea that it was going to take twenty years out of the middle—or what I hope is the middle of my writing life. I am not sorry I did, but I don't think I would have had the nerve to do that, if I had known.

Newcomb: Do you know what it is in you as a person or as a writer that has a rage for symmetry in *The Civil War: A Narrative* and in your novels?

Foote: No, I don't. I don't know what that is. I told you before that I never knew what I was going to do with my life if I hadn't been a writer. There was a time when the one thing other than writing that I have ever been really interested in was architecture. I used to love to draw plans of houses and things. I never knew how they were going to look after they got built, but I did know the arrangement of the rooms which was what interested me.

Newcomb: Strange. Back to the question of characterization in the *Narrative*: did you know which characters were going to be heroes—a kind of old-fashioned word—when you began writing?

Foote: I found out some strange things. When you are writing a novel, if you get hot, as you call it, the characters tend to take over. They rear up on their own hind legs and do things that you hadn't expected them to do. So did the characters in *The Civil War*, in the sense that some people most of the Civil War buffs have contempt for turned out to be warm, nice people. Some of the people that were great heroes turned out to look to me like scamps. And that same thing happens in the novel, so I am very pleased that that happened. This is not a question of delivering some judgment on them and making them conform to my judgment. I wouldn't do that—that's a bad kind of distortion. That's what happens in romantic novels, for which I have nothing but contempt. But they did rear up on their hind legs, the same way a character does in a novel.

Newcomb: I am thinking of individuals such as Princess One-Eyed. I had never heard of her until I read *The Civil War: A Narrative*, or Pat Cleburne, a general from Arkansas. First of all, someone mildly interested in the war could assume there never was a general from Arkansas and that Arkansas was never in the war, but here is this man and we meet him in volume I. Did you like him then, because it's obvious . . . ?

Foote: Yes, Pat Cleburne is a lot of people's favorite. Cleburne, in his lifetime, was sometimes called the Stonewall Jackson of the West. He's been nearly forgotten now, but he probably was the most accomplished division commander in either army. Pat Cleburne's division, which was made up of Arkansans, Mississippians, and Texans, was a pistol-hot outfit. They were something—they never gave up one yard of ground, except under orders to give way, and they never failed to take any objective assigned to them, except at Franklin where Cleburne was killed.

Newcomb: When one reads the *Narrative*, one wants to know where is Pat Cleburne. Where is this old friend? I talked to a woman who read this, and she had to put it down; she wept. One doesn't pick up *The Civil War* to see which side is going to win or to see if this General Grant is going to survive, but if one has never heard of Pat Cleburne, and one wants to know did he die in 1918 in his bed, and you find this man was killed in battle and you say there was a waste; there was a good man. This is what I mean by characters.

Foote: Well, I hope so. That's a supreme compliment which I am happy to receive. I wanted that very much. That's the way it affected me, so I wanted it to affect other people that way. You meet a lot of people in the course of writing something like that and you can acquire an enormous affection for them, and when they get killed you can be greatly saddened, just as their soldiers were saddened by their loss. I found another thing in the war that is funny. There are certain real scamps, bad men. Lincoln's secretary of war, Edwin Stanton, was a bad man—really a bad man—a coward, a bully, many bad things, and I acquired great affection for him, such as Dickens may have had for Bill Sikes. He livened the page; there he is shaking with fear. He is marvelous; I like him very much. There are some others I didn't like. I acquired a growing distaste and dislike for Phil Sheridan on the Northern side, who was a blustery fellow I had no use for, and Joe Johnston on the Confederate side, one of the great Confederate heroes adored by his soldiers. I disliked him more and more as I went on, but I leaned over backwards to keep that from showing—and I hope that it didn't. I am sure it did, some.

Newcomb: I sensed it some as if the narrative voice was saying, well, the soldiers liked him so there must be something there, but I am not quite able to find it yet.

Foote: I am sure that came across. I tried to keep it from it, but I am sure it did.

Newcomb: What was it about somebody like Phil Sheridan?

Foote: It's his blustery quality, his complete willingness to throw a regiment away for the sake of a ribbon or little bit of a reputation. It was his prejudice against Southerners that got my back up some. He disliked all Southerners just because they were Southerners. He got kicked out of West Point for a year just for threatening a Virginian with a bayonet. I hope I didn't let that warp my judgment of Phil Sheridan as a soldier, but I did have a dislike for him.

Newcomb: Your novel is very well organized—here I am calling the Civil War narrative a novel—but it's organized in a symmetrical way. The subtitles always refer to a battle in the East and then a battle in the West. Does the symmetry ever get you in trouble?

Foote: I don't think so. I would not want the reader to be too conscious of it, but there is a foundation, a skeleton that I hope supports like the armature in a piece of sculpture. I hope those things are there for strength rather than for getting me into trouble. If you plan it well, you can put almost anything on it.

Newcomb: How about in the novels? Has the symmetry perhaps bound you?

Foote: I think that it has lead me into taking chances, into doing things that I would not have done if I wasn't conscious of a strong skeleton. I do not feel cramped by that at all. I feel set free by that, the way a man would be if he was doing a dance on a platform. He would do well to build that platform strongly before he started his jig. I feel that way about it. I am not worried about the platform collapsing on me if I try a high kick or something.

Newcomb: Another characteristic—here we are for television trying to talk about something that is one million six hundred thousand words and we can't sit and read those—but I am trying to give a sense of what went on there. I think the first thing one noticed in review after review as the three volumes appeared is how readable they are. A person might be easily intimidated by the size of the three volumes and yet they do read smoothly—too quickly in places—you don't want this to end. I am seeing things as I read, and I think many reviewers noted this too. Once I heard Saul Bellow introduced as the only novelist who doesn't write with his eye on the movie rights and I thought more's the pity. Is this characteristic of you, that you are a visual writer?

Foote: I hope I'm a visual writer, but actually my main concern is with commas, semicolons, dashes, and periods and those things. I interest myself in the verbal aspect of it, and, of course, that is supposed to conjure up the picture, but I concentrate on what makes the picture come rather than the picture that's going to come.

Newcomb: Maybe that is what makes it so visual.

Foote: I hope so, and I think that if it does, it does.

Newcomb: One can see when he reads *The Civil War* and then starts to look elsewhere that other writing is so much less visual.

Foote: Most historians are, I am afraid, so concerned with finding out what happened that they make the enormous mistake of equating facts with truth. No great column of facts can ever pose as the truth. Truth is order imposed on those facts; truth is the breath of life breathed into facts. It is *not* the facts. You can't get the truth from facts. The truth is the way you feel about it. It's made me question our judgment on great American political figures, for example. I remember the Kennedy years—both of them—and I don't think history will ever get any true view of John Kennedy and what he meant to us at the time he was alive, because the facts don't support what we felt. What we felt about Kennedy cannot be expressed with facts. It was a feeling and that is going to be very difficult for future generations. They may be able to quote what some of us had to say about him, but that is not enough, either. It was a feeling that has to be communicated and some future historian is—in the course of writing the history of the United States—going to get to the Kennedy years and just be plumb mystified. What in the world was going on? He looks like a pretty ordinary little gent to me, and historians are not going to understand what he was. They are not going to understand that he followed Eisenhower when everybody was so weary of this big Kewpie doll sitting in the White House. They are not going to understand the reaction. It makes you question history when you see how much you cannot do.

Newcomb: What is the relationship of the historian to the novelist?

Foote: Well, the chief virtue a novelist has is he at least recognizes—from the start, I hope—that he has got to be a good writer. Historians—a lot of professional historians—have a profound distrust of good writing. That may sound outrageous, but it's true. They mistrust anything that is well written. They think that it can't be serious if it's well written or something. Why should anyone pay any attention to prose rhythms, if what he wants to do is tell the facts? I claim the opposite: I claim that the rhythm and the prose communicate the truth as much as the facts, but the historians don't.

Newcomb: Then both of them are after the truth, the historian and the novelist?

Foote: Right. In the note—I guess to Volume I—I said the historian and the novelist are after *exactly* the same thing, the truth, and not a different truth, the same truth, only they approach it by different methods. The historian gets his facts out of documents, books, and handwritten things, newspapers, congressional records. The novelist gets his out of his head, from his memory, and neither—if he is a good historian or a good novelist—would be false to those facts. The novelist would no more be false to his "facts" than the historian would be false to the facts he found in documents and they both want to tell us how it was.

Newcomb: And that's what the romantic novelist is false to?

Foote: He is as false as the bad or crooked historian.

Newcomb: Or one who is dogmatically trying to . . . ?

Foote: And one who distorts. Certain writers in our time have taught us a great deal. Hemingway is in a bad trough now. There is a great deal of contempt for Hemingway. They had better go back and read some Hemingway. There is a man who could write and teach you about writing. When you read a page of Hemingway, I don't care how lousy a husband he was or that he put a shotgun in his mouth when he couldn't take whatever it was any longer. You go back and read some Hemingway and you can learn how to write. If any historian in this country wrote a single page of history that had the clarity of a single page of Hemingway, that page of history would live forever. But he won't study Hemingway, he will think he is wasting his time if he reads Hemingway, and he is not. Hemingway will teach him how to write history. When Hemingway says the marlin came out of the water endlessly, he is saying something that historians will never be able to say.

Newcomb: And in just a few words.

Foote: Right.

Newcomb: Have the historians succumbed then to the social sciences?

Foote: Yes, I think they have. Something happened later they call cliometricians, or something like that, where they use computers to find out what's happening. It's disastrous. They will find that out sooner or later and correct it.

Newcomb: Garbage in, garbage out.

Foote: Yeah. They are going to lose sight of what it means to be a man. In fact, Cleburne is not going to be a breathing human being, he is going to be a factor. That's happened to us. A soldier is no longer an entity with a rifle; he's a blip on a radar screen and you destroy him by pressing a button—at least in theory. Writers are certainly never going to see human beings as a blip on a radar screen. They had better not. Maybe that would be some kind of novel; it wouldn't be my kind, though.

Newcomb: Well, maybe so. In the *War*, you haven't confined yourself to battles . . .

Foote: I think Lincoln's backstairs maneuverings with Chase are just as interesting as the Battle of Fredericksburg to me and deserving of the same kind of study and attention. He'd chop a man's head off without the man knowing that the axe had come anywhere near him. It's beautiful to watch him work. I often thought during the Faubus time in Little Rock, with Eisenhower up in Washington—I was writing *The Civil War* then—and I got to imagining how Lincoln would have handled that situation. Faubus would never have known what would have happened to him. Lincoln would have chopped his legs off. Eisenhower couldn't do anything but send in paratroopers; Lincoln would have him tied up in a neat little bundle in no time at all because he would have known what Faubus was doing. Eisenhower didn't. When Faubus went up to see Eisenhower about a meeting, agreeing that they'd get this thing all worked out, Faubus was snowing him totally and Eisenhower believed him. There is a marvelous photograph of them parting with a handshake after that meeting and Faubus has his chin up. Eisenhower has his down and Faubus had him. He had just finished skinning him. He wouldn't have done that to Lincoln. Talk about historians, some of them are psychiatrists now. I was talking to a psychiatrist in New York—whose name is marvelous—his name was Smiley Blanton and he told me he understood I was interested in the Civil War, and he has always been fascinated by it, and he'd like to talk to me a little about it. I said I would be delighted and he said the person who interested him most was Sherman. He said, "Sherman was so obviously a man with various psychoses that if I could have gotten hold of Sherman at anytime between his twentieth and thirtieth birthday, I could have straightened all of these things out and spared the world a great deal of suffering." I couldn't believe I was hearing him, because I know Sherman and I knew *him* for what he had just finished telling me. Sherman would have wrapped him up in a neat little package and dropped him out of the window there. Smiley Blanton thought that he would straighten Sherman out. I don't know—psychiatrists must be spooky people if they think that they can go around straightening people like Sherman out.

Newcomb: If I recall from the *War*, Sherman would be down for almost the count and just come back as a matter of course.

Foote: Absolutely.

Newcomb: Never give it a thought. There is a job to be done.

Foote: He is an enormously interesting man to write about. He lost his son while he was coming from Vicksburg to Memphis on a boat. His son had come down with yellow fever and died on the boat before they got to Memphis. When Sherman got into Memphis here, they put the son in a sealed casket to send him back up to Ohio to bury him. Anyway, Sherman came ashore and said, "The world is over for me. I no longer have any interest in life. The war is no concern to me; I just wish I was in the grave with my dear boy." He was walking around looking like that and he got on the train to go see Grant somewhere. When they got out to Collierville, the train came under an attack—it's what's now called the Battle of Collierville—and Sherman's spirits went right over the roof. He was just the same man he was before his boy ever got sick. That's the way he was. In fact, he had all of the old pizzazz right as soon as the bullets starting cracking over his head. He was just as good a man as he ever was.

Newcomb: You seem taken with him, and yet for Southerners in Georgia he has always been a kind of Lucifer . . .

Foote: Sure! Sherman had a hard time understanding why his southern friends wouldn't speak to him after the war. He explained that he shortened the war and prevented it from being a lot worse than it was by attacking civilians who were supporting the war. He had a great fondness for Southerners—he liked them. Sherman spent much of his life in the South, and especially liked South Carolina. He loved that section. He said that his campaign in Georgia was so successful because he had learned the terrain as a lieutenant there going around sketching the beautiful countryside, not knowing that he was preparing himself for fighting his way through it.

Newcomb: Oh, my word! I wasn't aware of that.

Foote: He is something.

Newcomb: Have you ever been tempted to follow up any of these figures or is the war behind you?

Foote: No, nonfiction is behind me. I get letters from various publishers wanting me to write various things. I either don't answer them at all or say hell, no, or stay out of that. I'd be trapped for another twenty years away from my novel—if I had another twenty years.

Newcomb: Did you ever in that twenty-years' span say what have I gotten myself into?

Foote: No, I was enjoying myself too much. I tell you the beautiful thing about writing about a subject that big, there is no cramping. I never felt cramped. I felt as free as I ever felt writing a novel, and I did not mind the research, which was very much like outlining and note-taking and everything for a novel. No, I never did. In my spare time, I might have thought, "My God, I could have written eight more novels by now!" But that was just spare-time thinking. Everybody does a little of that every now and then.

Newcomb: And then, after the *War* you just went right back to the novels?

Foote: Yeah. I can't imagine living without working—that would be unthinkable for me. I don't know what I would do with my life. I don't have any hobbies; I don't play golf, don't play polker, don't belong to any clubs, don't do anything but write and enjoy my home.

Newcomb: Is it just coincidence that the first novel after the *War* more or less takes up in the '50s?

Foote: No, it's not a coincidence at all. The world practically stopped for me along about 1960 or so. By the time the Hippies came on the scene, I didn't want any more to do with the scene. When they started talking about relevance, I tuned out. I don't like people who don't see that Milton is relevant. I don't like people who think Latin is not worth studying because you will never use it. I don't want the world to stop and let me off. It's just that my interest stops short there.

Newcomb: And yet, in terms of history, your last novel before you started on the *War*, was bringing us up into the '50s—the Delta in the '50s—and now your last novel, *September September* brings us back to the '50s.

Foote: It's a little more precise there and here you get structure again. The reason I wrote *The Civil War* was—having written those five novels, I had a strong feeling of having completed a stage of my life. Those five made a unit in a sense, and I wanted a pause to assess what I wanted to do next. It was going to be different, so I thought I'd use this two-year Civil War thing as a pause and an assessment when it stretched to twenty. But that's exactly what I did. Now I am back to novels and I hope—God willing—to be able to write five more.

Newcomb: Is *The Civil War: A Narrative* what you envisioned?

Foote: It really is. I know that is a sort of heresy. We never accomplish what we set out to do, and, of course, I didn't accomplish everything I set out to do, but I really am satisfied with that. I got it in the past now and I can look at it and I don't think I could have done better. So I am satisfied. I don't want another go at it. That's it. It sits there on the shelf.

Newcomb: Your father died when you were very young.

Foote: Right. I was not quite six.

Newcomb: So does this have an effect on how you see, how you perceive what went on around you. Your friends, the Percys, did not have a father in the home . . . is that correct?

Foote: Their father died just before they moved to Greenville as early teenage boys, but Mr. Will was a true father to them, so they had a father figure anyhow. I not only lost my father before I was six, but I was an only child too, so I had a really hard time knowing what it would be like to have a brother or sister and many of the main characters in my books are only children often. I didn't notice that until later. It's because—I suppose—I'm avoiding writing about something I don't know from my own sensation. I think I've gotten old enough now to be able to know what it would be like to have a brother or sister, but in the younger part of my writing life I don't think I had a very good notion of how you would feel towards your sister or your brother. The Mississippi Delta was a splendid place to have grown up and I have enormous affection for it which will be with me as long as I live, but that doesn't keep me from seeing the great ills. I remember someone—it was a great shock to me—I had left the Delta, maybe ten years before, someone asked Bobby Kennedy in the early '60s, what he would have done if he had not gone into politics. He said, "I would have done one or two things. I would have gone out to Dakota and worked for the Indians who were so mistreated and abused or I would have gone to the Mississippi Delta and worked for the Negro." And it came home to me particularly hard because it seemed to me to be a direct criticism of me. Of course, he wasn't conscious of my being alive, but I had left the Delta, you see, where I could perhaps have done some good. And it hurt me to think that I had turned my back on something that Bobby Kennedy had been willing to devote his whole life to. You grow up in a thing and you're not inclined to see the evil as clearly as you would if you were visiting that place. It seems so much a part and parcel of the life, especially when it contributes to your comfort, as it did to mine. The race question is the big thing.

Appomattox for Shelby Foote

William Thomas/1978

From *The Commercial Appeal* Mid-South Magazine [Memphis], 19 March1978, 22-25. Reprinted by permission of *The Commercial Appeal.*

He looks like The Southern Author in spite of himself. At 61, his hair is gray and distinguished, his beard is trim and scholarly, his manner is quiet and thoughtful, his clothes are casual, and he has more pipes lying around than a strong man could light and smoke in a week.

To many people, these are the marks of authorship.

But to Shelby Foote, the image of himself as the pipe-smoking writer is particularly distasteful. "I hate it so much," he says, in a voice made in the Mississippi Delta, "I hate it so much that I have refused to be photographed with a pipe in my mouth."

The truth is Foote also smokes cigars—but only when he's sitting down.

"For some reason," he says, "I cannot walk around with a lighted cigar."

No matter. Under any circumstances, Foote is Memphis' man of letters—and it is for this reason interviewers seek him out, especially now that he has produced his first novel in more than 20 years.

In some ways, it's as if those years had never happened, for all the effect they've had on Foote and his life-style.

For example: he still answers his door openly and without suspicion, the way people used to do before tales of neighborhood crime made them so nervous that they started jumping at every knock. The first thing he says to visitors is "hello." The second is: "Coffee?" Then he leads the way into the kitchen and spoons instant coffee into two cups, adds boiling water, pours cream from a can of condensed milk and takes off through the house for the place where the books are written.

It is a large, comfortable room at the back of the house at 542 East Parkway South, where Foote lives with his wife, Gwyn.

The room has a fireplace, a bed, an Oriental rug, two black leather swivel chairs, a typewriter, a table, a straight chair, a great number of books and classical records, a fishing rod, a model airplane, a French cavalry bugle, three old-time Mason fruit jars, a World War II helmet, a box of White Owl cigars, several racks of pipes, an M-I rifle mounted on a copy of Picasso's antiwar painting, "Guernica," a large drawing of three men by Carroll Cloar and a long desk at which Foote writes up to eight hours a day when he's doing good.

There are also a few visible reminders of Foote's encounter with the Civil War—a good copy of a Confederate soldier's cap, two hand-drawn battle maps, a single shelf of books and two small photographs of the top generals, U. S. Grant and Robert E. Lee, the latter taken at his home following the surrender at Appomattox when the last thing he wanted was his picture made.

Otherwise, there is little about the room to show that this is where the "last romantic war" was resurrected and re-examined with such care that it took 20 years to tell the story.

"Afterwards, I was very conscious of the need to shake the war," says Foote, who completed the last volume of his triology on May Day, 1974. "Since then, I have been quite consciously emptying my mind of all the information I ever had about the war. I don't even know, anymore, when Stonewall Jackson was born."

Eager to get back to writing novels, which is where he started, Foote did other things to forget the war that had occupied his thinking since 1954.

"I took down from the walls all of the pictures of the generals that I had kept there while writing the history. I took down the big maps that showed the whole country during the war years, and the hundreds of notes that I'd put on the wall to remember who said what when. Finally, I gathered up nearly all of the books, 500 or 600 of them, put them in boxes and took them down to the library in Greenville (his hometown) and gave them to them."

Then, Foote stepped out of the 1860s and stepped into the 1950s—specifically, the fall of 1957, the period in which his new novel, *September September* is set.

In Foote's eyes, that was quite a month. It began with the introduction of the Edsel automobile on Sept. 4, and it ended with the Russians putting up Sputnik on Oct. 4. In between, the schools were integrated in Little Rock, Arkansas, and nothing has been quite the same since.

Although Foote's book takes place against the backdrop of the Little Rock crisis, it was Sputnik that stirred him the most.

"This was a profound shock to me because it destroyed a basic belief that I had held since I was a child. I reached consciousness in the 1920s and grew up in the '30s. Nobody that didn't live then can quite believe today how much science was worshipped. We thought the scientists were going to have the answer to everything. When you saw cities of the future, it all worked beautifully, just beautifully. There was no energy problem, no congestion, no pollution. We thought medicine was going to solve every disease. We really believed those things.

"We also believed that a scientist, who was the hero of those times, had to be a free man. If his mind was not free to go into channels it wanted to, he would not be able to do his work; he would be so distracted—and ground down that he could not be an outward-thinking person. But then the Sputnik was put up by what we were told were slave scientists captured in Germany, taken to Russia, and placed in laboratories under guard. That was a lick because it destroyed my belief that man has to be free to make great scientific advances.

"Anyway, my point is this: It was the Sputnik going up that I saw as the exact lip of an enormous crater that yawned, and now we are separated by that date."

So Foote proceeded to forget everything he had so painstakingly learned about the Civil War years and went about the job of soaking up all he could about the fall of 1957.

Convincing people that he was through with the Civil War wasn't easy.

"All sorts of lucrative offers involving money and fame came in. People wanted me to do articles and lectures and interviews and god knows what all about the Civil War. I consistently said 'no' to every one of them. Somebody even wanted me to do a history of the Revolutionary War, for god's sakes. I didn't even answer that one. I figured I did my time and I wanted out. It is not true that there is no discharge from that (Civil) war. I got my discharge."

Foote is not the only writer who has been exhausted by the Civil

War. "I wrote to Bruce Catton (*A Stillness at Appomattox*) and said I hoped he could go ahead with his biography of Grant through the presidential years," Foote says. "He wrote back and said, 'I will not go ahead with anything; I am now 103 years old; the Civil War's got me so tied up that I have become a very aged veteran.' "

Nevertheless, when he returned to the novel, Foote used the same methods for his fiction that he had used to produce the narrative history of the war. "I now believe the historian and novelist are after the same thing—that is to tell how it was," he said.

"I researched this novel far more than I had ever done before because I had learned how to do it. The first thing I did was go down to the newspaper office and, with a fine-tooth comb and a notebook, learn everything I could about September 1957, from the files of *The Commercial Appeal* and the *Press-Scimitar.* I even knew what time the sun came up, what time it set, how much it rained and when the autumnal equinox occurred. And I discovered some very curious things:

"For example, the strongest American influence on me is Faulkner, and I discovered that Faulkner's 60th birthday was Sept. 25, 1957, and so I introduced that fact into the story. One of the characters remarks that Faulkner is 60 years old today. The peculiar thing about it was that I wrote that on my own 60th birthday."

Not only did Foote research his novel with the same care that he took with the Civil War, he used the same tools to do the actual writing—an old-fashioned dipped pen, Sheaffer's Script Ink and whatever blotters he can find these days. In a technological age, pen and ink is not easy to come by.

"The problem is," says Foote, "they don't make my ink anymore, they don't make my pen points anymore and they don't make blotters anymore. I used to get ink in pints and quarts. Now, I have to go out and buy little 2-ounce bottles, a dozen at a time, and pour them into an old quart bottle. Fountain pens almost don't exist anymore. And blotters: I used to go to any insurance office and get a double armload of blotters with advertising on them. Now, you can't even buy them in stationery stores.

"Maybe I'll go back to sanding a goose quill, in full retreat. It might sound strange, but one of the great finds of my life took place when I went in an old stationery store in New York and discovered two gross of No. 313 probate penpoints. They're my kind of points."

As he did with the three Civil War books, Foote has his original copy of the novel completely written out in longhand. Although it is a fairly short novel—it runs a little over 100,000 words—it took him just over 13 months. If Foote had not known his setting so well—briefly, it has to do with a kidnapping that takes place in Memphis—it probably would have taken longer.

"What I was trying to do was write a short novel to get my hand back in," says Foote, whose first book, *Tournament,* was published 30 years ago. He wrote one novel a year for five years. One of them, *Follow Me Down,* was attacked by the American Legion as a dirty book. Some members took it out to the city dump to burn it along with D. H. Lawrence's *Lady Chatterley's Lover.* One of the hidden ironies in the new novel is the news that *Huckleberry Finn* was banned in New York, which, says Foote, was a nice bit of counterpoint: "They had one kind of bigotry down here and another kind of bigotry up there."

When Foote wound up his history of the Civil War, he celebrated by opening a special bottle of wine (Mouton Rothschild, '59) and treating himself to a reading of Proust's *Remembrance of Things Past.* When he completed the novel, he decided to go to New York for the publication date and to read the Proust work.

"I always give myself a reward when I finish something," he says, "and the reward I give myself is always the same thing. I read *Remembrance of Things Past.* That's my big prize. I think I've read it nine times, now. It's like a two-month vacation because it takes that long to read Proust. I like it better than going to Palm Beach."

Also, it is one way Foote prepares himself for another writing job.

"Reading good writers is your university," he says. "That's where you say, 'ahh, so that's how you do it.' And the more times you read a thing, the more you learn. When you know where a writer's going, you can better appreciate how he goes about getting there. And the bigger the writer the more you can learn. Dickens and Shakespeare can really teach you how to write."

In an age of television, it is fascinating if not surprising advice from a man of letters. The interesting thing is that Foote also watches the tube. However, he does it for different reasons than most:

"I flop down on the bed in a half-dead state and watch that inane stuff come off the tube as a good way of resting and getting sleepy. Richard Nixon was a great favorite of mine. Every time he would come on the screen, I would go to sleep. It was very strange and fascinating, too. You know, here was the criminal himself facing 100 million people—and I'd go to sleep."

Although Foote wrote his latest novel as a kind of warm-up for a bigger book that he has been thinking about for a long time, *September September* has been selected as a Book-of-the-Month Club alternate and his agent is trying to sell the story to Hollywood.

"God knows what will come of all that," he says. "It would be funny if the thing made a lot of money and I had that huge load on my back. I have had one absolute standard attitude toward money all my life—that is the utter need for spending it as soon as possible so it wouldn't be loaded on my back.

"An old jazz musician said a good thing one time. He said what you need to write the blues is no money in the bank and nobody loving you. So I feel an obligation to get rid of the money and alienate people so I won't be either rich or loved."

Foote plans to start his next novel in the spring.

"I'm still setting it in my mind," he says, "but the title will be *Two Gates to the City,* and it will be about my section of the Mississippi, the Delta, in the late '40s and on through to the mid-'60s. It's about three cousins and their grandfather. It's a family novel—I don't mean it's a saga, I mean it's about a family. It's going to be extremely difficult in a lot of ways because it's not all action like this one (the present novel).

"You can fail miserably with the best intentions in the world. But you can't worry about that. I've had this book in my head for a long time—all through my *Civil War.* The people are all worked out. I have extensive outlines that I did 25 years ago. A lot of it will change, of course, because I've changed. But I believe this:

"It will be worth a grown man's time."

Interview with Shelby Foote

Dick Cavett/1979

Permission to transcribe and print this interview courtesy Daphne Productions, Inc.

Cavett: Good evening again from New Orleans. When President Carter toured the Gettysburg battlefield not too long ago, his guide was the man who is my guest tonight, Shelby Foote. The president was certainly in good hands because Mr. Foote is a novelist who took a twenty-year break from fiction to write a three-volume narrative history of the Civil War and it brilliantly brings to life not only the great battles—Gettysburg and so on—but the whole panorama of the war. Mr. Foote's novels like *Shiloh, Follow Me Down, September September,* usually deal with the South and Southern history which makes sense, since he is a Southerner—born in Mississippi, now lives in Memphis—and Mr. Foote, we are delighted that you have made the trip down the river to be with me. Did you actually come down the river?

Foote: No, I flew down.

Cavett: Okay. You are a novelist and yet you are about—well, maybe, fifty percent of the time referred to as a historian, but I think you prefer the label, novelist, writer . . .

Foote: Writer is the best professional name, really.

Cavett: But you did take twenty years to work on the three-volume work?

Foote: Yes, I didn't *start* to take twenty years, but I took twenty years. The original contract called for a short history of the Civil War.

Cavett: Was the original contract yellowed by the time . . . ?

Foote: Yes, it was. I asked them if I could go ahead and they said go, so I went.

Cavett: The same people were still running the publishing house?

Foote: *(Laughs)* Bennett Cerf.

Cavett: What is it? This sounds like such a wide-eyed, dumb question, but why is the Civil War *still* so grabbing and appealing whereas so many other wars don't have the cachet?

Foote: There are many answers. Churchill called it the last of the old-fashioned, romantic wars and the first of the modern wars, so that they coincide. I think, honestly, the reason we Americans are so attracted to it is that innately, anyhow, we understand it was the Civil War which made our country what our country is rather than the Revolution. The Revolution started us out, but the Civil War decided which way we were going and I think there is a strong sense of that in almost anybody that knows anything about it.

Cavett: Is there anyway of conceiving of the country—could you write a novel, for example, in which the Civil War had not taken place and what America was today without it?

Foote: No. Walker Percy does some speculating on that in *The Last Gentleman* and instead of Lincolns he sees Sewards being driven around the country and so forth, but it's for fun.

Cavett: Are there some myths about the Civil War? It's always fun to see a myth exploded—some myths that still cling regardless—despite your writing? I know Lincoln is so sanctified that it's almost boring. He had become a sanctified bore in some way. But we learn from you, and I guess it was known somewhat before, that he was not all that benevolent, kindly and doting as he is sometimes portrayed.

Foote: It's almost impossible to overpraise Lincoln. He's beyond our comprehension and as big a man as anyone wants to think he was. But the sanctification of him has covered up some of his most important points. He had qualities that people don't recognize because they are hidden under the saintliness. He had a certain steeliness and an ability to analyze himself that's almost incredible in any human being. And he had absolutely no humility, but he had a covering modesty. He's one of the few men I've ever read about who could abide having another man think he was a fool. If someone thinks that I'm a fool, I'm going to be very fast to disabuse him of that notion. Lincoln would sit back and wait for his opportunity to demonstrate when it would really count. If an opponent of some sort thought he was a fool, Lincoln had him exactly where he wanted him. He could do things like that. This steely quality to his mind that would enable him to analyze a situation and analyze his own position in that situation is one of the most remarkable things about him. The saintliness has covered up another side to him. I've forgotten the figures now of how many warrants for execution Lincoln signed during the Civil War. Lincoln was known as the man who wouldn't let a little soldier boy who slept on his post be shot. He signed a great many warrants for execution. Jefferson Davis never signed one.

Cavett: Is that true—not one?

Foote: Not one.

Cavett: That is a fascinating fact.

Foote: Davis said the poorest use could be made of a soldier is to shoot him.

Cavett: Especially when he's one of yours.

Foote: Yeah, that's right.

Cavett: Lincoln—now in those cases where he signed those, was it that he familiarized himself with the case and decided this man should die?

Foote: Well, the comparison of Lincoln-Davis really isn't fair. In the Union Army, you couldn't shoot a man without the president's signature—as you can't now except in flagrant cases. But he did have to do something like approve of it by putting his signature to the court's findings before the man could be executed. It's unfortunate that I've forgotten the figures. I've forgotten how many Indians were hanged in one day at Mankato? They had a gaudy hanging that Lincoln authorized. Now he cut the list down from two hundred and something down to twenty-six or whatever it was, but they hung them all in one day there by Lincoln's signature.

Cavett: Yes. There are the native Americans who are still bitter about that, who don't like the fact that this man is on our money.

Foote: Right. I would think so. He did, though, in that case go through the list and very carefully rule out anybody he felt that he could rule out as not having been guilty of an actual atrocity.

Cavett: Yes, that's what I wondered: in all of these that he signed, did he trouble to stay up late and study the case, as they say?

Foote: He did. The best sign of what the war did to Lincoln is the Brady photographs. You see photos of him the first year, second year, third year, fourth year in office and the man aged at least twenty years in those four years.

Cavett: Yeah, they appear to be five years apart, the pictures.

Foote: Right. Right.

Cavett: It's always hard for me in reading about the Civil War not to somehow root for the South in the way that as a kid you were for the Indians.

Foote: Right.

Cavett: I don't know what the parallel is or why it is. It isn't just that the South is more colorful, more romantic and all of those labels that have been attached to it.

Foote: I think you are demonstrating a very usual American tendency which is to root for the underdog.

Cavett: Well, that may be it, but I have seen underdogs I didn't like.

Foote: So have I.

Cavett: I always find myself pulling for the South to come out if not ahead, better than they did.

Foote: A good quality is what you discounted. It's the colorfulness, the individuality which continued to operate from high rank to lower rank, the raucous sense of humor, things like that. They are attractive and they pull you toward them.

Cavett: By the way, am I the only person who doesn't know what the rebel yell actually sounds like? I've always heard it referred to.

Foote: If you knew what it sounded like you'd be the only person who *did* know what it sounded like. It's gone.

Cavett: It's lost.

Foote: It's totally lost. It's been described, but it's been described in so many different ways that it's hard to tell what it was. The basis for it some say was the fox hunt yip on horseback chasing a fox, "Yoicks!" and so forth. But it seems to have been almost a scream, very high in the throat and with no brain behind it—and a truly terrifying thing. One of the best descriptions I've ever heard was given by a Northern soldier and he did not describe the yell, he described the sensations when you heard the yell. He said it's like a corkscrew up your back when you hear that thing and it's coming at you.

Cavett: It'd be fascinating to know exactly what it was and how it was produced. Could everybody do it or was it like the Tarzan yell?

Foote: Everybody could do it. They asked an old veteran at a U. D. C. [United Daughters of the Confederacy] banquet to give it for them and he said, "It can't be given except at a dead charge against the enemy and to ask me to do it here with a stomach full of food and a mouth full of false teeth is ridiculous. It can't be done." *(Laughs)*

Cavett: And that was our last chance to find out?

Foote: That's right. He's gone now.

Cavett: Well, is it also my imagination or is it the movies or the way fiction is put together that gives you the impression that Southern generals and officers, in general, were much more colorful, romantic, chivalrous?

Foote: Yes. I think so on total, but there are an awful lot of romantic, chivalrous ones on the Northern side too. Those men had been pretty good friends before the war, especially the West Pointers. I think, though, you would have to say that it was Jeb Stuart with the red-lined cape and the plume in his hat and all that. Phil Sheridan was a pretty colorful fellow, but unfortunately, he was only about five feet four inches tall which made it harder for him, but they said he looked like a giant up on that horse.

Cavett: Were there people that, in doing research, you ended up despising, that you thought were heroes before?

Foote: I hope I didn't go so far as to despise them. There were two generals that I took a dislike to. One of them was Phil Sheridan; the other one was Joe Johnston, on the Southern side. I liked them personally in some ways, but I got exasperated with them. Sheridan was going around punching his fist in his palm, saying, "Smash 'em up! Smash 'em up!" which sounded too much like Patton to please me. And Joe Johnston—every time he got into position—backed up, and I got exasperated with his retreating tactics.

Cavett: It's interesting to me. I could never quite get it into my head that the Indian Wars were going on at the same time as the Civil War. You always think that somehow history stops for the Civil War.

Foote: Yes, I was surprised to find that out, too. Of course, when you think about it the Indians, if they ever had a chance to get away with anything, it was while the army was busy fighting this huge war in the East.

Cavett: Yes, if they had taken Washington, for example, that would be an interesting development.

Foote: (*Laughs*) Yes.

Cavett: Did you know that during—well, I don't know whose administration—a lot of the Plains Indians were taken to Washington to meet with the president—this happened many times—to meet with the president—and they couldn't believe how many white men there were and each place they went they thought this same group of white men were being moved around with them because they couldn't believe these were all new ones. The Sioux word for white men is *wasichu* meaning "They are everywhere." Well, we seem to have strayed here. But the Civil War gave us General Custer, didn't it?

Foote: It certainly did.

Cavett: What does "brevet" mean?

Foote: It means honorary rank. You are awarded that rank without receiving it on paper, but you can wear the stars, but you don't get paid. That's about what it amounts to.

Cavett: What would it have taken for the war to go the other way, for the South to win?

Foote: It would have taken more than the South ever had. The North fought that war with one hand, the other hand behind its back. If circumstances had called for it, the North simply would have brought that other hand out from behind its back. One thing you have to realize how much the North did in addition to fight that war. Vassar, M.I.T.—I can't remember the long list of universities and colleges that were established during the war. The Homestead Act was in full blast. The West was settled during the war. The North by no means exerted its last ounce of energy and the South very nearly did. There was no way. I think anything the South could have done on its own would never have won that war. The one chance would have been intervention by England or France and there was no chance for that.

Cavett: That was never a real possibility, was it?

Foote: Not when Abraham Lincoln defined the war as a war in defense of slavery on the other side. That was the genius of Lincoln, defining the war that way. He swung that tarbrush and that tar never has come off.

Cavett: By the way, the incident they can never resist in movies of the period in which they say, "Mr. Lincoln, what song would you like to hear?" and he strokes his beard and says there's one that's always appealed to me, a wonderful melody, it's called "Dixie." And they strike it up and there are cheers. Did that ever happen?

Foote: Yes. It happened at the very end. He called for the band to play "Dixie" when the news came from Appomattox. He said the song had been recaptured and the Attorney General advised him it was federal property now and he'd like to hear the band play it. And they played it.

Cavett: Do we know who wrote it?

Foote: I don't think they really know who wrote it. There's some talk about Daniel Emmett and this, that, and the other, but I don't think they know who wrote it, or Christy's Minstrels? I don't know who wrote it.

Cavett: So no estate is getting wealthy every time "Dixie" is struck up? What is meant by the phrase that the Civil War was or wasn't our first modern war, depending on which side you're on?

Foote: Simple things. It was the first war in which the railroad truly was an important factor and it was from the start—First Manassas or Bull Run, as it's called. The railroads brought Joe Johnston's troops down from the valley to take part in the battle and were very important. It was the first war in which the telegraph played an important part. And there were various inventions, the submarine. Lee himself invented the railway gun. He mounted a cannon on a flat and took it out to the railroad line and fired from it.

Cavett: Does the Gatling gun come from the Civil War?

Foote: No. I think it was afterwards. I wouldn't be surprised if it had been sort of invented during the war but it was never used. The repeating rifle was, but not the Gatling gun, I think.

Cavett: One of the things you first learn as a kid in school—statistics people are fond of tossing out at cocktail parties—is that more people were killed in the Civil War than in all the other wars put together before and since.

Foote: That was true up to Vietnam and maybe halfway through Korea.

Cavett: Now, why the excessive carnage?

Foote: It's really quite simple. The weapons were way ahead of the tactics. The Civil War musket wasn't a musket, it was a true rifled weapon. It was muzzle loading, but a good man could get off four shots in a minute. That's not slow shooting. And yet they still massed their men and advanced on an objective. And you can imagine what a mass of men would run into when they tried to take men who were entrenched up on a hill. You see what happened at Gettysburg. There were fifty percent casualties in that charge.

Cavett: It's unbelievable.

Foote: Yeah.

Cavett: Well, I suppose twenty years spent on the subject, you would just as soon we change the subject now perhaps to something else.

Foote: Yeah.

Cavett: You wouldn't mind.

Foote: I've been busy for three years; now I'm forgetting everything I knew about the Civil War. It's true.

Cavett: Well, I'm glad you haven't lost all of it. Tell me why so many great writers are from the Mississippi Delta.

Foote: There's lots of frivolous answers such as, there's nothing else to do down there, but . . .

Cavett: We know that isn't true.

Foote: No, I think that it's partly accidental. I come from a little town in Mississippi called Greenville, that's on the river there and there are seven or eight published writers either living there or have lived there, and I credit it all to one man, William Alexander Percy, who was a writer. It was not that there were literary coteries—there were not—but, by example, he showed that you could be a writer.

Cavett: Is that *Lanterns on the Levee* Percy?

Foote: Yes, that's right. Leroy Percy's adopted father, Walker Percy's adopted father, too. It was by example. I sometimes think that if Will Percy had grown up and lived in Greenwood, it would have been Greenwood where the writers came from.

Cavett: Seven is remarkable when you consider. I think in a recent story to do with John Updike, he pointed out that about a hundred people in America make their living as writers at any given time, not including new-journalists, of course, but writers in that sense.

Foote: Creative writers or something.

Cavett: To have seven from one town . . .

Foote: We don't all necessarily make a living, but we're published.

Cavett: Maybe that's the largest percentage. There is something though still to be explained about it, because the percentages are so high and, I know, my wife comes from the heart of that area, as you know, and all of her friends talk well enough that their conversation could simply be taken down and put on the Broadway stage or somewhere and their letters are publishable and they're not writing majors or English majors. There's something about language.

Foote: There's a good appreciation of a good story. I can remember and it doesn't matter how often you've heard it—an aunt of mine saying to her husband—"Tell about that time you were in Yazoo City." She's heard it fifty times, but she loves to hear it again and knows how other people will enjoy it. There may be something in the fact that the one Southern art—and it's as dead as the Rebel yell—was oratory back in the old days and there's something about the organization of a speech and the delivery of a speech and the rolling periods and so forth that tie into writing and it may be survival of some part of that art in the South.

Cavett: Well, I'm certainly glad it's there. It's a wonderful thing and I do have the feeling that you could just ring a doorbell and say you're going to have to make your living as a writer to almost anyone in, say Greenwood, Mississippi, and if they had to, they could do it. But I know there is more to writing than that. And speaking of writing, would you show us what's inside this volume?

[Foote displays a bound volume of *The Civil War: A Narrative* in his own handwriting.]

Foote: I do a final draft of everything I write.

Cavett: I thought that was a reproduction of some sort, but this is actually your handwriting as the pen is put to paper.

Foote: That's right. It doesn't have anything to do with anything, except pleasing myself to do it, really.

Cavett: Did you learn that in the Greenville public schools?

Foote: No, No.

Cavett: What style of writing is that?

Foote: I don't know. It's the way I write and people have a great deal of trouble reading it until they get used to it and then they can read it easy because no two letters are alike.

Cavett: At first glance, it doesn't appear to be English. From here it could be Arabic or something.

Foote: Right.

Cavett: And moving in on it, I can see everything quite clearly.

Foote: Right.

Cavett: About your work habits. Are you still at it seven days a week?

Foote: No, since I've gotten old, I work six days a week. I used to work seven. And there was a good reason for that. I think a lot of writers know that when you stop you have to start again and it's like a steam engine, if you've got a head of steam on and you stop, you got to build up another head of steam. I used to be alarmed to find that if I laid off one day, it's take me two to get started again. If I laid off three days, it would take six.

Cavett: Like a musician or an athlete—you just fall back?

Foote: I think so. You have to build up this head of steam and go. And stopping means losing your steam and starting up again. Hemingway was interesting on that. He always said you ought to quit for the day when you know what the next sentence is so that when you sit down the next day you can write that sentence and then you're going.

Cavett: That's right. He believed in having a little impulse left just before he knocked off for the day.

Foote: That's right. Good advice.

Cavett: You're not one of the people who contributes to the sort of dissolution of the interest in Hemingway? Awkward way of saying it . . . Hemingway's in fairly ill repute a lot now.

Foote: Yes, he is.

Cavett: He's almost considered a dismissable joke in certain academic circles.

Foote: That's right. The dislike of Hemingway is curiously personal. I am a constant defender of Hemingway against people who run him down. I think my favorite modern writer is William Faulkner who has influenced me more than any other writer, but if I had to say what writer's work is going to live or if I could find a single page in literature that I would say I knew was imperishable, it would come from Hemingway. It can never die. It can be detracted, but they can never destroy that.

Cavett: You go back to those books, the power's still there?

Foote: That's right.

Cavett: But it's almost as though there's a movement afoot to unseat him.

Foote: That's right. Now they are right when they attack him on certain lines. He certainly never wrote a good novel, by a long shot, but I'm talking about the quality of the writing, the ability to communicate sensation and the cleanness of it. It's beautiful writing and it is writing a writer can learn from—truly learn from.

Cavett: Do you divide writers into those groups—the ones you can learn from and the ones you can't?

Foote: Yes, I think so.

Cavett: A great genius, they say, has very little to learn from someone else.

Foote: I've heard that. I don't think that's true.

Cavett: You don't turn to *War and Peace* to find out how to write a novel but maybe to a lesser novel.

Foote: I think there's some truth in it. But I learned an awful lot from William Shakespeare and Marcel Proust and it taught me a great deal.

Cavett: You're on the seventh go through Proust, I believe, or is it the seventeenth?

Foote: Every time I do something I feel really good about, like finish *The Civil War*, I reward myself by reading Proust again. I've done it about, I think, eight times now.

Cavett: The whole shelf of Proust.

Foote: Yes, that's the way to read it.

Cavett: Couldn't put it down? Tell about meeting William Faulkner, would you?

Foote: Yes. Mr. Faulkner was very different from the conception of him as a standoffish, secretive man. He was not that way. He was outgoing, friendly, almost cavalier in manner and very glad to talk about his work, once he was convinced you weren't trying to pry into his private life, which I certainly wasn't. And a congenial companion. He was given to moods of silence. I was perfectly willing to give him that. But he was not like the conception of a man who's standoffish at all. He was not that way.

Cavett: Would you tell how you actually first me him? I believe you and Walker Percy had a slight disagreement on whether his privacy should be invaded?

Foote: We did. Walker and I were driving up to Sewanee to spend some time and I wanted to go by Oxford and meet William Faulkner.

We were about eighteen, I think. And Walker said, "I'm not going in there and bother that man." And I said, he's a writer. It's all right, we'll go see him. And he said, "Well, *you* can go knock on his door. *I'm* not going to do it." So I pulled up in the yard there and got out of the car. There was a whole bunch of dogs—dalmations, fox terriers, bird dogs—I waded through them up to the door and knocked on the door and the door opened. It was Faulkner and he said, "Yes?" And I said, Mr. Faulkner, I'm from Greenville and I'm wondering where to get a copy of your first book, *The Marble Faun.* That was my cover story, if he bought it, and he came out and said, "I don't know where you can get one. Maybe Leland Hayward could find you one. I can give you his address." He said, "Where are you from?" And I said, I'm from Greenville over there. And he said, "Come on let's walk down away here." We walked through some cedars and he said, "I just finished a book about your country over there." And I said, what's it called? He said, "It's called *If I Forget Thee, Jerusalem."* I didn't know what to make of that and I said that's nice and went on. I kept waiting from then on for *If I Forget Thee, Jerusalem* to come out and it wasn't until about five or six years ago that I learned that the original title of *The Wild Palms* was *If I Forget Thee, Jerusalem.* So he had finished *The Wild Palms* that day.

Cavett: And you were the only one to know that at that point? Was he drunk when you met him?

Foote: No. I've spent other times with him—couple of days riding around in cars and we would go get ourselves a bottle of whiskey and drink it, but he was never the slightest bit drunk. No.

Cavett: I hope the story's true that when he was working in Hollywood, he didn't like his office very much and they said, well, you can certainly work at home, then when they couldn't find him, it turned out he had gone back to Mississippi.

Foote: It *is* true. He said he liked to work at home and home meant one thing to him. Just like Robert E. Lee saying my country. He meant Virginia. Home meant Oxford, Mississippi.

Cavett: "My country" then was smaller in size. Will your next novel be about the Delta, as is rumored?

Foote: Yes. I'm going to write a great, big thing called *Two Gates* *to the City.* It's about a Delta family—not a saga—about a family engaged in a problem at once.

Cavett: When you say you're going to write it, you mean you have not put pen to paper yet?

Foote: I haven't started the start-to-finish writing. I'm just pushing the organization of the thing around and adjusting the people to suit me and all.

Cavett: If we broke into your writing room, what would we find in terms of that novel now? Graphs, charts?

Foote: You'd find diagrams. And short biographies of characters that I want to keep in mind and suggestions for turns of plot and eras to be looked into. Things like that.

Cavett: Do you have a title for it yet, or is it bad luck to reveal it?

Foote: No. *Two Gates to the City.*

Cavett: There must be some classical reference in that? Is it Troy?

Foote: *The Seven Gates of Thebes* is part of it and there's an old Negro spiritual, "Seven Gates to the City," isn't there? "Hallelujah . . . "

Cavett: That sounds right.

Foote: Right, it's a spiritual. This has to do with an old way of life and a new way of life. And so on.

Cavett: When they say the Civil War is still being fought in the South, what does that really mean today?

Foote: It doesn't mean much to me. I used to go up to New York and I'd be in a nightclub or some place and I'd be with a group of people and one of them would say, "Aren't you from Mississippi?" And I'd say yes. They would say, "Why can't you people stop fighting the Civil War?" And I hadn't mentioned the Civil War. It was always somebody else mentioning it.

Cavett: Throw it at you immediately. There are still deep and bitter feelings, though, about what was done to the land and the homes.

Foote: Yeah. Some of it is somewhat justified. We never treated a defeated enemy as harshly as the South was treated. If you disenfranchised everybody who had any rank or held any office . . . Some of it was pretty heavy.

Cavett: I'm sorry to say that we have come to the end of, for me, a very interesting half-hour and I wish we had more time.

Foote: I enjoyed being here.

Cavett: It was a great pleasure. And we will see you all. The gentleman's name is Shelby Foote, should you have joined us in the last few seconds. We will see you all tomorrow night. Goodnight. Thank you.

Shelby Foote

John Griffin Jones/1979

From *Mississippi Writers Talking*, I (Jackson: University Press of Mississippi, 1982), 37-92. Reprinted by permission of the University Press of Mississippi and John Griffin Jones.

One of his first things he said to me when I arrived at his home in Memphis was, "I don't do these things very much," but he granted me two afternoons with him in his study. Both days I sat on an ottoman by some cardboard boxes containing a typed, unbound draft of the third volume of his *The Civil War: A Narrative*—with which, he said, he built his fires—while he rode a swivel chair at his desk. He wore bedroom slippers and khaki slacks, and kept his hands in constant motion loading and lighting, relighting and cleaning his pipe. Occasionally he would reach high into his bookshelves for a crumpled pack of Chesterfield Kings. The small pictures of Union and Confederate leaders and the passages of dialogue or official communication among them printed on note cards were absent from the wall above his desk, signaling his return to fiction. Both his voice and his thin face, covered by a thick, close-cropped gray beard, had the distinctive character of another era. I found it difficult to separate him from the deep traditions of which he spoke.

Jones: This is John Jones with the Mississippi Department of Archives and History, about to interview Mr. Shelby Foote. Today is Thursday, August 16, 1979, and we're at Mr. Foote's house in Memphis, Tennessee, on Parkway. I suppose it's best if we start at the beginning, if you could tell me some of your early background, when and where you were born.

Foote: Well, I was born in Greenville, Mississippi, at the Greenville Sanatorium on the seventeenth of November, 1916, in room 31 although it was room 13. They don't have room 13s in hospitals, I guess. The doctor was Dr. A. G. Payne. My daddy was working for a gin down in Rolling Fork and came up on a freight train when he heard my mother had gone into labor.

Jones: What did your daddy do?

Foote: He didn't do anything until after he got married. He was sort of a rich man's son that never thought he would do anything in this world. About the time he got married, his father lost all his money. My mother's father, Morris Rosenstock, got him a job as a shipping clerk with Armour and Company there in Greenville. That was about 1915 or so. He just suddenly caught fire and he lived another seven or eight years. By the time seven years were up he was manager of all the Armour and Companies in the South. But he died in Mobile, Alabama, in September of 1922.

Foote: So your mother raised you?

Jones: Yes. I was not quite six years old when he died and my mother never remarried. She did indeed raise me. We lived back in Greenville until I was—well, to get it straight, while my father was alive we lived in various places because he was rising up the business ladder. We lived in Vicksburg, Jackson, Pensacola, and he had just been transferred to Mobile at the time he died. He got a promotion each time. He'd had a good life. He was born in 1890, a planter's son. He was more interested in hunting and gambling and drinking whiskey and fooling around than he was in anything else, until he and mother got married.

Jones: Born at Mount Holly?

Foote: No. He was born at Mounds Plantation near Rolling Fork. He's buried there now. He lived at Mount Holly through his boyhood. My grandfather had three or four plantations down there. There was Mount Holly, Mounds, Egremont, and one called Hardscrabble. My Daddy grew up with that kind of life. His father had come from Macon, Mississippi—this is Huger Lee Foote I'm talking about, my father's father. His father was Hezekiah William Foote from Macon, Mississippi, a wealthy man there. He had been a Colonel in the Confederate army, was at Shiloh—in fact, got the tail shot off his horse at Shiloh. My father never had any intentions of doing anything with his life, so far as I know, until he and my mother got married. He did not go to a university. He went to Brannam and Hughes to school, and when college time came around he wasn't interested in that; he didn't go, he stayed around home. By the time he would have been a junior or senior in college he was getting married.

Jones: So your grandfather was the first Foote in the Greenville area?

Foote: Yes, he was the first one. He was the youngest son of old Hezekiah William, and his father sent him to Chillicothe Business College up in Ohio. I still can't imagine some Southern boy going to Chillicothe Business College. But his father sent him there—to learn bookkeeping, I suppose, and that kind of thing—and then sent him over to the Delta to manage four plantations. Mounds Plantation was one, where my father was born, and another was Mount Holly where they lived soon after that. Mount Holly was his favorite of all the places he was running for his father, so as soon as he began to run those places he began paying his father for Mount Holly. He wanted to buy it from him. He made the last payment the year the old man died, and then it was left him in his will.

Jones: I've heard that story.

Foote: That's hard.

Jones: And who gambled it away?

Foote: He did. He finally sold Mount Holly and moved to town and spent all his time gambling, some at the Elks Club there in Greenville, but he also went many places. I've talked with old men who knew him in poker games all over that region. He died of apparent cancer. I'm sure it was cancer; I'm not sure whether it was stomach or intestines or what it was. I remember them telling me he was sitting on a pillow during the last of his poker playing days. He also had one of the first operations that was known as the Murphy Button; something to do with an intestinal bypass. It was a daring technique in those days. My mother has told me about seeing him. He died a year before I was born. She told me about seeing him, but when she knew him best he was already in the hospital, lying up in bed there. My first novel *Tournament* is written out of sort of a conception of him, but it's only a conception. It's not even founded much on fact. I'd never seen him, I'd never talked about him a great deal with his widow or my mother, except for small things.

Jones: Was the Foote family always centered in Mississippi? When did they come down to this area?

Foote: They were originally in Virginia, went from there to Chester

County, South Carolina, and from there across Alabama to the black prairie region of Mississippi, where my great-grandfather settled. He was, I've heard, the first man in Mississippi to bring in blooded cattle, to raise pedigree cattle. There's no trace of him left around Macon, no kinfolks even. I go there every now and then; I like to see the old man buried in the cemetery there—he's got an obelisk over his grave, and his four wives are buried around him, one to each of the four main points of the compass.

Jones: Is your mother still in Greenville?

Foote: She died ten years ago but she lived there nearly all her life.

Jones: Are there any of your close relatives in Greenville?

Foote: I have an aunt, Elizabeth Foote. I have another aunt, Katherine, her older sister, who's paralytic and in a nursing home in Greenville, and that's all.

Jones: What about the governor in the 1850s, Henry Stuart Foote, is he related?

Foote: He's a distant cousin, not close kin.

Jones: Where was he from?

Foote: Well, it's rather confusing. He's really a Tennessean. There is a connection though, he and my great-grandfather were among two of the founders of Vanderbilt, so they were connected that way. I don't know the exact kinship of old Hezekiah William to Henry Stuart Foote. Henry Stuart Foote's an interesting man. He was sort of a renegade. He left the Confederacy and went abroad.

Jones: Did he?

Foote: Yes. He was a fiery man, something of a blowhard, I think, and a mortal enemy of Jefferson Davis's, before the war and during it.

Jones: Had a fist fight with him, didn't he?

Foote: Yes, it was at a boarding house in Washington. He made a remark that Davis took exception to, about a young lady or something. Those fist fights never amounted to much; like any two fifty-year-old men swinging away at each other.

Jones: Well, he was quite a duelist in his time, too, wasn't he?

Foote: Yes. You never know how serious those things are. There's a scene of him in the Confederate Senate, or House, I've forgotten which. He was attacked by a fellow member, a man named Dargan, I believe, from Alabama, with a Bowie knife. Foote managed to scramble out of the way, and some of the other Senators grabbed Dargan and pinned him to the floor, and Foote came back within range and said, "I defy the steel of the assassin!"

Jones: When you were growing up in Greenville, was your family literary?

Foote: No, my family was not literary on either side. I've done some speculating about that and there are several answers to where the devil the literary thing came from. So far as blood goes, and kinship, if it comes from anywhere it comes from my mother's father who was born in Vienna, Austria, and left there when he was seventeen years old and came to this country, probably to escape conscription; we don't really know why because he wouldn't talk about it. He was a Viennese Jew. His name was Rosenstock. He came over here when he was seventeen, and how he got to Mississippi from probably landing in New York I do not know. But anyway he came down the river and settled here and was keeping books on a plantation at Avon for a man named Peters, who was a planter there at Avon. This man Peters had a redheaded daughter who was a true belle, a beautiful woman. I've got some of her trinkets, and my grandfather married her. How a Jew bookkeeper managed to marry the daughter of a planter I don't know, but he swung it somehow. He had three daughters by her and she died bearing the third one. My mother was the middle daughter of the three. The oldest one had a great influence on me because I loved her very much and she was very fond of me and we were close. Her name was Maude. The younger daughter was named Minnie, and I suppose strident is one of the kindest words you can use to describe her. She's still living in Nashville, I think; a dreadful woman. My mother—I couldn't say too many nice things about her. She supported me in every sense all my life. A lot of bad things happened to me and she stood by me through all of them. She got discouraged I'm sure from time to time, but she never reproached me for any of my mistakes. I could see her disappointment. But she never said what I would have said in her place: "There you go again. You're always acting like this." She never did that. The best way to describe her attitude toward me, and it's by no means a complete description, is that she never once hurt my feelings. It is a very strange thing to be that close to someone and never hurt their feelings. I hurt her feelings many times, in anger, in scorn. But she never hurt mine, though she had plenty of reason to.

Jones: What did she think about your work?

Foote: She liked it, and she was happy that I had found what I wanted to do. She would have been happy no matter what I'd done, if I enjoyed doing it.

Jones: At what age do you think that the notion of becoming a novelist and writer came to you?

Foote: It came to me, thank God, not too soon. I was editor of the high school paper there in Greenville, *The Pica,* it's called, so that I suppose I had some literary pretensions. But it didn't interfere with my life before then or even at that time. It took over my life later on. I lived a very normal Delta boyhood in spite of an interest in books. Incidentally, my first interest in books ran from *Bunny Brown and his Sister Sue* through *Tom Swift* up through *Tarzan.* So I've always been glad that I enjoyed dances and helling around the Delta. It's where I got much of the material I use now, so that I'm glad that I didn't become a recluse. When I got to be about sixteen or seventeen I discovered good reading and found out there was another whole world I had scarcely suspected up to then. The real thing that happened to me, I can almost pinpoint it, was when I was about twelve years old. For some reason or other, not having anything to do with school, I read *David Copperfield.* I had done a lot of reading of what I suppose can only be called trash. But reading *David Copperfield* I suddenly got aware that there was a world, if anything, more real than the real world. There was something about that book that made me realize what art is, I suppose, translating now. It made a tremendous impression on me. I didn't then and there rush in to read the rest of Dickens nor fan out into reading other things, but it was the first real clue I had as to the existence of this other world. I had a delayed reaction to it because I was about sixteen or seventeen before I came around to really reading. When I did finally come around to it, for the next five or six years I read quite literally almost everything I could get my hands on, especially modern things. I heard somewhere, probably from Will Percy, that the most important three novels of the twentieth century were Thomas Mann's *Magic Mountain,* Joyce's *Ulysses* and Proust's *Remembrance of Things Past.*

So, the first few months after my seventeenth birthday when my mother gave me the Proust, I read those novels because I considered that I should read them. It was a great time; I was like a colt in clover with that stuff. It was marvelous. That's what, if anything, made me a writer. The other strong influence was the Percy family. I remember I was about fourteen, something like that, out at the country club, swimming, and Will Percy came over. He'd been playing golf—he was a dreadful golfer, but he liked to play occasionally in those days—he came over and said, "Some kinsmen of mine are coming here to spend the summer with me. There are three boys in the group and the two older boys are about your age. I hope you'll come over to the house often and help them enjoy themselves while they're here." I said, "Mr. Will, I'll be glad to." That was the first I heard of Walker, LeRoy, and Phinizy. Soon afterwards they arrived and I began to go over to their house and they began to come over to my house, and we became good and close friends, which we have been ever since.

Jones: I have read that a lot of people think that the fact that there wasn't ever a lynching in Washington County, and the fact that the Klan never gained a foot in the local politics . . .

Foote: Yes.

Jones: And even the fact that Hodding Carter could come there and write freely his type of journalism, was due to the atmosphere that the Percy family created.

Foote: There's a lot of truth in that, but there are other factors. The Percy influence was the main current sociological bar to the Klan. They set a style and an adherence to truth and justice that the Klan could have no part in, and people subscribed to that, so they had a high example in the community to go by, to guide them. They had other things too, though. Jews had always been prominent in Greenville. I was amazed to find anti-Semitism outside of Greenville in the Delta itself and, of course, elsewhere in the country. I was amazed to hear that Jews couldn't belong to the country club in Greenwood. I didn't know what to make of that because there were more Jews than any one religion in the founders of the country club in Greenville. It surprised me greatly. That, too, was a factor. Jews were among the most prominent people in town. If anybody knew Jake Stein and they heard somebody talking anti-Semitic they knew how absurd it was because they knew what a fine man Jake Stein was, and others too. It never caught on. But the Percys must not be underrated in their influence in that fight. Senator Percy was strongly anti-Klan and expressed himself so at every opportunity. Mr. Will as a young man did what he could in that direction, too. In *Lanterns on the Levee,* he tells about the election that was held and how the Klan candidates were defeated. There are still prominent men in Greenville who were members of the Klan, and old citizens know who they are and don't feel too kindly toward them to this day. It was not really as horrendous a thing as it sounds now. The Klan was political, almost social. I don't think that they intended to lynch anybody or put anybody in ovens or anything like that. Most of the members of it were politicians who were looking for bloc votes.

Jones: I heard you say on the ETV "Climate for Genius" series that had Mr. Will and the Percy family lived in Greenwood, then that would have been the place where the literary renaissance took place.

Foote: Yes. Well, now, that's something else. As to my becoming a writer—I said how I got interested in books on my own and everything else—well, Mr. Will had a lot to do with that, too, because he was something quite rare. He was a very good teacher, not a teacher in the sense of lecturing you, though when he got to talking it was very much like lecturing, sometimes. But it was by example. Here was a man who was a world traveler, who was widely read, who knew about the cultured forms of life on other continents, who had experienced the company of some of the fine writers of our time, and he would talk about it in a way that made you not only know the reality of it, but also appreciate the beauty of present day literature and past. I've heard Mr. Will talk about Keats, for example, in a way that made you wish the conversation would hurry up and get over so you could go home and read some Keats. He had that effect on you when he talked about it. He was a great admirer of Browning, too, which I am to this day, partly because of Mr. Will's influence. He had some blind spots, some serious ones with regard to modern literature. He had a low opinion of Faulkner, and he didn't think John Crowe Ransom was much of a poet. They had gone in a way different from his, so he didn't follow them. Surely he was wrong on that. It is a shortcoming on his part not to have been able to see the excellence of Faulkner and Ransom. But what he did like he could make you see why, and make you like it too. He didn't have any literary influence on me, his writing didn't influence my writing, but he was a marvelous example of a man who had availed himself of what good literature has to offer; not only literature, but also music and the dance, painting. He had been almost everywhere and seen almost everything. He was one of the few people I knew who before the war, the Second World War, had been, for example, to Japan and lived there for a time, and loved it very much, crazy about the Japanese.

Jones: But his character was one which was very affecting, wasn't it?

Foote: Right. He had a capacity for great anger. You mustn't think Mr. Will was all sweetness and light. He could get as mad as anyone I've ever known in my life. When the boys and I would get into some kind of trouble and break something—once we broke a fine Venetian chandelier. It was Roy's job to go down and inform him that the chandelier was broken, and I went with him. Mr. Will had a law office down at the Weinberg building in those days. We went down to the law office and stood around—we were about seventeen, I guess—and waited for Mr. Will to come out. He came out and Roy said, "Uh, Uncle Will, that chandelier in the library, I'm afraid it got broken." Mr. Will said, "What do you mean 'it got broken?' " It turned out that I had put some tennis balls in it and the youngest boy, Phinizy, had to turn it to get them and it unscrewed from the thing it was fastened to and came crashing down. Mr. Will said, "Goddamnit, people who don't know how to take care of good property shouldn't be allowed around it!"—just furious. Roy and I we were scared to death of him. I don't know exactly what we thought he was going to do, but his anger was a fearsome thing to be around.

Jones: All the boys felt very close to him?

Foote: Absolutely. Sure. They called him Uncle Will and you see a lot of people referring to him as their uncle. He was their second cousin, their father's cousin. Their grandfather and Mr. Will's father had been brothers; that was the relationship.

Jones: What type of effect do you think that Will Percy and his writing has had on Walker?

Foote: That's an interesting question, because Mr. Will's values are not Walker's values. Walker would find the old Grecian, Roman stoicism perhaps admirable as broadsword virtues, but he doesn't think that's the path to heaven. He would have no satisfaction in it as a solution to what makes a man or what makes his soul. He would find some admiration for those qualities in a man as to character, but as to what made him really a man, Walker would find those unsatisfactory. That's partly because of the difference in their ages. Certain things were satisfactory fifty years ago that no longer are. The attitude toward the Negro, for instance, takes some understanding. Mr. Will, and Senator Percy before him, believed that the best thing any man could do was do his best in his circumstances and be a shining example, I suppose you'd call it, to the people around him. Therefore, the Negro's solution to his oppression and its various problems was to excel in spite of them so that when he made a claim for decent treatment and fair treatment, it had to be respected because of his excellence. That's basically the Booker T. Washington view: "Let your buckets down where you are." By the time Mr. Will came along, people were beginning to see that that might be a pretty good rule for the world at large, but it's not a good rule in a country where all men are supposed to be equal from the outset. A man is not supposed to have to prove he's equal in this country. That was one of the flaws in it. The other was that some of us poor souls are not equipped to do what superior men like Booker T. Washington can do. And it's a dreadful thing to see the government itself passing laws discriminating against you. So this solution of individual excellence was not a satisfactory solution, and Walker would never have found it so. Senator Percy now, before Will Percy, Will Percy's father, he came at the end of his life, as a result of political failures—he lost any popular election he ever ran for—to believe that, as he said, "Shooting at the stars had always seemed to (him) to be pretty poor marksmanship." A man should succeed in his own area. Take his own little postage stamp piece of the country and be a good man inside that, and he would have done what he was put on this earth for. How much of that is sour grapes I don't know. I do know that he enjoyed his term as Senator back in the days when he was elected by the Legislature, and I'm sure he would have liked to have gone on with that. And I think that this late view about "shooting for the stars" is an expression of his disappointment more than anything else, although it was his outlook at the end of his life. I remember Senator

Percy, but only vaguely. I remember him as a dignified gentleman with a white mustache playing golf mainly out at the club. I remember his wife, Miss Camille, a marvelous woman, had a deep voice, very likeable. But they were dead a couple of years before the boys came.

Jones: Yes.

Foote: Yes.

Jones: He died in 1929.

Foote: Was it that early?

Jones: Yes.

Foote: Yes.

Jones: Walker is the oldest brother?

Foote: Yes, but he's only about a year older than LeRoy, a year and a few months.

Jones: And then how much younger is Phinizy?

Foote: Phinizy is about two years younger than LeRoy, maybe two and a half.

Jones: You were good friends with Walker all the way through college?

Foote: We went to Chapel Hill together.

Jones: Yes.

Foote: Then he went on to medical school at Columbia.

Jones: Did you finish at Chapel Hill?

Foote: No, I only went two years. I knew by the time I had been up there about six weeks that I didn't want a degree or anything like that. So I just took what courses I wanted to, and by two years I'd had plenty of it. I've always been glad I didn't stay.

Jones: And at that time you had decided that you wanted to write?

Foote: Well, I certainly hadn't decided I wanted to do anything else. Nobody ever really decides he wants to write. I think I knew that, and aside from jobs in mills and cotton gins and things like that, all the other jobs I'd ever had were as a reporter or something like that.

Jones: At this time did Walker have any idea that he might write?

Foote: He was intent on becoming a doctor, but he was writing. He wrote poetry, both of us wrote a good deal of poetry back in those days and you can go back in the files of *The Pica* and read some of it I'm afraid. But, yeah, we were both writing, and when I got to Chapel Hill I wrote for the *Carolina Magazine*. Walker was so busy getting his science degree that he didn't have much time, but he too wrote a few things for the magazine, reviews of books and general articles on the movies, things like that.

Jones: Knowing Walker like you do, what do you think of the characters he's created: Binx Bolling, Will Barrett, Dr. Tom More. . .

Foote: Well, my judgement of Walker's work is really interfered with. When I read Walker I can hear him talking, and I know some of the stories he's told and some of the experiences we've had together that went into the books. He's not an autobiographical writer in the ordinary sense of Tom Wolfe, of somebody like that, but he does use things out of his life. I read him; I'm a great admirer of his work. I think he's a substantial artist of our time.

Jones: I've read in an article or some place where he said, "You can be sure that I didn't learn to write by sitting at the feet of old men on the front porch listening to them tell stories."

Foote: Right.

Jones: How would you rate that influence on you?

Foote: I would rate it highly. I learned a great deal from listening to old men on the front porch, and so did Walker. He just meant that writing is not something that is picked up out of the air—which, of course, it's not. But he didn't mean by that to slight his material. The material was there for him and he absorbed a great deal of it listening to people talk.

Jones: When did you write for the *Delta Democrat-Times?*

Foote: I never really worked for the *Delta Democrat-Times*. I worked for the *Delta Star.*

Jones: Before they merged.

Foote: Hodding Carter came to Greenville and started the *Delta Star,* and I was a reporter on the *Star.* It was Hodding himself who worked harder than anybody, unless maybe it was his wife Betty who worked harder than he did, and then Donald Weatherbee was the managing editor who worked very hard, then I was the reporter who did not work very hard.

Jones: This was after you got back from college?

Foote: Yes, right after. One of the reasons I didn't go back to school—the main one was I didn't want to, but there was another one—was that the war was heating up in Europe. We all saw it coming. When it started in September of 1939 I joined the Mississippi National Guard, knowing that we'd be put into federal service pretty soon. We didn't go into federal service until November of '40. But during that year I was in the National Guard at home there. We met once a week and went to summer camp, and I knew I was biding my time until we went into service. I was very much in favor of our getting into the war because of Hitler. It was during that year that I worked mostly at the *Delta Star* and I also wrote the first draft of my first novel *Tournament* at that time.

Jones: It seems like your experience as a reporter has affected you, it comes out in your writing—*Follow Me Down*.

Foote: Sure, it would. *Follow Me Down,* for example, is an attempt to show the reaction of a town to a crime of passion, including the court trial. There were such crimes and I attended many such trials, as a reporter and just as a spectator. So, yeah, all that goes into it.

Jones: Was there any factual base behind *Follow Me Down?*

Foote: Yes. There was a man named Floyd Myers who drowned a girl named Emma Jean somebody, I've forgotten her name, and was tried for it and did get life imprisonment at Parchman. That was merely the basis for it. They didn't live on the island or anything like that, but he did drown her in Lake Ferguson there at home. There was that much to it. And I did attend his trial, which I learned a lot from.

Jones: What about the Parker Nowell character?

Foote: He's based in part on a lawyer named Ben Wilkes who was Myers's lawyer in that case, only in part though. Ben Wilkes didn't have a wife who ran off with somebody else. He certainly didn't listen to any thousand dollar phonograph and all that kind of thing. But Nowell was in part based on him. Nobody uses a real character entirely on his own in a book. You use parts of four or five people to make a character. And so I did with Parker Nowell. Nowell's phonograph, for instance, belonged to Mr. Will, which, incidentally, Mr. Will could never operate. He had less mechanical ability than anyone I've ever known in my life. He couldn't operate an automatic pencil. Walker and LeRoy and Phin got together one Christmas. He liked to listen to the radio, but he never could operate one. So, push button radios came out about 1936 or so. It had push buttons on it for getting the different stations. Below, where the push button was, there were celluloid tabs that a light shown through, and you could take a pencil and write WQXR or whatever on the little tabs. The boys showed him how to operate it, said, "All you have to do is push this button and that shows you the station." They came in the next day and he had used a pencil and pushed the pencil through the celluloid things. He could never operate anything. He couldn't drive a car. He could never operate anything mechanical. He was funny, faced with a mechanical problem.

Jones: He was a small man physically, wasn't he?

Foote: Yes. You didn't think of him as small, but he certainly was, just as you didn't think of Faulkner being small and Faulkner was smaller than Mr. Will. Mr. Will would make personal judgments against artists. He didn't think they were exempt from the rules that required you to be well-mannered. Faulkner came over there once in the late twenties, I guess it was. Mr. Will had a tennis court in the back there, and he took tennis pretty seriously. It was the one sport he really did take seriously. Faulkner had been drinking and got out on the tennis court and made a fool of himself. Faulkner never had Mr. Will's admiration as a writer or a man or anything else after that display on the tennis court; he'd shake his head about it every time he would remember it. He didn't think anything good could come from anybody who would do a thing like that.

Jones: Were you at home when Mr. Will died?

Foote: I was at officer candidate school at Fort Sill, Oklahoma, and I got a leave, a furlough, just before I went there. I was a sergeant in the 114th Field Artillery and I got to go to officer candidate school, and on the way there I got to spend a few days at home. Mr. Will was in the hospital dying then. I had seen him earlier when his health had started failing. He had an ailment known as aphasia. His words would jumble up; he would mean to say one thing and say another. Sometimes what he said didn't make sense. He spent that last year in great distress, I now realize. He seldom dressed—he would usually have on a dressing gown. I can remember seeing him standing around—it was only when I came home on weekend leaves and things like that—but I remember being with him there one day and he said something, and I laughed. He said, "You mustn't laugh when

I make mistakes, I have an ailment that makes me make those mistakes." It is very sad to me. It was a tragic death, in a way. It's especially poignant because a couple of years before that, before it ever hit him, he told me once he thought the worst death any man ever died was Maurice Ravel, who had just died about that time, and Ravel had aphasia. He said the particular horror was that Ravel's thoughts, as he understood it, were quite clear, but he could not express them. He could think music, but he couldn't write it down or play it on the piano. And that seemed to him like a particular hell on earth. Then within two years—I think Ravel died in '37 or '38—a couple of years after that there was Mr. Will going through what Ravel had gone through and what he described as a particular hell on earth. It was very sad. He died while I was at Fort Sill. I remember getting a telegram from my mother about his death in the spring of '42.

Jones: Was he suffering that illness when he was writing *Lanterns on the Levee?*

Foote: No, he had finished *Lanterns on the Levee.* He wrote *Lanterns on the Levee* on big, yellow legal tablets, and his secretary, whose name was Mitchell Finch, typed them for him. He, of course, couldn't have begun to type anything. He wrote it in pencil on these yellow sheets and Mitchell Finch would type them up for him. I remember he got me to read a couple of the chapters that he was particularly delighted with. They read to me, in those early drafts, like he was finally writing down what he had been telling us for so many years, and they were not as effective written down as they had been verbally, orally. But when I saw them in print I saw how good they were. But in that form, typed, except that they were pretty close to the exact way he phrased things talking, they didn't seem as good to me. Then when they got in print I could see how good they were. *Lanterns on the Levee* is a beautiful book in many ways.

Jones: Yes, I think so.

Foote: It is, however, a plea for and a summation of the conservative position, and, as such, it's not hard to discredit it. Many of the evils that I grew up with are defended in that position, and would never have been corrected with that position. The most persuasive thing about it is his gentleness, his honesty, and his fairness. I don't mean to shortchange any of those qualities in him. They were all there in as full force as in any man I've ever known.

But I think most of us can see now that men in those days didn't really address themselves to the problems that were on hand. A thing that people might not know about him though, if they took him simply as some stereotype conservative, was his insistence on respect for Negroes at all times. I remember once I was over there sitting out in the living room reading and the doorbell rang and I went to it and there was a black man standing there, rather well-dressed and everything, and he said, "I've come to see Mr. William A. Percy," and I said, "Just a minute." I went back—Mr. Will was in his study back there—and I said, "Mr. Will, there's a nigger out here to see you." Mr. Will looked at me real hard and said, "Tell Dr. so-and-so to come right in." I had not meant anything by it, just a Mississippi boy talking, but he was quick to correct me on that kind of talk. And quite right. But he was closed off from anything he might think of as radical. Langston Hughes came down home and was addressing one of the Negro church congregations there, and the minister, who had known Mr. Will and Mr. Will liked, asked Mr. Will if he would introduce him. Mr. Will said he'd be glad to. So he went down there and it was an all-black congregation and Mr. Will introduced Langston Hughes as a fellow poet and an admirable writer. And then Langston Hughes, with Mr. Will sitting there, made what Mr. Will could only think of as a communist speech, I guess, or something. Anyway, he was furious at having been drawn into introducing a radical like Langston Hughes. Of course, Langston Hughes was not a radical, but he sounded radical to Mr. Will. I guess Hughes wanted people to stand up and demand their rights, and Mr. Will wanted them to earn them. I keep making it sound like he was a dark, double-dyed conservative. In some ways he was, but he was not looked on as a conservative by the community. They thought Mr. Will was practically a "mixer," as they call them nowadays. They didn't think it was right that he would receive Negroes in his home and discuss seriously the sociological and other problems with them. That was looked on as a pretty wild thing to do in those days.

Jones: He looked upon Negroes and the aristocracy as the true inheritors of the Delta.

Foote: That's right, that's right. There was nothing really unusual about that view; Faulkner expressed it sometimes. He said, "The white people have already lost their heads; it depends now on whether the Negroes can keep theirs." Oh, yeah. Their virtues, to Mr. Will, had almost nothing to do with freedom, it had to do with dignity, and suffering injustice in a better way than most people can. It would take a lot of thinking about before you would presume to sit in judgment on Mr. Will's views, but they are the views of the people who created a system that had a great deal wrong with it.

Jones: I sometimes feel that what Mr. Will was, Walker is working against.

Foote: Well, that's right; he is. But he's working against what's wrong with it. He's still admiring of what is right with it. I guess the best example of Mr. Will himself in Walker's fiction is in *The Moviegoer.* The aunt in that expresses the virtues Mr. Will believed in, and Walker obviously, at least Binx Bolling obviously, sees the inadequacy of those virtues. That's one of the things the book is about.

Jones: Your earliest influences were Proust, Mr. Will, and who else?

Foote: Certainly William Faulkner. *Light in August* was one of the first current novels I read. It came out around 1932 when I started reading earnestly. I read *Light in August* and I was tremendously impressed by it, and also puzzled by it. I've never written a letter to an author saying how much I liked his work or didn't like his work, but I had a very strong inclination to sit down and write Mr. Faulkner a letter saying, "You had such a good story to tell, why didn't you tell it instead of confusing me the way you did?" I've always been glad I didn't write that letter.

Jones: Did you come to know him?

Foote: Yes. I was with Faulkner maybe five, six times; spent the night in his house once, took a trip with him up to Shiloh once, had dinner with him and Miss Estelle a couple of times. I liked him very much. He was a friendly, even outgoing man with certain reticences. His reticences never bothered me; I figured a man with that big a genius strapped to his back would be bound to have some pretty hard times.

Jones: But you didn't see any great incongruities in him?

Foote: No, I didn't. I've read where other people did; I didn't. He seemed like William Faulkner to me, man and writer. I did not find any gap between the two. The man wasn't as great as the writer, but

I'm sure that's nearly always true of great writers. I simply liked him. He was a good companion, a likeable man, a great deal of humor, a gracious host, and seemed like a fine husband—which I later found out he was not. But I liked him.

Jones: It seems to people, especially in my generation, the things that are taught to you about him are all rather dark concerning his personality.

Foote: Yep. Those things are rather hard to judge when you are young and a person's reputation is not overwhelming at that point. You'd just see him for what he was and you liked him or you didn't like him.

Jones: Was he interested in the Civil War, too?

Foote: Yes, he was interested in the Civil War, but only in an amateurish way. He didn't know much about it. Faulkner was never interested in the facts, the hard background, statistics, any of that. But he had a very fine if somewhat romantic view of the War, and he knew the general shape of it far better than most so-called buffs. He had a real good eye for terrain. I walked him over the field at Shiloh, surely one of the most confusing fields of the War, and he caught on to it fast. And I don't think he had ever been there before.

Jones: We talked earlier about how old people, sitting around talking and telling stories that even I still hear, influenced you a great deal. Were there stories passed around in your family about the War?

Foote: No; very few. I only saw about two or three Civil War veterans in my whole lifetime, and they had probably been drummer boys or something. Not much talk about the War. There were certain things left over from the War. There were old maiden aunts whose sweethearts had been killed in the War. There were widows of Confederate soldiers around; they'd married the old men when they were fairly young and the men were old. There were customs that were very much a part of it, although you didn't realize them too well. For example, we never celebrated the Fourth of July because that was the day Vicksburg fell. I remember there was one family—it was very unusual to have outsiders, even in Greenville in those days—but there was a family there from Ohio and on the Fourth of July they all got in their car and went up on the levee and had a picnic and they forgot to set the brakes and the car rolled down the levee and fell in the river. Everybody said it served them right for celebrating the Fourth of July.

Jones: Confederate history is something that has just always fascinated you?

Foote: Yes. I read background material on the Civil War at certain phases of my life the way other people read detective stories. It did fascinate me. The actual mechanics of the battles and everything interested me. I wanted to find out what happened. And certain people: Stonewall Jackson, Bedford Forrest, Robert E. Lee, interested me. I wanted to know about their lives. I would read biographies of them—Henderson's *Jackson* was one of the first that drew me to it, and Robert Self Henry's *Story of the Confederacy* was an important book for me as a young man, a child, really.

Jones: When you were in the Second World War, did you have combat experience?

Foote: No. I was in the Fifth Division, a regular Army division, and we were stationed in Northern Ireland during the training period for the year leading up to the invasion. I had a serious run-in with a colonel in my battalion, and out of that a serious run-in with the general of the whole damn brigade, and as a result of their watching and waiting they jumped on me for falsifying a trip ticket about a trip to Belfast and brought me before a general court-martial, and I was dismissed from the Army for falsifying a government document. It was a real con job. What happened was they had a rule that you could not use a government vehicle for pleasure beyond the range of fifty miles, and our battalion was fifty-two miles from Belfast. The other two battalions were inside the circumference. So, we commonly changed our trip ticket to forty-eight miles instead of fifty-two. Anyway, that was the thing I was charged with. It was just a simple con job. I came on home, worked for Associated Press for about three months in New York, and then joined the Marine Corps. I was in the Marine Corps a year, including combat intelligence school at Camp Lejeune, and then was in California waiting to go over when they dropped the bomb, and I got out on points. I had plenty of points because I had four years in the Army and a year in the Marine Corps. I was a captain in the Army and a private in the Marine Corps. The other Marines used to say, "You used to be a captain, didn't you? You ought to make a pretty good Marine private."

Jones: It would seem like you had some combat experience just because of the way you write so vividly about the Civil War battles.

Foote: Well, the Army experience itself was very useful to me. I learned a great many maneuvers of all kinds, and I did study hard the use of artillery and tactics.

Jones: Tell me the story of how you came to write the trilogy. Originally it didn't start off to be that, did it?

Foote: No, it started off to be a short history of the Civil War. Random House wanted me to do it and Bennett Cerf was happy about it and I signed a contract for a short history of the Civil War. It was going to be about 200,000 words, not a long book at all. But I hadn't any more than started before I saw I wasn't the one to write any short history of the Civil War; just a summary of what happened really didn't interest me. But I was enormously interested in the whole thing. So, about the time I got started—in fact, I hadn't done much more than block out what I call the plot—when I saw it was going to take a lot more space than that. My editor at Random House then was Robert Linscott, a very nice man, and I wrote him and told him I'd like to go spread-eagle, whole-hog on the thing. It must have been a terrible shock to him, but he saw Cerf and whoever else he had to see and made his recommendations; they considered it, I suppose—I never heard any of that; he just wrote back and said, "Go ahead." So I did. What was really upsetting to them, this was supposed to be the first volume in an historical series they were going to do: one on the Civil War, one on the Revolution, and so forth. This first one turned into a gigantic trilogy, so they didn't try any more.

Jones: Immediately you saw how enormous your task was going to be?

Foote: Yes.

Jones: And at that time did you realize that you were going to put your fiction down for twenty years?

Foote: No, I had no idea. I knew how big it was going to be, but I thought I could write it fast. I thought it would take me two years instead of one to write a volume. Actually, it turned out it took me five years on each on the first two and ten years on the third.

Jones: And did you put down your fiction during that time?

Foote: Absolutely. I've never in my life been able to do but one thing at a time.

Jones: What were your sources, besides the *Official Records?*

Foote: Well, as you say, the *Official Records* were the main thing, but my sources were probably not over 250, 300 books. And I didn't use letters or things like that, manuscript stuff. I stuck to printed material.

Jones: Where did you get the insights that made it a narrative?

Foote: From learning how to write novels.

Jones: Is that right?

Foote: That's exactly what it is. Novelists know instinctively not to do things that historians do all the time. It's what makes historians such poor reading, and I'm not talking about being entertaining, I'm talking about what makes you dissatisfied with an historian, a dry, unskilled historian's history. There are great historians, I'm not talking about them. There has never been a greater novelist or writer of any kind than Tacitus, for instance, who was a great historian by any standards; Gibbon, Thucydides. It's just that a lot of modern historians are scared to death to suggest that life has a plot. They've got to take it apart and have a chapter on slavery, a chapter on "The Armies Meet," chapters on this, that, and the other. There's something almost low-life about trying to write about events from a human point of view. So they say. The result is they have no real understanding of the Civil War because they don't understand what Lincoln's problems were. They don't see them as problems impinging on a man; they see them as theoretical problems. I'm not saying what they do has no validity; I am saying it has no art. Of course, without their work I could have done nothing. They get along without me very well, but I couldn't get along without them.

Jones: Regimental histories, I've heard you say, played a large part.

Foote: Yes. They are not to be trusted for facts, but they are to be greatly admired for incidentals: how soldiers felt, what they did, sometimes humor, which is a necessary ingredient. I sometimes think that there's never been a single page of very great writing that did not have humor in it. It may be dark humor, it may be sardonic, it may be this and that and the other, but there's always humor in any good writing. There's scarcely a passage in Shakespeare that doesn't have humor in it, even if it's just a crazy juxtaposition of two words.

Jones: In your opinion, has history overrated or underrated any figures from the War?

Foote: Absolutely. The underrating of Jefferson Davis is almost like a giant conspiracy. Davis was a warm, friendly, outgoing man. When you read about him in history he sounds like a cold-blooded prig. It is almost unexplainable. It's just hard to believe how this gigantic conspiracy got formed, because some very fine historians think of Davis as a stiff, unbending man. He was not, not at all; he was the opposite of that. I just think, somehow, they don't pay any attention to things like his letters to his wife or those things, his fondness for his children. They would begin to question those things if they understood better the kind of man he really was.

Jones: Do you feel like he made the largest contribution to the Confederate war effort?

Foote: No, I wouldn't say that. Robert E. Lee is certainly a rival in that regard. He was the hardest working man in the Confederacy, I think—Jefferson Davis was. I agree with what Lee said; he said he didn't think anyone could have done a better job than Davis did, and so far as he personally was concerned he didn't know anyone who could have done as well. Davis had his shortcomings; he was too testy in his dealings with men like Joe Johnston and Beauregard. But I agree with Lee that, in sum, he did a better job than anybody else I know would have done.

Jones: What about on the Union side, who do you think was the most important individual?

Foote: Well, in this case there's no doubt at all because Lincoln was. But Lincoln was a genius. He was a true political genius, and those are rare. It's one of Mr. Davis's misfortunes to be compared to Lincoln. Almost nobody can be compared to Lincoln.

Jones: Do you think Davis had the foremost intellect of his time?

Foote: No, Davis was not even an intellectual, though most people think he was. He was not. His tastes were really quite simple. In poetry his favorite poet was Robert Burns, who is a good poet, but certainly not of heavy intellect. He had little humor, too little humor, far too little humor, although he had more than most people realize. No, Davis had determination, will, and enormous integrity. If he gave a man his word there was no way he could be persuaded to go back on it. Lincoln would break his word to his best friend on earth, in two minutes, if it would help the Union cause to do it. And he never kept his word beyond the point where the conditions under which he gave it pertained. His enormous flexibility, his pragmatism, were incredible.

Jones: Do you think Davis could have served the Confederacy better as commander of the Mississippi troops?

Foote: No, I think Davis was right where he belonged. I've never been satisfied that Davis would have been a first-rate soldier. He was too intelligent for that, if you see what I mean. A good general ought to be a little stupid, to keep from getting rattled. There was a genius on the Confederate side all right, but it wasn't Davis or Lee, it was Bedford Forrest. I once told General Forrest's granddaughter that I had thought long and hard about these matters and I had decided that there were two authentic geniuses in the Civil War; one was her grandfather, Bedford Forrest, and the other was Abraham Lincoln. There was a pause at the other end of the telephone. Finally she said, "You know, we never thought much of Mr. Lincoln in my family." She didn't like that coupling, that comparison, at all, and didn't think much of me for making it.

Jones: What about individuals in the war who were overrated?

Foote: Well, there are a lot of those, but it's hard to know who is doing the overrating and does it matter and all that.

Jones: Yes.

Foote: There are generals I don't like personally; Joe Johnston's one of them. Phil Sheridan's another. But I don't say from that they were overrated, it is just that they had flaws that rubbed me the wrong way. I hope I didn't let that show in the book, though I'm sure it did to some degree. A historian has a great fondness for scoundrels. Edwin Stanton was a scoundrel, but he's very useful to me. He livens a page, picks it up. So too, just as there can't be any good without evil, he makes a good contrast for some other people who wouldn't show up as well if you didn't have Stanton to compare them to.

Jones: What about the notion that the North fought the War with one hand behind its back, do you think that's accurate?

Foote: Yes, I often say that, and I think it's quite true. In the course of the War, the North passed and acted on the Homestead Act. They developed the West while the War was going on. Incredible inventions were made during the Civil War—wars always bring on inventions—but things that you don't think of like the fountain pen, or the machine that sewed the uppers to the soles of shoes, were made where one person could do the work of forty people. There were many things like that. Some of our finest institutions of education were founded during the Civil War: Vassar, M.I.T., and a lot more. My point in this is that the North was doing all those things and fighting the War at the same time. If they had had to do more to win the War, they simply would have done a great deal more instead of these other things they were doing. The Confederacy put close to everything it had into that War, but the North, as I said, fought it with one hand tied behind its back, on purpose. And they got rich in the process—selling their wheat crop to England, for instance.

Jones: So to think that the War was lost at Vicksburg, or the War was lost at Gettysburg, is completely erroneous.

Foote: If I had to pick any one point at which I said the War was lost—and I never would—I would say Fort Donelson.

Jones: In '62.

Foote: Yes, way early; February of '62. It did about four different things: it caused the loss of Tennessee and Kentucky—in the sense that Kentucky was never going to be recovered. It led to the isolation of the Transmississippi. Above all, it marked the emergence of U. S. Grant, the man who was going to win the War. But Donelson was reversible at Shiloh, except they didn't reverse it, so that you slip back and say, "No, Shiloh was the decisive point," and then, "No, if we had done this at Gettysburg," and you keep on with these might-have-beens and you wind up nowhere. I think the truth of the matter is there was no way the South could have won that war. The one outside chance was British recognition, and help, and we were not going to get that, especially after Lincoln defined the War as a war against slavery. The English people would never have put up with their leaders taking them into a war that had been defined on those terms.

Jones: But isn't it true that there was a point where England and France, especially Napoleon III who had recommended it, were considering intervention?

Foote: Napoleon III wanted to intervene for his own reasons, primarily to get Confederate cotton, I think, also to weaken a growing opponent, and perhaps some political maneuvering to get England involved so that strength could be drawn off that way. But the high point that is often pointed to in recognition is a British cabinet meeting that went on about the time the Battle of Sharpsburg, or what the Union people called Antietam, was being fought. When the results of that reached England, Lee was in retreat and the time had passed when they could have recognized them. But I'm not at all convinced that if Lee had been successful in that invasion the British would have recognized and engaged in the War. That was a big step they weren't about to take. You have to remember certain consequences to England if they had come into that war. The War of 1812 had wiped the British merchant fleet off the seas, and the Northern navy would have done the same thing in the 1860s. England wasn't about to be crippled that greatly at a time when French power was growing and the Germans were a threat from another direction and all this was going on. There couldn't be any kind of winner in that kind of thing. And the English have never been famous for pulling anybody's chestnuts out of the fire. They had general admiration for the Confederates, but that admiration wasn't about to be translated into terms of anybody going over and fighting, or risking their fleet.

Jones: Even if things had worked out where Lee would have won at Gettysburg and had gone down and taken Washington, that, in your opinion, wouldn't have affected the ultimate outcome?

Foote: Well, it's problematical, of course, but not very profitable to speculate on.

Jones: Yes. Today, do you still visit the battlefields?

Foote: Very seldom. If I happen to be close to one I might drop by to see it. I get a particular satisfaction out of doing it because I feel that it sort of belongs to me now that I've written about it—all writers feel that. But not much anymore. I've been determined to wash the Civil War out of my head ever since I finished that third volume, and I've pretty well done it, too. I don't remember now where Stonewall Jackson was born.

Jones: Did you take President Carter around the battlefield at Gettysburg?

Foote: Yes, and Sharpsburg and Harpers Ferry, all three of them.

Jones: When was that?

Foote: July of '78.

Jones: Was he knowledgeable about the War?

Foote: Yes, not beyond the average good buff, but he knew the War and was very interested, particularly in what Georgia troops did—a natural thing, and likable. I liked Carter very much; still do.

Jones: Was it hard for you to get back into the field of fiction after twenty years on the War?

Foote: Writing is always hard work, but no, it wasn't any harder writing *September September* than it had been writing *The Civil War.*

Jones: Tell me where the idea for *September September* came from.

Foote: I really don't know; it's not based on anything. There was no case like that here or anything like it. I wanted to get my hand back in by writing a short, action novel; so I did. I researched it hard, the way I'd done in history. The whole book takes place in the month of September in 1957, which I could remember because I was in Memphis, and I went down and read the *Commercial Appeal* and the *Press-Scimitar* for the month of September 1957, as a way of starting. I took notes on what the temperatures were and how much rain fell on the various days, phases of the moon, changes that have been made in the city since then. So I wanted it to be accurate, but I always wanted that, in my earlier books too. The headlines and things that are quoted in *September* are right out of the two papers.

Jones: Seems like you have sort of mellowed from *Follow Me Down* to *September September*. Both of them are about a crime; yet in *September September* no one gets murdered.

Foote: Yes. What's more, I have a lot more tolerance of people's shortcomings than I had back in those days, I think, because I've discovered a good many of them in myself.

Jones: I personally enjoyed *September September* very much.

Foote: I'm glad. I expected it to be a runaway bestseller, which it certainly was not. Everybody always thinks something's going to be a runaway best-seller. I've been lately reading about Faulkner; he thought *Absalom, Absalom!* was going to take off like a rocket. It certainly did not. It came out about the same time as *Gone With the Wind,* in the same year, anyhow. I don't know whether Faulkner ever read *Gone With the Wind* or not. He said, "No story needs to be a thousand pages long!" I don't think he ever read *Gone With the Wind.*

Jones: I read once where a reporter had asked him who he had been reading presently, and he said, "I don't read my contemporaries," and walked across the room and proceeded to tell some writer that their work was directly related to this other writer's work.

Foote: Right. The only book I actually saw him read was a book called *Bugles in the Afternoon* by Ernest Haycox, a western. But he was an avid reader. I've talked with him about other books, but that's the only book I ever actually saw him read.

Jones: Let me ask you a pretty nebulous question that I think has a lot to do with what your fiction shows. What effect do you think the Southern defeat in the Civil War has had on us and our ideology and our character?

Foote: Profound effect. In the movie *Patton*, Patton stands up in front of an enormous American flag and says, "We Americans have never lost a war, and will never lose a war as long as we keep our qualities." Patton was from Virginia, and when he said, "We Americans have never lost a war," I couldn't believe he knew what he was saying. He had lost a war. Southerners are in close touch with some things that the rest of the country doesn't know much about, and one of them is military defeat. And it wasn't just defeat; it was grinding defeat. Without being annihilated, very few sides in a war have ever been trounced as thoroughly as the Confederacy was trounced. We were really beaten in that war; we were beaten far worse than the Germans were in either of the world wars, for instance. We were ground down into the ground, and then ground down some more after it was over. Southerners who are at all aware of their history—and even if they aren't it's part of their heritage—are among the people on earth who know best what defeat is, and it has a great deal to do with the way we see the world. We are also thoroughly familiar with injustice, which can be recognized at a hundred yards from our treatment of the blacks over the century, so that a lot of American ideals are bound to sound pretty absurd to an observant Southerner who has been in touch with the underside of the American character. It's very important, the fact that we were defeated in a war.

Jones: We've talked for about an hour and a half and I've got more questions that I'd like to ask you, but I think at this point it would be good if we either took a break or I came back tomorrow.

Jones: This is John Jones with the Mississippi Department of Archives and History, back for a second interview with Mr. Shelby Foote. Today is Friday, August 17, 1979, and we are at Mr. Foote's house in Memphis. Yesterday we touched on some things that I would like to pick up on today. Following Faulkner's death in '62, didn't you go to the University of Virginia as writer-in-residence?

Foote: Not really. I've been truly writer-in-residence at Hollins College for one semester, and while I was at Hollins I simply went down to Virginia for four or five days and sat in on some question-and-answer things and gave a reading in one of the auditoriums. I was not writer-in-residence at Virginia though; I was writer-in-residence at Hollins. I don't believe in writers having much to do with college campuses, or intellectuals for that matter, but it was a way of paying my daughter's tuition at Hollins. I made enough money to pay her way through school, and that's why I did it. I also gave a series of lectures here at Memphis State, about eight or ten lectures, I've forgotten. That was to pick up eating money while I was writing the third volume of the War. The Hollins job I took sort of in between the second and third volumes.

Jones: What exactly does a writer-in-residence do?

Foote: He usually teaches creative writing; that's usually his job. But since I didn't and don't believe creative writing can be taught, I taught a course on the modern novel. It was funny, too. I had four or five novels, I've forgotten which; they were Hemingway's *In Our Time,* Fitzgerald's *Tender is the Night,* Faulkner's *The Hamlet*, and I wound up with George Eliot's *Middlemarch*, which is my favorite English novel and I claim is a very modern novel. But after I started teaching these girls, who were twenty and twenty-one—they were all seniors or graduate students—I realized that every one of those novels had been written before those girls were born. Time had really caught up with me. But a writer-in-residence usually sort of gives the students a chance to get to know a working writer. I suppose it had some value; my advice to them always was stay away from writers. But I enjoyed doing it. For one thing, I had very little use for the young people of the sixties. They were talking what sounded to me to be an awful lot of foolishness. For example, they wanted to know if a thing was "relevant," and if it wasn't "relevant" they didn't want to have anything to do with it. It turned out that a lot of things that mean the most to me weren't "relevant," like Milton and Browning. That set me off. I also did not like their music, any of it. I never thought much of social protest in the forms they favored. I don't have any basic objection to blowing up buildings and things, but I don't like a lot of spouting off and running around with rifles lifted in the air and giving salutes and things. Those were the prejudices I went there with. I was pleased to learn that though I never lost my objection to any of those things that I just listed, I did like the young people very much; they were likeable in back of all I considered horrendous. They were likeable people. So it did me that amount of good. I still believe strongly that a college campus is a dreadful place for a working, creative writer.

Jones: You don't feel like you can combine academics and creativity?

Foote: It might be done by somebody, but he'd have to write about academic things, I would think—which is not a very satisfactory subject for a novelist. The main objection to it I had was a general sharing of intellectual concerns. People would sit around drinking all night long, talking about their work in progress, which I never would under any circumstances do. I can't imagine any writer talking about what he's trying to write about. I once saw a very foolish criticism, I think by Malcolm Cowley, of William Faulkner. He was talking about the unevenness of Faulkner's writing, that there was a good deal of erratic and even halfbaked stuff in Faulkner, and his prescription for Faulkner was that he wished he could have had intellectual friends to talk with and then he wouldn't have had to commit all that foolishness in his work, he could have committed the foolishness in conversation with his friends. I don't know whether it ever occurred to Cowley, but he could have also committed the nonfoolishness in the presence of friends. These people I got to know, I liked them personally, poets and people like that who were writers-in-residence—they certainly were not writing any poetry; they were making a living. A lot of them had a wife and two or three children and they had to make a living, I suppose. It's hard to turn down fifteen or twenty thousand dollars a year and a house to live in, but it's not any way to live when you're a writer.

Jones: Did Mr. Faulkner feel the same way about it?

Foote: Well, he did become writer-in-residence at Virginia for two years. I've always thought that Faulkner, by that time, had decided that he had done his work and deserved some rest and amusement. And he was a vain man, as indeed all of us are, and I think he enjoyed the adulation and the company of young people. There's another thing about Faulkner—once the Nobel Prize came along, the public moved to meet him with respect. Before that, he had been an object of contempt, especially in his own town. He got the reputation of being extraordinarily stand-offish. I've heard that once, in objection to something that happened after *Sanctuary* came out, people would drive into his gate and around the driveway and stare at him. He didn't like that; he thought it was rude. He put up signs telling them to keep out, but they'd come in anyway. So, one day he was sitting on the gallery having a drink, and this carload of tourists, I guess you'd call them, came in to stare at him. He jumped on the banister and urinated into the flower bed in full view of these people, and they took off in a hurry. But I think when people moved toward him in any genial way he was genial in return. I know that, because he knew that I wasn't interested in any secrets out of his private life, and if I had been interested I wouldn't have presumed to ask him about them; he knew that. In my relationship with him he was one of the most genial, outgoing men I've ever known—delighted to talk about his work. He had no objection at all to talking about his work, and I talked with him a good deal about it.

Jones: Do you think he resented the way the people of Oxford saw him? Going to school up there you hear all kinds of wild stories.

Foote: Yes, I think he did resent it, and he had every right to resent it. When I was a young man, back in the thirties, you'd be in Oxford and you'd ask directions on how to get to his house, and people would turn their heads to the side and spit into the street. They didn't like him being there, and they didn't want anything to do with anybody who wanted anything to do with him. It was that bad. Also consider some of the Tom Wolfe syndrome. Wolfe, you know, was told that if he ever returned to Asheville they'd lynch him. They wouldn't have, but they told him that. Well, some people in Oxford thought Faulkner's stories of miscegenation and all that kind of thing were giving the Glorious South a bad name, and they resented that. I never had much of that trouble. I had some general resentment by people that I didn't punch a clock, but that's about all it amounted to. Anything I did, like I had a big white boxer, weighed over a hundred pounds—I was very fond of him, he was with me all the time—a lot of people thought that was a total affectation to have this big white dog that you go around with.

Jones: Where were you living then?
Foote: Greenville.
Jones: Did you work on your trilogy when you were working at Hollins?
Foote: I've never done any work away from my home. I did do some research and take some notes and things like that, but I hadn't any more than started on that Hollins job, which I had agreed to, than my mother came down with cancer, and I had to commute between Hollins and here almost every weekend. She was in the hospital here in Memphis, and at home here too. She left Greenville and came up here to be with us during all this treatment. I had planned to do a good deal of work—I was up there by myself; my wife stayed here with our child—but because of my mother's critical illness during that time I didn't.
Jones: Was that the major reason you took ten years on your third volume?
Foote: Well, when I finished the second volume I thought I had another five years to go on and I accepted this Ford Foundation grant with the Arena Stage in Washington as a sort of vacation, a way of resting up for starting the third volume. I enjoyed it. We got a townhouse in Georgetown with a swimming pool and all that. We spent Mr. Ford's money right and left. We were there about, I don't know, six or eight months, and it was very pleasant, and that six or eight months I deliberately used as a vacation. Following the Washington thing we had the brilliant idea of going down to the Alabama coast and building a house on the Gulf there. There were two things wrong with that: one, I got crossways with the Ku Klux Klan down there during the George Wallace days, and the other was we had an architect here in Memphis named Adalotte design a house for us. It was a three-story house with a nine-foot gallery all the way around the two top stories. It was a beautiful house; but we found that in a sixty-mile-an-hour wind it would fly. So we had a lot of delays on that, and finally decided not to build it.
Jones: What kind of pressure did you get in Alabama from the Klan?
Foote: It wasn't bad. It was the kind of pressure anybody would run into down there if he let it be known what his feelings were, different from theirs. They considered that their backs were to the

wall and they even translated themselves into terms of being modern-day Confederates, which is what they were not, and I told them every time I had any kind of confrontation with one of them or saw them with a Confederate flag; I told them they were a disgrace to the flag, that everything they stood for was almost exactly the opposite of everything the Confederacy had stood for, that the Confederacy believed in law and order above all things. Its main hope was to get in front of the courts, while they were cussing the courts and wanting not to have anything to do with them and wanting to disobey the orders of the courts. I created a good deal of resentment against myself down there until they decided I was crazy and then they were more sympathetic.

Jones: You've said you've spent the last five years or so trying to wash the Civil War out of your head.

Foote: Yes.

Jones: Do you feel like your fiction is a more lasting literary contribution?

Foote: I don't know how I feel about that; I don't know that it is more lasting. It could be that I have more pride in and affection for my fiction than I have for my history because it all came out of my head rather than out of documents. But I'm satisfied with that job I did on the War; those three volumes suit me; I'm proud of them, and willing to stand by them. I'm also protective of the novels because most people think that the history is my serious work and the novels are not up to that standard. I disagree with that, violently.

Jones: Do you get more pleasure out of working with fiction?

Foote: No, they're not that different, writing history and writing fiction. All the same problems are there. Somewhere in one of the bibliographical notes I said it doesn't much matter if facts come out of documents or out of your head, they are still things you work with and respect. You are looking for the truth, and, as I said also, it's not a different truth, it's the same truth. You try and find out the truth, and it doesn't really make that much difference—to the person writing it, anyhow—whether you made up the facts, which you then must respect, or you found them in documents, which you must respect. I never felt cramped at all while writing the history. I felt just as free as I feel when I'm writing a novel. It's true, I couldn't make up the color of a man's eyes, but I could find out what color they were. It just meant a little harder work.

Jones: You didn't have any facts in the trilogy that weren't completely documented?

Foote: Absolutely not. If the work didn't have absolute historical integrity it would have been a total waste of time. There would be no point whatsoever in doing a novelistic treatment in the sense of inventing scenes that would explain Robert E. Lee or how Stonewall Jackson looked. All that has to come out of fact, and the whole thing would have been vitiated if I had invented anything or distorted anything. It wouldn't do. I've never known a modern historical instance where the truth wasn't superior to anybody's distortion. I would be willing for that book to be subjected to any kind of iron rule about accuracy. If I didn't do that, I would say that it was not worthwhile.

Jones: I was always fascinated by the incidentals in the narrative. You knew exactly at what point Stonewall Jackson was leaning up against a tree sucking on a lemon.

Foote: That's right. Those things are all in the documents. Nothing flatters me more than to have someone ask me if I made up some scene, because I hope it sounds as if a novelist wrote it, but I didn't make up anything in it. I may have done some conjectures of which I do very little in that book, and my interpretation of why somebody did something or the future effect of what had been done in the past is a contribution, I hope. But any facts in there are facts, whether it's the weather or the color of somebody's hair and eyes or his height and weight or his age or what his schooling was, what his voice sounded like; all those things are accurate. I'm not saying I didn't make some errors and mistakes, I'm sure I did. But they were as accurate as I knew how to make them.

Jones: What about when you were writing, did you read one sequence ahead in the *Official Records* or would you get a whole overall view and write from that?

Foote: I did a whole overall view, reread some of my favorite books, read other books that I had not read, biographies, general histories of the War, studies of individual campaigns, always the *Official Records of the War of the Rebellion,* that 128-volume monster. I read all that and that gave me the information with which to plot the whole three-volume work. Having done that and having straight in my mind how the plot was going, I then researched each individual incident as I came to it. I would generally research at night and write in the daytime.

Jones: But you could sit down and write the complete scene freehand?

Foote: Yes. I would have notes stuck up on the bulletin board for quotations or so I could remember what book something was in. I never had a typist or an assistant or a research person or anything like that. I did it all myself, and I couldn't have done it any other way. I couldn't have asked somebody to go find something in a book for me; I would have gone crazy waiting for them to find it, for one thing. And I certainly didn't want anybody turning out a whole bunch of notes for me, so I didn't want any kind of secretarial assistant. I didn't even want anybody typing it because that gave me another chance to improve it—each copy you make is that much better. But I would be sitting down writing a scene and I would remember something that happened and that somebody said something at that point; then I would scratch my head and remember what book it was in, and then when I went over and got the book I would remember that it was about two-thirds of the way down the page on the left-hand side, and I would find it. Sometimes I would be stopped dead cold in my tracks for two hours while I tried to remember what book and what part of that book it was in. But that was my way of doing it, and it suited me. Any short cut would have been an interference.

Jones: What about the criticism you got on the trilogy, was it mainly that you took too much of a Southern bias?

Foote: There was a little bit of that. There was some objection to winding up on the note of Jefferson Davis, for instance, as a continuation of this war against Jefferson Davis which was waged from 1861 to 1979, and will continue to be waged. There was a little bit of that, but to tell you the truth I saw very little criticism of anything about those books. It was all praise. There was no attack on it, almost none. I saw, I'd be guessing if I'd say, four or five hundred reviews, and practically none of them, some of them were lightweight and slight, but nobody really attacked it, said "No, no, no." Some people were disappointed by the treatment I gave certain characters, favorites of theirs. I remember a very good historian named Vandiver had some objections to my depiction of Stonewall Jackson at the Seven Days, but that was just a difference of opinion; it was not a direct attack on any facts I had.

Jones: He said something about Stonewall Jackson delaying on the way to Mechanicsville or Gaines Mill?

Foote: He said that Jackson didn't delay, he did exactly what he was supposed to do.

Jones: Ordered.

Foote: Yes. Some truth in that, but it wasn't Jackson in his spread-eagle style, God knows. And Lee always wanted men to do more than they were told to do. In fact he said he learned from General Scott to bring the armies together, bring all his units together on the field; then the battle was up to them.

Jones: And you don't think you'll ever involve yourself in another novel or any type of history of the War?

Foote: I doubt it. Originally I thought I would do a short novel early in my writing life on a Civil War subject and that was to be *Shiloh*. I wrote that. Then in the middle of my writing life I hoped to do a big historical novel on the Siege of Vicksburg, and at the end of my writing life I wanted to write another short novel on the Battle of Brice's Crossroads, all of them basically Mississippi battles—Shiloh, of course, being just across the state line—but I won't write the Vicksburg novel and probably won't write the Brice's Crossroads novel; I've been there, you see. T. S. Eliot said an interesting thing that all writers know to be true. He said, it's in one of the *Four Quartets,* he said that writing—you're trying to do a thing that you don't know how to do, and, he said, it winds up a general mess of imprecision. Having done it you have learned how to do it, but having done it you're no longer interested in doing it again. That's the tragedy—if you know how to do it, it's because you've tried and bungled, but now that you've learned how, you are no longer interested because you wouldn't be learning. Many people think that writers are wise men who can impart to them the truth or some profound philosophy of life. It is not so. A writer is a skilled craftsman who discovers things along with the reader, and what you do with a good writer is you share the search; you are not being imparted wisdom, or if you are being imparted wisdom, it's a wisdom that came to him just as it came to you reading it.

Jones: That's a good point. Can you tell us something about other things you learned in writing the trilogy about the uniqueness of a Southern heritage?

Foote: I'll tell you a very simple thing that I got out of writing about the War that tremendous long time. It started at the very beginning and continued through the writing. I acquired a knowledge of and a love for Southern geography. It's great when you learn about the rivers and the mountains and the way the South physically is. That's a thing that is important to us. People do draw from their physical backgrounds. Whether you live in the mountains or on the seacoast makes a big difference in what kind of person you are. There are other things too. I'm from the Mississippi Delta which has a forty-foot top soil and is often said to be the richest farming land in the world—it's not, but it's often said to be—and I've known some people out in the hills too, and I've discovered that there's sort of an inverse ratio between the richness of the soil and the providence of the people who live on it. People who live down in the Delta don't worry too much about the future because the soil is so rich they don't have to, I guess. It's like Hawaiians; when they get hungry they can reach up and pull a pineapple off the tree. An Eskimo, if he stops thinking about food for two hours in a row, would starve to death, and so he knows to think about it and to do something about it. Out in the hills of Mississippi you'll see people canning vegetables and doing all kinds of things looking forward to a hard winter. Down in the Delta they just go down to the supermarket and buy a can of beans. It's funny. George Washington Carver, one of the finest men I ever met, came to Greenville in the early or middle thirties to lecture to a big Negro gathering there celebrating one hundred years of progress or something, and he reproached them something awful. He said, "I've seen Buick automobiles in the yard of a house where you can study botany through the floor and astronomy through the roof." He wanted them to be frugal and look after themselves; be good, solid citizens. Dr. Carver was a fine man. I remember his speaking. I covered it as a reporter on the newspaper there as a high school boy when I was working for the paper in the summertime. I remember one thing that made a great impression on me. First, Dr. Carver did. I've seen about five or six great men in my life, and Dr. Carver was certainly one of them. Another one was a psychiatrist named Harry Stack Sullivan who came down and visited the Percy family back in the thirties. But what I remember about the Carver visit was there would be audiences of five or six hundred people—it was in the very hot summertime—and every person in that audience was dressed. They all had on ties and coats, and they were very proud. They were all black, no white people there, or scarcely any. I remember how proud they were and they showed their pride through dressing up, and it was hot. This was Mississippi in July or August, I think, when there was no air-conditioning ever heard of. They were great in that respect.

Jones: Did Mr. Will bring him to town?

Foote: He brought Harry Stack Sullivan, but not George Washington Carver. That was done by the blacks at home there; they brought him over from Georgia. I guess after the death of Booker T. Washington, Carver was probably the best known Negro in the country, because of his work with what he called, "the lowly peanut." He was a wonderful man.

Jones: Who else did Mr. Will bring to town that had an effect on you?

Foote: Oh, I'm trying to think of the many people I met at the Percy house. I remember Roark Bradford was there one time, a very funny man, really funny. Dave Cohn stayed there at the Percy house for about a year writing a book. He came on a visit and stayed a year. He was from Greenville and he'd been in New Orleans as manager of Sears Roebuck or something. By the time he was a little over forty years old he figured he'd worked enough and made enough money to live on and he didn't want to be a businessman any more, he wanted to be a writer. He came back home and went to see Mr. Will about it, and Mr. Will said, "It's all well enough to say you want to be a writer, but writers write. That's what you have to do, not talk about it." And Dave said he thought he would, and Mr. Will said, "Well, fine. Why don't you stay here at this house? You can get it done." Dave Cohn stayed there and in less than a year wrote *God Shakes Creation,* probably his best book, and he wrote seven or eight more. I like Dave Cohn's work.

He had a good ear. He was very good on blacks. He wasn't ashamed at all to see the absurd side of them, which Roark Bradford had pointed out so well by then. Dave was also interesting about certain provincial aspects of Memphis. It was Dave in *God Shakes Creation* who said, "The Delta begins in the lobby of the Peabody Hotel and ends on Catfish Row in Vicksburg." He was always welcome at the Peabody; they were glad to see him—he stayed there whenever he was in Memphis—but they never even gave him a cup of coffee, and he thought it was rather amusing that they had so little appreciation of this publicity. Any New York hotel would have put him up and fed him for years. The Pontchartrain in New Orleans would too. But not in Memphis.

Jones: Reading that type of thing and Hodding Carter's work, you get a different sense of the Delta than you do in your work. Your work is closer to Faulkner.

Foote: Yes; more influenced by Faulkner certainly. The Delta is generally misunderstood. For some reason we in the Delta think we are the aristocrats of Mississippi simply because we've had more money than most other sections of Mississippi. At the time I'm talking about there was damn little anybody had, but the Delta was better off than other sections. And we thought of ourselves as the aristocrats, with pure blood lines and all that foolishness. Actually the Delta is a great melting pot—God Almighty's a big dollar mark. It's not at all the way it's portrayed, say, in the work of Tennessee Williams. I've never understood Williams writing about the Delta when he had Columbus on the Tombigbee River, which is a much better place to write about than the Delta. What I mean is it is much better for Tennessee Williams to write about Columbus because he knew it, and he didn't know the Delta. I've always been interested—more than say Faulkner was—in the actual historical shaping of a society, the events which caused people to be the way they are, and their conflict with those events. I'll probably never write anything past the mid-sixties. I kind of stopped looking, about that time.

Jones: Are you going to return to Greenville in your work again?

Foote: Yes. I'm writing a big long family novel right now called *Two Gates to the City.* It's about a family in the Delta. It's not an historical novel. It's about a group of people, probably in the late forties. It's not a saga by any means. It's a family novel in the same sense as, say, *The Brothers Karamazov.*

Jones: What do you think is the truth behind the fact that so many writers come from Mississippi?

Foote: That's a question that's often asked, and there is no easy answer. There are good flippant answers, such as there's nothing else to do down there, so you write. There are only two movies in town so you haven't got much to do. You go to court and watch a trial. My day was before television, so that didn't take up an awful lot of people's time. I've seen recently that the average American boy watches something like six hours a day. It's unbelievable. And you have to subtract that from a lot of things, that six hours out of the waking eighteen. You've got six of that and six of school and six eating or something, you don't have much left for reading or doing many of the things I did when I was a boy.

Jones: So you think something basic is changing?

Foote: Oh, yes, a lot of things are changing. I always hesitate to say it's for the worse, no matter how worse it looks to me, because I've heard these dithyrambs before from people saying it's a miserable damn time. When our leading writers were Fitzgerald, Faulkner, Hemingway and Dos Passos, people were saying, "There are no good writers around anymore; Dreiser's dead," and so on.

Jones: But do you see something changing in the Southern character?

Foote: I'm sure it must change. For one thing, when I grew up we had a peasantry. That being gone has a profound effect on things. Imagine Russian novels without a peasantry. Imagine Faulknerian novels without blacks. Well, sure it's changed. That's not necessarily for the bad though; we'll just have to wait and see. You're always at the mercy of history, of events, as to whether you have good writers or not. You can't turn them out by any formula; you can't provide a society that will result in good writers. In fact there's a curious paradox there. Our best writers have come out of dreadful times, and out of dreadful systems. Mozart and Beethoven, Bach and Haydn composed under what was largely a patronage system—the worst of all systems, supposedly, but it produced some terrific work.

Jones: I read in a 1952 interview that somebody did with you where you said that you didn't have any other hobbies, that writing was your religion. Is that still the case with you?

Foote: Yes, yes, I don't play golf or even poker. I don't belong to any clubs or anything; don't do anything but write.

Jones: Do you write everyday now?

Foote: Try to, yes. I'm a slow writer, 500 words is a good day, but I always worked seven days a week. I don't do that anymore; I take off Sunday and I don't work eight hours a day like I used to, I work five or six hours. I've written and published over two million words, and so if I'm tired I feel I have a right to be.

Jones: Who do you think that today is writing the best fiction, besides Walker and you?

Foote: You mean for the whole country?

Jones: Yes.

Foote: There's some I like a lot. There is no one I think measures up to the big men before our time, certainly not Mailer or Styron or Capote, but there are writers I like. I think John Updike is a skillful writer. My favorite writer among people who have come along after me is Cormac McCarthy; I like his work a great deal. He had a new novel out about two months ago called *Suttree* that I like a lot. That's his fourth book. I like McCarthy's work very much. There's a South American writer that I put off reading and finally read about two months ago that I am really crazy about. His name is García Márquez. He wrote a book called *One Hundred Years of Solitude*. It's one of the finest novels I've ever read in my life, unbelievably funny. It's got a huge, mythic sort of Faulknerian quality to it. I like it very much. That book came out in 1970 and I didn't read it until eight or nine years later. I called Walker right after I finished it. I was so pleased with it, I said, "Walker, Jesus Christ and God Almighty, I've discovered a very great novel!" He said, "Hey, what is it?" I said, "It's called *One Hundred Years of Solitude* by García Márquez," and Walker said, "You son of a bitch, I did my best to get you to read that book five or six years ago and you wouldn't do it." I'd forgotten he ever said anything about it. It's a good book though.

There's a big gap in my reading of novels caused by my Civil War reading. I read very few novels during those years. I would go back and read *The Brothers Karamazov* or *The Magic Mountain*, but I wasn't reading modern novels, except writers that I was particularly interested in like John O'Hara or Styron and Mailer. Something has happened to writers in our time that's very serious. When they get early fame they get torn on the bias; they get pulled crossways. It's no easy thing to be twenty-six or seven years old and be on the cover of *Time* magazine and have people clamoring after you all the time. You get to believing the extravagant praise, you get to appearing on television talk shows, you get to attending conferences and all that kind of stuff. I don't know why they let themselves in for it, but it appears to be unavoidable. There're some who have managed to avoid it; Salinger steered away from it; but he appears to have gone down the chute even without it. I don't know. It's a hard time, though, because of instantaneous communications and the tremendous growth of television and that kind of thing. It really gets at you. I'm certainly comparatively obscure; and yet you wouldn't believe the amount of stuff that comes into this house—people wanting me to read and comment on their novels or do interviews or write for travel magazines, all this kind of stuff. And there's a lot of big money flying around. I'm not surprised that a lot of people are seduced by it. It's wrong. I have no idea about what to do about it. There are pressures out of nowhere, such as being writer-in-residence somewhere. A young writer learning his craft has got no business being a writer-in-residence. When I was coming up, there was nobody that wanted me on any college campus whatsoever, but now they want all these young boys and a lot of them are on campuses and they're not doing a damn thing but laying the coeds. It's a bad scene, particularly for poets. Practically every poet you know is on a college campus somewhere if he's under sixty years old. It's had a bad effect, I think. He ought to be out in the world, writing about what he sees out there, not on a college campus. There are also all kinds of grants and things that are very bad. I ought to be in favor of anything that would help my fellow writers, and me too. I've had three Guggenheims and a Ford Foundation grant, but they were for purposes of researching the War when I had to travel and buy books, which I'd have a hard time doing without Mr. Guggenheim's money and Mr. Ford's money. But I still think it's bad, particularly for young writers who are learning their craft. No matter how pitifully poor and small the living is that you earn with your pen, you get a tremendous strength by earning your living by your pen. If you're living off government money or grant money, you lose that, and it's a big loss. Now I'm talking particularly about a young writer. After you get a little soft in the belly and the head, I suppose such money doesn't do you much harm. But it diverts you from what should be your pride, it diverts you from what should be your concern. Wondering where your next meal is coming from is a splendid thing for a writer; it's not bad, it doesn't cripple him up, it doesn't keep him from working. Going out and having a job as a common laborer or a timekeeper or something like that is a hell of a lot better way to reinforce your income than teaching on a college campus. Writers used to know that. You can't imagine Hemingway or Fitzgerald or the early Faulkner or John O'Hara or any of those people doing any of those things. They simply did not do them. There was very little opportunity to do them, but they didn't do them. They knew it would interfere with their work, and they put their work first, not their wife and children.

Clinton Bagley [Greenville resident]: Do you think this can help at a later date? Miss Welty gives the W.P.A. credit.

Foote: The W.P.A. did fine work. That was something else. People were starving and people couldn't go out and dig ditches; there was nobody digging ditches or anything. The W.P.A. gave you just a little bit of money, enough to keep you from starving, and those people did some good work. But there, once again, I'm talking about major writers: Faulkner, Hemingway, and Fitzgerald weren't on W.P.A., they were home working. They didn't even have time to go down and earn a little bread to put on the table, they were busy writing. Some of those three were making pretty good money; Hemingway, for instance. But that wasn't their concern. Their concern was getting their writing done, and learning how to do it.

Jones: What about the future of the Southern novel? It seems like a lot of things we always thought of as Northern qualities have come down on us.

Foote: Yes, there's a good deal of homogenization going on. When you're traveling and stop in a Holiday Inn, you can't tell by the looks of the room whether you're in Minnesota or Mississippi. When you go into a restaurant to eat you can't tell where you are. Regional food, regional lodgings, all that is pretty well over. And so I suppose, as a result of radio and the jet plane and those things, we'll all be evened out more and more as time goes on. When I was a boy, people didn't know how to pronounce Roosevelt's name, they called him Roosevelt (vowel sound as in shoot). It was double O, and they had never heard anybody say it. So you had strong regional characteristics simply because of a lack of communication with the rest of the country. I think the attempt to preserve a heritage—not as a brake on progress, but as a matter of pride in that heritage—is a very valuable thing and should be hugged onto. I approve very much of these latest things such as you're doing here, trying to catch the time and fix it with the use of tape recorders and various other things, and the preservation of documents that would be destroyed. The Department of Archives and History there in Jackson has done some marvelous work on preserving things that would have been lost without it. But you can't have pride in your heritage if you don't know the heritage. I was driving through Mississippi, I think it was on a Monday, and I can't remember what year it was [1963], but I heard on the automobile radio that there'd been a bomb set off in a church in Birmingham the day before, and three little Negro girls had been killed. So I was going through a place called Prentiss, Mississippi, and I pulled into a roadside restaurant-cafe to get a newspaper to try to find out what had happened. I went in and the proprietor was standing behind the cash register talking to a Mississippi highway patrolman. There was a waitress down the counter there. I went up to the proprietor and said, "Do you have a morning paper?" and he said, "We're all sold out." I said, "I wanted to find out something if I could about this Birmingham explosion, a bombing or something in a church over there." He said, "Yeah, that was all in the paper this morning. I guess those niggers will learn sooner or later." I said, "Well, I must not have heard it right on the radio. It said three little girls were killed." He said, "That's right," and I said, "Thank you, anyhow," and went and sat down at the counter. The waitress came over and I said, "I just want a cup of coffee," and she went to get the coffee. I turned back around to the proprietor and said, "This town is called Prentiss,"—I've left out one thing he said. "We've got to preserve our heritage," was one of the things he said in the extenuation of this bombing and everything else; his notion that we had to hold the blacks down if we were going to preserve our heritage, because it would be destroyed. Anyway, while she was getting me the coffee I turned back to him and the patrolman and I said, "This town is called Prentiss; is it named for Sergeant S. Prentiss?" He said, "I don't know," and I said, "It seems likely, but it might have been some other family name, Prentiss or something." He said to the waitress, "You know how Prentiss got its name?" She said, "No, I don't know," and the highway patrolman said he didn't have any idea. That showed you how much their heritage meant to them. It was a strange business though. There's a lot of ugliness down here. Yet I know from my experiences in the North and in the South that that same man, if I had been broken down on the side of the road with car trouble or something, he would stop, get the jack out of his car and help me, get all greasy and dirty, and would not have expected anything more than a "thank you" for doing it. It's a curious mixup of traits. Most of the evil comes from ignorance. It seems that the good is inherent and the evil is acquired. I have a candidate to blame for all this. I think the planter is the "nigger in this woodpile." He's the son of a bitch who set the system up so he could rule the roost, and he managed to keep everybody under him quiet by promising them about this open society where they could be planters someday and live the way he lived. Sometimes I'm amazed at his genius, at how well the whole thing was designed. Even the giving of Christmas presents to plantation workers was designed to demean them. Almost everything about day-to-day life on the plantation—and I speak with some knowledge because I come from a long line of planters—was designed to hold these people down so that he could live the way he did. I don't know if people would even believe it nowadays, but it was quite common for a cook who worked seven days a week, all day, fixing breakfast, dinner and supper, to make three dollars, three-fifty and four dollars a week. What she got for that was money, which she used to pay her house rent, usually about five dollars a month for the cabin she lived in with no plumbing, and cast-off clothes, and food to take home to her husband and children at night. That can't be a good system. That's bound to be a bad system. And the people who were paying that to her, in many cases, were making a great deal of money. Something was very wrong at the core of it, not only in slavery days but in those days too, which practically amounted to peonage. My grandfather and two other men at home, including Senator Percy—it was my grandfather, Senator Percy and O. B. Crittenden—had a plantation across the river, where the bridge goes now, called Sunnyside. They brought in Italian and Sicilian workers; paid their passage over on the boat. The three men nearly got into serious trouble with the federal government because a Catholic priest who was ministering to those people saw what was being done to them. It amounted to peonage; they had to work off their passage and it never worked out so that they got clear. The three men were very nearly prosecuted for peonage, but they managed to get from under it by the fact that Theodore Roosevelt had met Senator Percy as a young man when he came down to my part of the country on a bear hunt with my other grandfather. This was my mother's father who was in on the plantation; his name was Rosenstock. My other grandfather Foote had had Roosevelt down here on a bear hunt, and they got to talking, "What are we going to do when we're not hunting with President Roosevelt? How are we going to talk with him? We'll bore him to death." So my grandfather said, "We'll ask Percy along; he can talk with him." So, as a result of that relationship they were able to get the indictment quashed, or anyhow not prosecuted on condition that they let the people go.

Jones: Mr. Foote, I've kept you long enough. Before I cut this off I want to say how much I appreciate your talking with me. It's been an honor to meet you.

A Colloquium with Shelby Foote

Helen White and Redding Sugg/1981

From the *Southern Humanities Review*, 4 (Fall 1981), 281-299.
Reprinted by permission.

The colloquium presented here [held at Auburn University, 5 February 1981] brought together the novelist/historian Shelby Foote and two commentators on his work, Dr. Helen White and Dr. Redding Sugg. The commentators are co-authors of an article about Mr. Foote's three-volume history, *The Civil War*, and of a volume on Mr. Foote to be published in the Twayne U. S. Authors series. In the colloquium which follows, the commentators provide background information on Mr. Foote's work and set the stage for his informal responses to their questions.

The Editors

White: Few literary artists can have been so consistent in their view of their talent and their material or so faithful in carrying out their early projects as Shelby Foote. His work is very much of a piece, and the orderliness of his literary career is reflected in the meticulous craftsmanship of his books. He declared in youth a distinctly "modernist" vocation as a writer, specifically of novels, and still, with D. H. Lawrence, regards the novel as "the one bright book of life." He in no way abandoned his vocation when he applied himself to history and, like Gibbon, devoted twenty years to a literary masterpiece which is also history. His fundamental commitment is to narrative art, whether factual or fictional. Since the publication in 1974 of the third and final volume of *The Civil War*, he has resumed the writing of novels.

Sugg: Publication of *The Civil War* intervened, volume by volume, between his fifth novel (1954) and his sixth (1978). During his first phase as a novelist, Mr. Foote published five novels which were a substantial beginning of a Faulknerian recreation of his native

Washington County with its seat at Greenville, Mississippi, under the names Jordan County and Bristol.

His first novel, *Tournament* (1949), viewed the scene from the vantage of 1910 or thereabouts, with renderings of the early nineteenth century and emphasis on the 1880s and after. He then took soundings at other periods: the late 1940s in *Follow Me Down* (1950), a tragic novel of poor whites; the 1920s and 1930s in *Love in a Dry Season* (1951), a mordant comedy of the upper class; and then the whole range of time since before the white man came to that country in *Jordan County* (1954), a novel which also includes treatments of Indians and blacks. In 1952, Mr. Foote published what is probably still his best known novel, *Shiloh,* a recreation of the battle of Shiloh; this novel, though not set in Jordan County, is tied to it by a character from there.

White: The early novels, except the first, are still in print and starting a second life as Mr. Foote adds to the Jordan County canon.

Sugg: The one novel of Jordan County which will not be reprinted is the first one, *Tournament*; though patently a young man's first novel, it is nevertheless rich and appealing. It introduces settings, personages, and themes with which Mr. Foote continues to work. Since it is increasingly hard to come by, let me ask Mr. Foote to give an account of it and discuss his reasons for keeping it out of print.

Foote: Yes. It is rather embarrassing to sit here in the vortex of all this praise, and I will now demonstrate that it is not deserved. But I will say of *Tournament* that it was a young man's attempt to deal with what he imagined might have been his grandfather's life. Since my grandfather died two years before I was born, I'd just heard about him, of course. But the book was an attempt to use the framework of his life as a novel. The main character of the book is nothing like my grandfather, but I used the facts of my grandfather's life to peg the story on. It was an attempt to understand the homeland I came out of. I knew then, way back in the dark ages of the '30s, there was something dreadfully wrong with that land that needed looking into—though I knew of many things that were good about it and could be enjoyed. So I tried to examine it. Looking back on the novel with the perspective of the years, I see now that I instinctively did what was right for my purposes; I was laying the ground-work for things I wanted to do later on.

Mainly, though, I was thrashing around in the wilds of the English language—happy as a colt in clover, learning how to write, and being pleased with things that I achieved. Some of the things I was most pleased with I would blush to look at now, but I had a good time doing it. I was at Chapel Hill when the war clouds were heading up in Europe, and I left school at the end of two years believing we were going to be in a war. I joined the Mississippi National Guard about the time Hitler went into Poland—making my protest—and spent that year, before we went into federal service, writing this novel *Tournament*. When I finished it, I sent it to an editor at Knopf who was William Alexander Percy's editor, and he kept it a couple of weeks and sent it back to me and said that they had read it around the office there and liked it very much but didn't think it would sell, it just showed promise, and the best thing I could do would be to put it away and come back to it after I had written a second or possibly third novel which they would be most interested in looking at. That sounded like good advice to me, so I put it away. But before I could start the second novel, we were in federal service.

When I came home five years later from the war, I got the novel out of the closet where I had put it and looked through it and some of it still looked pretty good to me and some of it looked God-awful; the Knopf editor had given me good advice. The first thing I did was make an extract from it for a short story that was, to my surprise, accepted right off by the *Saturday Evening Post*. So I wrote a story about twice that length and sent it to the *Post* and they took that too. And I wrote one three times that length and sent it to the *Post* and got back a letter informing me that the *Post* did not publish stories about incest. That was the last connection I ever had with the *Saturday Evening Post*. I do take some satisfaction, however, in the fact that it died before I did.

But by the time I had worked on the novel and put it into shape. While I was doing that, I wrote *Shiloh* and sent it to a publisher in New York who was absolutely delighted with it but said it wouldn't possibly sell—what else did I have? And I said well, I am hard at work on a novel about the Mississippi Delta that begins in Reconstruction and comes up to about 1914 or so, and they said they would be delighted to publish it sight unseen—it sounded like a good subject. So I took *Tournament* out and finished polishing it up and sent it to them, and that was *Tournament's* history. It is out of print now and, for all I care, will stay out of print. But I look on it as a sort of mother lode out of which I take anything I want—I cannibalize it for all kinds of uses and have gone back to it often in writing other novels and will continue to do that through the one I am writing now.

Sugg: The novel which supersedes *Tournament* as the most available introduction to Mr. Foote's fiction is the one called *Jordan County*. This was a technical departure in Mr. Foote's conservative, classicist work. The first three novels of his fictional county and the novel *Shiloh* are notable for tight construction, executed according to clear though complex outlines. The novel *Jordan County*, however, is made up of linked stories and novellas arranged in reverse chronological order from about 1950 back to the 1790s, although there's no attempt at complete coverage. This arrangement, together with the subtitle, *A Landscape in Narrative,* implies the program according to which Mr. Foote is still working and which was adumbrated in *Tournament*. Mr. Foote, will you explain that subtitle and give your view of the group of early novels as looked at from the vantage you reached with *Jordan County?*

Foote: I was quite consciously trying to cover this county—a county I had more or less discovered for myself by basing it on my home county, Washington County, in Mississippi. It has an industrial north, an agrarian south, and a capital on a river. In each of the novels I tried to reach into some segment of that county with the intention of writing, over the years, a whole series of novels more or less in the manner of Balzac or Zola to show what life there was like over the span of the two hundred or so years that it was sitting there. *Follow Me Down*, the second novel—the first novel after *Tournament*—is a study of poor whites, farming people in the southern part of the county. It is a study of a crime of passion, an attempt to deal with a rather lurid subject and to deal with it through a series of monologues by the participants. It starts out with a group of three monologues, has a central section with three monologues, and a final section with three monologues. Through the first section you are becoming more deeply involved in the story because the people telling the story are themselves more deeply involved. The central section concerns the murdered girl and the man who murdered her. And in the last section you get *dis*involved because the people telling the story are less involved in the story that is being told, so that I hope what you get is a sense of penetrating to the heart of a horrendous thing and then emerging from it, fully clothed and in your right mind again.

The third novel, the one that followed *Follow Me Down,* is called *Love in a Dry Season. Dry Season* is an attempt to do two things: to deal with the so-called upper classes of the Mississippi Delta—a tremendously overrated class, incidentally; we are not all that "upper" down there—and also to deal with the period from about 1929 until the start of the Second World War, a period which is basically that of the Great Depression (and that is what is meant by the "dry season"—or at least one of the things that is meant by the "dry season"). It is a novel I remember with happiness because of a facility I seemed to have while writing it. I enjoyed writing it and I liked it partly because some of it, to me anyhow, was quite funny. When you ask a writer what is his favorite of all his books, he is not apt to answer you in terms of the specific gravity of a work or whether it has great importance or anything—he is apt to tell you that he likes something because he enjoyed *writing* it. I felt a particular free communication between my brain and hand. When I wanted to say something, it seemed to come out right, and that is such a happy experience that I treasure it greatly and therefore treasure the book.

After that came *Shiloh,* which had been written before *Follow Me Down. Shiloh* is an attempt to examine a battle through a series of monologues by people engaged on the southern side and on the northern side. Shiloh is one of the most confusing battles the world has ever experienced; I was trying to penetrate that confusion and at the same time communicate it. (Something else about the methods of writers—and, incidentally, about why they write stories—happened to me during the writing of *Shiloh.* It's a funny experience. I conceived the novel first as a story about a young Confederate soldier who went into battle for the first time and in the course of that battle gave his first rebel yell. It was to be a story about what it was like to be a young soldier and get caught up in the emotion of battle and give your first rebel yell—that's all it was. And it later became only part of the book. When I got to that section about the young Mississippi private going into a charge, he gave his first rebel yell and I had left it behind me before I knew I had written it. The whole reason for writing the book was over in about three lines and I didn't even know it was over until I had written it.)

Anyway, after *Shiloh* I took things that I had been writing over the years and wrote some new things to fit in among them; and in that fashion made *Jordan County*. The first story takes place about 1948, '49, or '50, and the last story takes place before the white man ever came to that country—and the stories in between attempt to cover various periods of the history of the county. There is a brief sketch for instance on Reconstruction, with a Negro narrator—it always seemed to me very strange that we have so little testimony from the blacks as to what Reconstruction was like, so I tried to look at it that way.

And having finished that block of five novels, especially having finished on that note, I felt it was important to move on to another form of writing. It seemed to me that if I hadn't actually exhausted it, I had at any rate used it enough; I wanted another form of novel. About that time, Bennett Cerf at Random House asked me if I would undertake a short history of the Civil War and it seemed to me to be a good way to spend about a year and a half coasting while I decided what form this next group of novels would take. We signed a contract for a short history of the Civil War which was to be about 200,000 words long. To show you how little I knew about the writing of history, I figured that I could write about twice as much history per year as I did fiction per year—fiction is hard work; history I figured, well, there's not much to that. So I started, and within about one week I saw that it was no part of my makeup, that nothing about me would be happy writing a little summary of the war. In fact, I might as well not write it. And then it began to open out for me and I was able to outline all three volumes.

My editor at Random House was a man named Robert Linscott, a truly lovely man. Anyway, I thought this all out, got the outline together, sent it up to him and said that, instead of a short history, I think I would rather do this three-volume thing, running about say 500,000 or 600,000 words a volume. I didn't hear anything for about ten days. I don't know how many meetings they had or who said what, but after a week or ten days a letter came back: "Go ahead; fine; much better that way." So there I was with this twenty-year project on my hands which I then thought would possibly be eight or nine years—but it expanded as I wrote. There's a French soup I've heard of; I've never had it—it's a job of compression and, as you move your spoon through it, the soup swells, and if you don't eat fast enough it overflows your bowl. I sometimes felt I was engaged in that during the writing of the war.

Sugg: Let me intervene a minute and turn you back briefly to *Tournament* before we continue with *The Civil War*. I think we ought to bring into play one or two of the names that run through your fiction—the name of the plantation, and at least that of Isaac. There is a highly symbolic plantation in these novels called Solitaire, based in part on a plantation in Mr. Foote's family down on Lake Washington—one of those loops of the Mississippi River that got cut off. People came up from Natchez and started the cotton kingdom from that end of the Delta. That name means something, and Isaac Jameson means something, and I'd like Mr. Foote to comment on them.

Foote: That goes back to my grandfather, too. He was the youngest son of about six or seven brothers in a place called Macon, Mississippi, out in the Black Prairie region. His own father, who was a substantial man, owned three plantations in the Delta and this last son he decided to make a Delta planter. He sent him to business school up north and down to Texas to study the cotton business in various places and then sent him over, at the age of about twenty-three or twenty-four, to run these three plantations. God knows how he did it, but he did, and he did a good job. One plantation was named Mounds, another one Hard Scrabble—I think they called it Hard Scramble—and the one he liked most, called Mount Holly. He worked very hard and lived at Mount Holly, and Mount Holly is the original of what I call Solitaire plantation. And when I say that, it sounds as if I am describing Mount Holly when I describe Solitaire. That is not true—it is not a literal description of it. (Incidentally, my grandfather went over to manage these three places for his father, and he loved Mount Holly so much that he wanted to buy it from his father. So he arranged out of his wages to buy Mount Holly by paying so much a year. The old man, his father, Hezekiah William Foote, lived a very long time and my grandfather made the last payment on Mount Holly the year his father died—then found that he had left it to him in his will.)

Mount Holly, then, was the basis for Solitaire, and the Jameson who is the sort of beginner of that region—the first white man—is based on a man named Irwin who was the first white man ever to see Lake Washington. He was a well-educated man—had been to school in Switzerland and God knows how many places, and he said that, despite having visited all the lakes in Switzerland, Lake Washington was the most beautiful lake he had ever seen. It is hard to believe now, when you go back, after all the poison that has been drained into it, killing the egrets and the fish and everything else, that it could ever have been so beautiful, but Irwin said it was and came back there to live with only about twelve slaves he took from his people down in Natchez. That is all part of the story I tried to tell.

You never know where names come from, just as you never know where symbolism comes from—and that is as it should be. Any writer who puts symbolism into his work on purpose, consciously, is apt to be a very bad writer. Those things had better come of their own accord. I remember I wrote a story about a jazz musician, and he is in a reformatory where they have an orchestra—a band—and the boy who played the cornet died of tuberculosis. The warden of the reformatory took the cornet and gave it to this boy and said, why don't you learn to play it? He accepted it as a gift and went back to start practicing, and he hugged it to his chest as he walked back. It was later called to my attention that this horn was full of tuberculosis germs which he was holding to his chest where the tuberculosis was going to take root. I assure you when I wrote it, I thought it was the most natural thing in the world for somebody to receive a prized possession and hug it to his chest. I do not for an instant deny the validity of the critic who pointed out the symbolism—I hope it is there; but I did not know it when I put it there. And that's the way it should be, I believe. If you start making outlines and putting in points where symbolism is going to crop up, you're likely to write a bad book because you are not going to be concerned about those things that make a book live, you are going to be concerned about those things that are your idea of what makes a good book—which is not the way to write. It is all right to read about the technique of writing, but when you sit down to a desk to write, you had better get all of that out of your head in a hurry.

White: Earlier, in our introductory remarks, we used the word "Faulknerian" to describe Mr. Foote's re-creation of Washington

County. Mr. Foote is indeed a legitimate heir of William Faulkner, but with acknowledged relations to other predecessors as well: Browning, Hemingway, Joyce, and Proust are among Mr. Foote's acknowledged ancestors in the art of writing. He is as distinctly the proprietor of his own "little postage stamp" of fictional territory as Faulkner was of Yoknapatawpha. The Delta is another world from Faulkner's Hill Country and Faulkner and Foote differ in narrative method, tone, and style, too. In differentiating their qualities, George Garrett, in *The Mississippi Quarterly, 1974-75,* has observed that Mr. Foote's prose "is characterized by a kind of classic clarity and condensation, often transparent, though the *materials* he deals with may be complex and dark" (p. 87). Mr. Foote, will you comment on your relationship with William Faulkner?

Foote: One way to comment on it is to tell you what I told him one time. I told him that I had every right to expect to be a far better writer than he was—because his models were Conrad and Sherwood Anderson, and mine were Marcel Proust and William Faulkner—and that my models were better than his models. He laughed at that and was kind enough not to say anything about its also depending on who was doing the writing.

The impact that I received from Faulkner was terrific for two or three or God knows how many reasons. One of them was that *Light in August* was, if not the very first, one of the first modern novels I ever read. I suppose almost everybody can remember his first modern novel, if he was lucky enough to read a good one—how different it was from what came before it and how it just knocked you off your feet. That was the way I felt about *Light in August.* At the time it came out, I believe in 1932, I was a high school freshman reading for the first time with any kind of perception, although I had already been impressed by various writers like Dickens. But this was the first modern thing that I'd read, so that Faulkner was my first impression of what the modern novel is.

Furthermore, Faulkner was showing me a country I knew well, and showing me how really little I knew it compared to him. So there was that added thing, and a third thing that certainly ought to be included—the language itself. It was my language—a demotic style of English I was thoroughly familiar with. I have often wondered who could appreciate a regional writer better: strangers or people who know the region. I sometimes think that we who know the region well are not surprised by some of the most beautiful things in it because we have been familiar with them all our lives. I never have gotten that straight in my mind—whether a Mississippian can read Faulkner with more appreciation than, say, a Minnesotan. It may not be so. But Faulkner to me meant a great deal because of those factors and perhaps others, too, not the least of which is his enormous skill as a writer. No writer that I know of, *no* writer that I know of, is a better communicator of sensation than William Faulkner is. He can tell you what it's like to be in the woods at dawn better than any writer I have ever encountered. I'd put him with Shakespeare in that regard. I think he is a very great writer—and when all this foolishness is shaken down and they stop praising him for all kinds of esoteric reasons, there will be a true realization of what a great writer he was. I think he will outlive the writers of our time because of this particular excellence.

I do not consider Faulkner the major influence on my work, however. I think my two favorite writers, for example, which means that they are indeed influential, are Tacitus and Marcel Proust. Proust to me is certainly the greatest writer of the twentieth century, and certainly one of the half dozen greatest writers of all times. I put Proust with Homer, Aeschylus, Dante, Shakespeare—but that's because he and I hook atoms, as I would say; I understand him because he responds to something in me. His idea of the way to tell a story makes me say yes, that's the way to tell a story, or delineate a character, or plot a novel, or demonstrate a thesis; anything you want to name, it seems to me that Proust does it better than almost anybody else, certainly anybody else in our time. Those influences are very important. A man *is* the sum of what he has read and seen, and you would do well not to miss any of the good in the world in the way of writing while you are learning your craft. That's where you learn it, from the writers who came before you.

Sugg: For particular reasons, Mr. Foote has accorded an honored place to William Alexander Percy as an elder fellow townsman and friend of his family and his own friend who provided what few small Southern cities could, a living model of the man of letters. The two share as their major theme the Delta planter and aristocrat, but the tone of Percy's *Lanterns on the Levee* is not to be found, except ironically, in *Jordan County*.

Foote: The Percys were tremendously important to my development as a man and as a writer. I have often said that if Will Percy had lived in Clarksdale or Greenwood or Hollandale or Shaw, it would have been Clarksdale or Greenwood or Hollandale or Shaw that would have been the Athens of the Delta, as Greenville sometimes likes to brag that it is. He did it not by having a literary coterie—he didn't have any such thing; there wasn't any passing of manuscripts from hand to hand and all that—he did it by two other methods. One was he was one of the greatest teachers I have ever known. He could read you a poem of Keats that, by the time he finished reading it, made you want to run home and be with Keats by yourself. It was that kind of thing that communicated his love of the thing that you accepted as a valid thing and wanted to possess for yourself. The other thing was that his was an example of a cultured house, in the sense of having books and music and the master of the house having been a well-traveled man in Europe and Asia and South America. It was a window through which you could see the world. No, it was even more than that—it was as if some of that other world had been brought in to this little town. What is more, he was a published writer. He had written a book. If he could do it, maybe you could.

About that time I was fourteen or fifteen years old, he brought three boys from Alabama to live with him. Their father had died and their mother died soon after. They were cousins of his; their father had been his first cousin. The close friendship between me and those boys was an important part of my life. My house was, I suppose you would call it, upper-class Delta, but their house was upper-class *world* because of Mr. Will. There were books around my house but they were mostly by Viña Delmar and Faith Baldwin, not to mention my own favorites like the Bobbsey Twins and Tom Swift and Tarzan. But this was something else. Throughout that period of adolescence, the high school years, I was at the Percy house almost as often as I was at my own house; I got to share in that, and I am sure it had an important influence on the turn my life took later. Will Percy was many things—a truly delightful man. That charm is communicated in *Lanterns on the Levee*. I differ with Mr. Will in almost every view he has of the planter aristocracy, of the rednecks from the hills, and of the position of the blacks—he and I would have fallen out almost certainly if we'd allowed ourselves to overtheorize about society and what's good and what's bad. But we didn't have a chance to; I didn't develop any opinions of my own until about the time he died. It was much the same way with his adopted son, Walker Percy, who is my best and lifelong friend. Mr. Will would have been delighted at our success, whatever it amounts to in this world, but he would have been regretful indeed of our views on all kinds of things.

White: The theme of the planter aristocrat, or rather the failure of the planter class to develop as a true aristocracy, is fundamental in Mr. Foote's fiction and can be particularly appreciated in one component of *Jordan County,* the story "Pillar of Fire," set before and during the Civil War. We take it as the central indispensable item in the canon, now that *Tournament* is out of consideration.

Here we meet Mr. Foote's eponymous hero, Isaac Jameson, the pioneer founder of the plantation named Solitaire. Mr. Foote's fiction has been more closely read by French critics than by American critics (see, e.g., the special issue of *Delta,* 1977, devoted to Foote, published at the Université Paul Valery at Montpellier), and the French make of Isaac Jameson an Adam in the Delta Eden. He is an impressive figure but implicated in the primal sin of the white man, the cruel exploitation of the Indian and the Negro in the service of King Cotton and the upholding of the cash nexus at the expense of human brotherhood. Fratricide and alienation are part of the heritage from Isaac, quite literally in the Civil War and then in attenuated failures of human relationships down to the modern generation.

Sugg: Instead of a necessarily abstract discussion, let's take this opportunity to hear a sample of Mr. Foote's prose, and note that all commentary is subordinate to the reading. There's a passage in "Pillar of Fire" which will serve the purpose; we turn to it for its felicity and richness of meaning, its prophecy, its condensation of the cycle of the Delta year. Mr. Foote, may we ask you to read the passage about Isaac's trek and his remarkable dream?

Foote: Well, this passage concerns Isaac Jameson's return to Lake Jordan. After he has seen the lake and remarked its beauty, he goes back to Natchez and takes from his wealthy family a little money and a few slaves and says they won't be bothered with him any more. He has given them a great deal of trouble over the years, so he returns to Lake Jordan and brings his slaves with him. His father had told him when he got the money:

> . . . "If you want to play prodigal it's all right with me. But mind you: when youre swilling with swine and chomping the husks, don't cut your eyes around in my direction. There wont be any lamp in the window, or fatted calf either. This is all."
>
> It was all Isaac wanted, apparently. Between sunup and nightfall of the following day—a Sunday, early in June—they rolled forty miles along the road connecting hamlets north of Natchez. Sundown of the third day they made camp on the near bank of the Yazoo, facing the Walnut Hills, and Wednesday they entered the delta, a flat land baked gray by the sun wherever it exposed itself, which was rare, from under the intertwined branches of sycamores and water oaks and cottonwoods and elms. Grass grew so thick that even the broad tires of the Conestoga left no mark of passage. Slow, circuitous creeks, covered with dusty scum and steaming in the heat, drained east and south, away from the river, each doubling back on itself in convulsive loops and coils like a snake fighting lice. For four days then, while the Negroes clutched desperately at seats and stanchions in a din of creaking wood and clattering metal (they had been warehouse hands, townspeople, and ones the brothers could easiest spare at that) the wagon lurched through thickets of scrub oak and stunted willow and over fallen trunks and rotted stumps. It had a pitching roll, like that of a ship riding a heavy swell, which actually did cause most of the Negroes to become seasick four hundred miles from salt water.
>
> They followed no trail, for there was no trail to follow. There was only Isaac, who rode on a claybank mare as far out front as visibility allowed, sometimes half a mile, sometimes ten feet, and even in the latter case they sometimes followed not the sight of him but the sound of snapping limbs and Isaac's cursing. Often they had to dismount with axes and chop through. Just before noon of the eighth day, Sunday again, they struck the southern end of a lake, veered right, then left, and continued northward along its eastern shore. Two hours later Isaac reined in the mare, and when the wagon drew abreast he signaled for a halt. A wind had risen, ruffling the lake; through the screen of cypresses the waves were bright like little hatchets in the sunlight. "All right," he said. "You can get the gear unloaded. We are home."
>
> Thus he began the fulfillment of a dream which had come to him the previous month. It was May then, the oaks tasseling; he and the

trappers had reached the lake at the close of day. While the sun went down, big and red across the water, they made camp on the grassy strip between the lake and the trees. Isaac lay rolled in his blanket, and all that night, surrounded by lake-country beauty—overhead the far, spangled reaches of sky, eastward the forest murmurs, the whisper of leaves and groan of limbs in the wind, the hoarse night-noises of animals, and westward, close at hand, the lapping of water—he dreamed. He dreamed an army of blacks marching upon the jungle, not halting to chop but walking steadily forward, swinging axes against the retreating green wall. Behind them the level fields lay stumpless and serene in watery sunlight, motionless until in the distance clanking trace chains and clacking singletrees announced the coming of the plowmen. Enormous lop-eared mules drew bulltongue plows across the green, and the long brown furrows of earth unrolled like threads off spools. What had been jungle became cultivated fields, and now the fields began to be striped with the pale green lines of plants soon burdened with squares, then purple-and-white dotted, then deep red with blooms, then shimmering white in the summer heat. In a long irregular line (they resembled skirmishers except for the singing; their sacks trailed from their shoulders like limp flags) the pickers passed over the fields, leaving them brown and desolate in the rain, and the stalks dissolved, going down into bottomless mud. Then in the dream there was quiet, autumnal death until the spring returned and the plowmen, and the dream began again. This was repeated three times with a mystical clarity.

"Wake up. Wake up, Ike."

"Dont," he said, drawing the edge of the blanket over his eyes.

"Wake up, Ike! It's time to roll."

In the faint dawn light the lake and forest had that same quality of unreality as in the dream. He was not certain he was awake until one of the trappers nudged him in the ribs with the toe of his mocassin and spoke again. "Ike! You want to sleep your life away?"

For a while he did not answer; he remained half-in half-out of the dream, which was still with him and which he knew already would always be with him. The trappers stood waiting, but he just lay there, looking out over the lake and at the forest. Then he sat up.

"You two go on," he told them. "This is where I stop."

White: Thank you, Mr. Foote. We ought now to look at *Shiloh,* both for its own sake as a work of lapidary elegance and as a transition to *The Civil War.* Although the fourth of Mr. Foote's books to be published, *Shiloh* was the second he composed. *Shiloh* is an exquisite instance of the historical novel in the most rigorous sense, based on systematic research, including reconnaissance of the battlefield, and containing characters both historical and invented.

Sugg: We would rank this book above Crane's *The Red Badge of Courage*, to which it is sometimes superficially compared. The two share the theme of the naive youth tested under fire, but this is only one of a number of equally important elements in *Shiloh*, and they are all subordinated to create an effect of the experience, the sensation of being in that battle.

White: If our assessment sounds unorthodox, let me quote William Faulkner, via Malcolm Franklin in *Bitterweeds*: Faulkner inquired whether his stepson had read *Shiloh* and said, "Well, Buddy, you should read it. It's the damnedest book I've ever read and one of the best." After presenting it as a gift, he added, "This is twice the book that *The Red Badge of Courage* is," and went on to comment that Mr. Foote wrote it as if he had been there himself—"he knows what he is talking about."

Foote: That is nice to hear, although Mr. Faulkner never said anything to me like that. He was a funny man about that. Somebody did an awful lot of work for him and someone else suggested that he ought to praise him for it because he would appreciate it so much. Faulkner said, "When a horse is running, you don't stop him to give him sugar."

Shiloh is an attempt to show a battle from the inside. It is in the line of work begun by Stendhal in *The Charterhouse of Parma*, where for really the first time a battle was described from the inside by a young man at the battle of Waterloo. Then it was continued by Tolstoy in *War and Peace*, where he too wrote of a battle as viewed by the people engaged. And then Stephen Crane wrote *The Red Badge*. I hope this is in that line. Writing about combat is a good subject for a young writer—it enables you to write *down;* you don't have to pump up the emotions you feel when a 155 millimeter shell is coming at you. You are not apt to overwrite about what you feel when that happens, so it gives you a chance to ride herd on what you are working on. Instead of trying to make it more than it is, you try to keep it from being as much as it is, or else the reader won't believe it. That was what I was partly trying to do with *Shiloh*.

Sugg: The material—the research—that *Shiloh* incorporates is virtually identical with that in the treatment of the battle in Volume I of *The Civil War.* Anybody interested in the minimal differences between fiction and narrative history will find comparison of the two versions enlightening. The novel is about twice as long as the section in the history, having to accommodate the fictional elements—mainly the invented characters through whom it is narrated.

White: The novel, as an art object, can be viewed as a closed system, but history refers to the world beyond the text of which the author is as much a part as the War and the records of it. Mr. Foote's artistic problem in the history was to contrive his own voice so as to serve as the inclusive narrator's tone and yet break into this from time to time recognizably as Shelby Foote.

Foote: This is in line with what I wanted to do anyhow. I have a strong feeling that all writers are looking for the truth and that it's an accident as to what form the search takes. If Proust had been from working-class people, he would have written working-class novels. And they'd have been I think just as good as the novels he wrote about French high society—or near-high society.

I don't know of any reason why a historian should not be as good a writer as a novelist. It doesn't often happen, because in my experience many historians have a profound mistrust of good writing. And I'm not just talking about fine writing. I mean good writing. They feel that it's somehow beneath their close attention. It distracts them from research, so that when you finish your research and you have your magnificent facts assembled, you shouldn't have wasted your time about how you're going to write about it. Just get those facts out in front of the people and you've told the truth. So they say, but I know that it's not true; Francis Butler Simkins used to remark that anyone who equates facts with truth doesn't know what the nature of truth is. It is the way those facts are presented, what they are embedded in, and the way the story is told that makes them true. If any historian in any single page of his voluminous life work would turn out one of those pages with the clarity and the truthfulness of a single page of the best of Hemingway, that page would live forever. And yet there seems to be contempt for the things that would make him live forever. He is content rather to find out facts and, having done that, think that he has finished his job, or nearly finished his job.

Do not misunderstand me—I have the greatest admiration for the people who discovered the facts that made it possible for me to write my book. Without them I'd have been nowhere. And do not think that I think all historians are bad writers. That is not true. I have said that one of my favorite writers who ever lived was Tacitus and Tacitus was writing history in the same way the best historians today write history. He didn't have to bother with bibliographies and footnotes but he was writing history in the sense of trying to tell the truth of what had come along before him and even during his life. He was a very great writer. And part of his greatness is the care that he took to arrive at the truth. That is the thing I stressed in the bibliographical note of the first volume of *The Civil War* and continued to stress all the way through.

The novelist and historian are after the same thing, the truth—not a different truth, the same truth—only they reach it by different routes. They try to come upon it in different ways, but at their best there is no reason why one should be a better writer than the other. If only the historian were willing to serve the sort of sweaty apprenticeship of learning how to do it, of learning how to handle the English language well enough to make his hand do what his brain says it wants done. Yet all too often that sweaty apprenticeship is skipped, and the result is nearly always disastrous. Our best historians—and I am speaking of men like Prescott—knew the value of learning how to write well so they could present their material in a way that wouldn't let it die. When we read Gibbon today, we are reading a great stylist. You are not apt to go to Gibbon for the facts, although Gibbon's facts are good. You go to Gibbon for the pleasure of reading it, and, of course, that's what makes a book live, no matter what its subject is. And we read it with pleasure because of the way he has written it. You get Gibbon's tone of voice, which is a very pleasant thing to be in the presence of and a very instructive one, too.

Sugg: During the twenty years that Mr. Foote was writing history, going his independent way as a professional writer, a number of scholars and specialists in the philosophy of history and literary theory and criticism published books, unknown to him we believe and in any case too late for him to use, for which *The Civil War* could serve as validation.

W. B. Gallie, for example, in a book called *Philosophy and the Historical Understanding* (New York: Schocken Books) which was published in 1964 when Mr. Foote published the second volume of *The Civil War*, has made a case for a logic of narrative being as persuasive as deductive logic. A formulation of his that sticks in the mind holds that, whereas we are accustomed to accept conclusions which follow *from* premises, narrative logic involves following—following a story, that is—*to* a conclusion. In writing history, one follows a story to a *known* conclusion. It is an artistic merit of Mr. Foote's history, inseparable, we think, from its value as history, that in arriving at a conclusion so very well known as Appomattox he knew how to order events, develop characters, create a feeling of contingency, maintain pace, and produce in the end all the effect of tragic drama—all in what Gallie calls "evidenced" narrative.

Another scholar who should be mentioned as especially pertinent is Leo Braudy, as is plain to see in the title of his book, *Narrative Form in History and Fiction* (Princeton University Press, 1970). Braudy credits Gibbon with having achieved in *The Decline and Fall of the Roman Empire* a narrative method intermediate between that of the novelist Henry Fielding in *Tom Jones*, for example, and that of David Hume in his *History of England.* What Braudy claims for *The Decline and Fall,* we claim for *The Civil War* also: namely "the shape of history" is in either case "preeminently a construction, a literary work with aesthetic rather than systematic order and coherence." Braudy's book could set a model for future studies of Mr. Foote's book in English departments, as well as in History departments.

White: Such studies might start from a remark Mr. Foote once made to the effect that when he writes either fiction or history, "it's words and commas and semicolons. . . . This results in a particular attention to details . . . " (*The Mississippi Quarterly, 1971,* p. 370). Great as the mass of *The Civil War* is, it is everywhere articulated and splendidly *wrought.* He once said he worked every paragraph as one might a sonnet.

Foote: That's a goal, that's what you try for. Someone said of Lincoln that the thing that characterized him in his greatness was that he "knew dangers that lurk in iotas." Nobody knows this better than a writer. He knows that it is being careful about small things that produces great things. Or if he is going to pretend to try to do something good, he is going to have to pay a lot of attention to small things. Of course, this gets back to the apprenticeship I was talking about, and especially to the application of the things you have learned in your apprenticeship, by reading and writing. It is very useful to use a novelist's method of learning how to look at things and see them the way Conrad, for instance, can teach you to do. If you are going to write about Abraham Lincoln it is a good thing to have a good notion of him in your mind. It is good to read Herndon who tells what Lincoln was like at home. It is good to read physical things—that when Lincoln sat down, he was not much taller than any other man; that his height was all in his legs, so that when he sat down, his knees were higher than his waist. If you placed a marble on his knee, Herndon said, that marble would roll down into his lap. Well, that is not very useful for explaining the excellence of the Gettysburg Address, but that is the kind of thing that a good historian will have in his mind when he is describing Lincoln crossing a room or talking with a friend or making jokes or weeping over the death of his son; they all go into it; he becomes real for you. Novelists frequently talk about characters in their books taking on a reality, or sometimes it is called "standing up on their hind legs." The historian should ask that of his characters, too, that they become very real to him—and whatever helps to make them real to you is a genuine help to you as a writer.

White: We found that *The Civil War* activated academic prejudice not only against narrative history but against specifically military history, regarded as a poor relation of political or social history. C. Vann Woodward pungently criticized his fellow academic historians' condescending attitude in his review of *The Civil War* in *The New York Review of Books* (6 March, 1975, p. 12), accusing them of not wishing to face the particularly bloody and intractable truth of battle.

Sugg: But on this head, too, the critical justification for *The Civil War* has come pat, in John Keegan's *The Face of Battle* (1976). His discussions of the reasons people have reservations about military history and the deficiencies of some famous titles in the field lead to a persuasive argument that military history can achieve both "the autonomy of an academic discipline" and—what Mr. Foote's work exemplifies—"the aesthetic freedom of genuine literature."

Apparently we do have a changing climate of opinion from which Mr. Foote's work has begun to benefit. *The American Historical Review* ignored Volume I of *The Civil War,* took a dismissive tone when Volume 2 appeared (J. I. Robertson, Jr., *AHR* 69, 791-92), and then on the publication of Volume 3 gave the entire work high praise (Robert Hartje, *AHR* 81, 975-76). The reviewer who was dismissive in the *American Historical Review* after Volume 2 reviewed the whole work upon publication of Volume 3, using the columns of *Civil War History* (21, 172-75), where he apologized handsomely not only for his own earlier obtuseness but for that of his profession.

White: I imagine that Mr. Foote is content to let *The Civil War* make its own way to posterity. Faithful to the program he laid out for himself in his teens, he is now well along on his return to Jordan County. Just as he was able to adapt his novelistic techniques to his purposes in writing history, so he applied the methods he developed in doing research for the history to help, as he put it, "get his hand back in" with fiction. His most recent novel, *September September,* is, though conceived as an action tale, based as firmly on painstaking research as *Shiloh* was.

Foote: It was a sort of secondary inertia that kept me going the way I had been going. When I finished *The Civil War* I didn't know whether to be glad or sorry, and I took a little while to rest up and try to decide which I was. Finally I decided it didn't make any difference which I was, and got back to work. But I wanted to write a novel laid, it seemed to me, in a very critical period, at the time the Russians put up the Sputnik. And it so happened that the Little Rock "explosion" occurred in the first days of September—I'm talking about Governor Faubus and the various Hooraws over at Central High School. Anyway, I wanted to examine that month of September which included the Little Rock trouble over at Central High and ended on the 4th of October with the Russians throwing up the Sputnik.

To me, the latter was a devastating experience. I've had some great disappointments and shocks in my life—one of them was that a civilized nation, one of the most civilized on the globe, could put six million people into ovens—that made me question the perfectibility of man, to say the least. The other thing, I had seen the forty-hour work-week come into being and I'd thought it was going to result in a flowering of culture throughout the land because people would have spare time in which art would make its demands. Instead they went out and bought motor boats or went bowling. That was a disappointment. But one of the greatest disappointments was the denial of the nature of freedom. I was born just before our entry into the First World War, and during my time, perhaps because of the Hearst newspapers, a lot of things encouraged me to think that science was going to be the salvation of us all. We were going to move on a frictionless earth and energy wasn't going to cost anything—it was going to work beautifully, the machines and everything else. But along with this I was taught another thing: that only free-born men, free to act with open minds, could make great scientific discoveries. This I believed as firmly as I believed anything; just as writers supposedly cannot work under slavery, so scientists wouldn't be able to. And then the greatest scientific advance of my time, I suppose, was the putting up of the Sputnik, which opened the space age, and it was done by slave labor in a slave country and quite literally by men who were almost convicts—captured German scientists—and it was a great shock to me. I wanted to look at what the world was like on the immediate eve of that.

The novel involves a story about the kidnapping of a little black boy in Memphis, Tennessee, and tells about the people who kidnapped him and the people he was kidnapped from, which gave me the first chance, in all my work, to deal with the black bourgeois. All the black people I had ever known had either been servants or doctors, none of them in the middle. They existed, but I had nothing to do with them, or the little bit I'd had to do with them discouraged me from ever having anything more to do with them. I found that they were doing nothing but imitating white people, and not doing a very good job of it. So I didn't like the black bourgeois much. I realized I wasn't going to be able to write about them if I didn't like them, so I went into it hard when I tried to write about the black bourgeois, which was a great gap in my work. And that was another one of my purposes—you see how selfish I am in my work; I want to please myself. I'm thinking about myself more than I am about you, which may be a serious flaw. We'll have to wait and see.

Sugg: Although Mr. Foote follows a policy of not discussing work in progress, he has stated that the novel he is now writing will be a major addition to the Jordan County cycle. The title of the new work,

Two Gates to the City, has been in his mind almost from the beginning of his career. Its point of departure is from a character in "Pillar of Fire"—a Union Army Lieutenant who directed the sacking of Solitaire and witnessed the death of Isaac Jameson. The Yankee officer returns to the Delta after the War and thus becomes another of the outsiders who make a recurrent motif in Mr. Foote's books. We shall be concerned with his descendants.

White: We have told Mr. Foote that in our reading of his books we have felt increasing and increasingly pleasurable suspense; we predict that, with the new novel, he is going to reach in the art of fiction, his abiding vocation, the heights already achieved and sufficient to guarantee his reputation in history.

An Interview with Shelby Foote

Richard Tillinghast/1983

From *Ploughshares* [Cambridge, MA.] 9 (2-3), 1983, 118-31.
Reprinted by permission.

Shelby Foote is the author of six novels—*Tournament, Follow Me Down, Love in a Dry Season, Shiloh, Jordan County,* and *September September*—as well as his magnificent historical work in three large volumes, *The Civil War: A Narrative,* which is already considered a classic. Mr. Foote lives in Memphis, Tennessee, where he consented to be interviewed last December. He is a strikingly handsome man, of medium height, with a closely trimmed gray beard—considerably younger looking than his sixty-six years. Reserved, but courteous and responsive, he speaks in the rich and mellifluous accent of a cultivated Mississippian. The interview was conducted one chilly Sunday afternoon in Mr. Foote's large study at the back of his comfortable, secluded brick house on East Parkway South, built in the 1930s in the style known in the East as "stockbroker Tudor."

Greenville, Mississippi, in the Mississippi Delta, where Shelby Foote was born and brought up, is famous for the writers it has produced. The first well-known author from Greenville was William Alexander Percy, whose *Lanterns on the Levee: Recollections of a Planter's Son* could be found, a generation ago, in every Southern home with the slightest pretense to literacy. More recently, Mr. Foote's close friend Walker Percy, whose father's cousin was William Alexander Percy, also came from Greenville.

The interview, which was too long to be printed here in its entirety, ranged over a number of subjects, one of the most interesting that I have omitted being Mr. Foote's reading of Continental novelists, including his favorites, Dostoyevsky and Proust.

RT: When readers who are unfamiliar with the South think of Mississippi, they think of Faulkner's Mississippi. What is the difference between the Delta, where you grew up, and Faulkner's hill country?

Shelby Foote: The difference is sociologically large. Once you get over into literature, though, you get into something else. The reason Faulkner is taken as a representative of Southern writing is really quite simple. He's the greatest Southern talent. And it goes beyond that. When somebody like me comes along and I'm eighteen years old and Faulkner's doing his best work, that influences me strongly. He's saying this is the way you can see your homeland, and the young writer says "By golly, that's the way I see my homeland." So Faulkner has a really great influence on you. But that influence is not as great as people say it is, simply because it's perfectly natural that I write somewhat like Faulkner since we're writing about somewhat the same thing, the same homeland.

RT: Let's talk a little about Greenville, your home town.

SF: Well, I was born there in November of 1916. It then had a population of about 12,000. It was the perfect size. One thing you have in a place that size is that everybody between the ages of about 15 to 18 is in the same school together. That is, everybody who was white was in the same high school together, and everybody who was black was in the same high school together.

RT: People with money didn't send their kids to private schools?

SF: Well, that's another happy accident. Nobody had any money. It was the Depression. I know of one boy—no, two—two at home who went to prep school. One got sent for disciplinary reasons, and the other got sent for snobbish reasons. Outside of those two boys I don't know of anybody who went off to school in those years. The result was that you not only had the huge advantage of getting to know all kinds of people in that way that adolescents get to know each other, you also spent the rest of your life in intimate association with people you knew that way. And it gave you an insight into all sorts and conditions of men. One of your best friends might have been the son of the president of the largest bank, and the other the son of the garbage collector. And you had a very close relationship involving hunting, swimming, running after girls, drinking, dancing, discovering books. It seemed to me to be a perfectly marvelous way to grow up.

RT: The way I've heard Greenville described, it completely goes against the Southern stereotypes.

SF: It fit the stereotypes in some fairly superficial ways and departed from them in the most important ways, I think. Mostly, not entirely: A good deal of that was due to the presence of William Alexander Percy. He was a published writer and a splendid teacher. He did it more by example than by anything else. It was a very exciting time to be around. There was never a lynching in Greenville; it never got swept off its feet that way. The Ku Klux Klan never made any headway, at a time when it was making headway almost everywhere else.

RT: Didn't that have an awful lot to do with the influence of Senator Percy, William Alexander Percy's father?

SF: Yes, it did have a great deal to do with it. In most places nobody would stand up to the Klan in politics. It represented too many votes for you to stand up to. You might explain to your friends that you thought the people in the Klan were a bunch of rednecks and nuts, but you didn't tell *them* that. In Greenville they did. For one thing, Senator Percy's wife was a Catholic, and the Klan was more anti-Catholic than it was anti-black or anti-Jew. So the lines were pretty sharply drawn. It was a wonderful place to grow up in other ways too. Not only was the town that way—diversity and homogeneity combined—but so was the whole region. The Mississippi Delta runs from Memphis to Vicksburg, about two hundred miles long. It's about sixty miles wide at the widest part. And it's a very different region from other parts of the South. It is not Anglo-Saxon. Pure bloodlines don't make any sense in the Mississippi Delta.

RT: Could you talk about that for a moment?

SF: It's really kind of simple in some ways. I've often thought there's an inverse ratio between the richness of the soil and the providence of the people who live on it. Out in the hills—Faulkner's country—people put up preserves and took good care of the houses and everything, and in the Mississippi Delta nobody puts anything up and they don't take care of their houses. They figure that if they need some pole beans they'll go down and buy them in a can. Even in my family, which was comparatively cultured, if you were entertaining company you wanted to impress, you gave them Del Monte peas, not peas out of the garden. A lot of it was wrong, but this up-and--down thing in the Delta was very swift because of the ease of credit and the richness of the soil. I've said this often before: There's not a family there that didn't have in a period of three generations ups and downs. The family on top would be on the bottom. The family on the bottom would be on the top. Easy credit corrupted the people on the top, and the ability to make it raised those on the bottom; the whole thing's on the boil all the time. You could see a hundred years of history in twenty years in the Delta.

RT: To me that seems unusual for the South, maybe for anywhere.

SF: There are other ways to account for it too. It was a true melting pot. There were enormous numbers of Italians, Chinese, and many others. It was possible to come down there and open a small store. You lived in the back of it and had a few articles on the shelves out front. Your children would be running the largest merchandising business in the Delta thirty years later. And that drew people from all over.

RT: How does your own family fit into this picture?

SF: One strong element in my family's background is my mother's father. He was a Viennese Jew who left home at the age of seventeen and came to this country. I still don't know how he wound up in the Delta, but he was keeping books on a plantation down at Avon, and married the daughter of the owner. I don't know what reaction the planter had to that. That's one of those things brought into the family. And where any literary interest came from, let alone talent, is not too difficult to find, because it certainly didn't come from any of the rest of my family. That's part of what I'm talking about.

RT: You're speaking more or less in terms of genes. But what about the social aspect of it? My experience growing up in Memphis and then moving to the Northeast is that Southern Jews are real different from Northern Jews. There's very little old-country "ethnicity" among Southern Jews—they're Southern before they're anything else.

SF: You see, they don't have to deal with the virulent brand of anti-Semitism the Northern Jews have to deal with . . . I remember being amazed to discover that they didn't take Jews in the Country Club in Greenwood [a town less than a hundred miles east of Greenville]. I couldn't believe that, because in the Country Club at home, there were probably more Jews than there were Baptists.

RT: I see what you mean. And that's a fascinating story in itself. But let's get back to an earlier subject: your work in relation to William Faulkner's. While I see many resemblances, it seems to me there's a different emphasis, in terms of the transition from the old times to modern times. In Faulkner there is clearly an age of heroes, but in the twentieth century what you have are mostly scoundrels, or in any case, lesser men. Whereas I don't see that sharp demarcation in your books.

SF: No, and I'm glad you don't, because people aren't like that. Faulkner's talent was of such a burning kind that he did not want it to be interfered with by doing anything like research or sometimes anything like thinking. He would start out to do something with a theory. I'm sure he created the Snopeses to represent a certain type of poor white, the common people in the hills. But when his talent turned loose on those people, they didn't represent anything but Snopeses. The Snopeses are so particular as to be a separate breed entirely to themselves. And he thought so too, after he created them. He once said to me: "People talk to me about genius. I don't know about that. But *one* time I had genius, and that was when I named those people Snopes."

RT: The heroic period in your Jordan County trilogy [*Follow Me Down, Jordan County, Love in a Dry Season*, published by Dial Press in one volume] only includes the men who went back there in the wilderness and carved out their places to begin with, because Major Barcroft, the patriarch in *Love in a Dry Season,* he's almost a comic character, isn't he?

SF: Yes. What I see is that the first people who came along were very hard working and brave. They had to be both. They set themselves up, and then they themselves, but above all their descendants, were corrupted by ease. Some of those people, those pioneer people, wouldn't bear too much looking at. They did some pretty dreadful things. But it was by way of surviving, which is very different from making financial deals that are highly questionable for the sake of getting rich.

RT: Isaac [the pioneer ancestor in *Jordan County*] has a dream, a visionary experience, the night before he finds his land. I find that very, very interesting.

SF: I wanted that in there, because it seemed to me it almost could not not be there. How could a man undertake such a thing without some kind of ideal, some kind of dream he was trying to fulfill? Otherwise he might as well have stayed in Natchez. No reason going into that crazy, wild country, exposing yourself to malaria and God knows what else, unless you had some real motive other than just to try to get rich. Being a person who would do that kind of thing would influence you in other ways. Isaac was opposed to the Civil War because he thought the War was wrong. And it seemed to me a thinking man would have thought the War was wrong on everything but constitutional issues. So that I do see those who followed being lesser men, because their challenges were less. And then finally you *really* get corruption, as in *Love in a Dry Season*. Those people might as well not be on this earth.

RT: That's my favorite book of yours, *Love in a Dry Season*.

SF: It is mine, in some ways. I was very happy while I was writing it, and it did seem to come out the way I wanted it to. I would think something and then my hand would write it the way I wanted it to go. That's a happy experience.

RT: The humor in the book snuck up on me. I was a little ways into it before I started realizing that a lot of things happening in it were very funny, almost farcical. I'm thinking of the triangle between Harley Drew, Amy, and Jeff, the blind man.

SF: That's one reason I'm so fond of it. I think it's funny, too, practically on every page, except some of the rather pathetic things about Amanda Barcroft.

RT: It seems to me that critics have tended to misread the book, taking for granted your disapproval of Harley Drew, who is admittedly in some sense almost a stage villain. But I sense a certain approval, even admiration in your attitude toward him—though of course he was an out and out scoundrel.

SF: That's right. Some of his traits could be called weaknesses. He hurt people, but he never would hurt anybody face to face.

RT: The way he schemed everything out. The fact that he won eight thousand dollars in that shipboard poker game, and then . . . He did some smart things, like spending a thousand dollars of it on clothes. That was a good move.

SF: Yes, you always have an admiration for somebody who's willing to take on the world; particularly if it's a higher world than his. I think that's totally admirable. Of course the way he goes about it is highly questionable. But Harley never did want to hurt anybody. He very much wanted to get whatever they had, and if hurting them was part of it, he'd be willing to do it, but not too much. He miscalculated right down the line.

RT: The Major's ploy was a good one, when Harley said "I'm in love with your daughter," and he said, "What color are her eyes?"

SF: I always thought that was a highly unfair question. I never know what color people's eyes are, including people that I'm in love with. What the hell difference does it make what color their eyes are? But he did skewer poor Harley on it. The Major did things that he did because of various things in his life that were irreversible. In the Major's position do you or do you not interfere with this man courting your daughter? I certainly would not want my daughter to marry Harley Drew. But on the other hand whom *is* she going to marry. What is going to happen to her? And what kind of life would she have had with him? That's difficult to say. The Major made it impossible for her to marry him, because Harley's not about to marry her without any money. Also, Barcroft had adopted very rigidly a code that he believed had been passed down to him.

RT: More a code than a reality. This is where I think a certain misreading of the book could get started. It's as though, automatically, a Southern novelist was going to admire the Major, a relic from the old days, and condemn an adventurer, a low-born scoundrel from the North.

SF: Exactly. Critics think all Southern novelists just love the South and every single thing about it. It ain't necessarily so.

RT: Bearing in mind what we have just been talking about, I'd have to say that you take a colder and more realistic look at the South than did Faulkner, who was much more a creator of myths.

SF: I think I do that too. But I do think that a quality of very great writing is that it converts tales into myths. Because myth is so much greater than fantasy, if you handle a fantasy right it will become a myth. One of my favorite modern writers now is Márquez. I was greatly pleased to see him get the Nobel Prize last year. *One Hundred Years of Solitude* is very strongly influenced by *The Hamlet,* and it has that quality of converting folk tales, almost, into myths.

RT: I gather you knew Faulkner rather well.

SF: We were together maybe five or six times. I spent the night at his house. We took a trip together. Incidentally, this business about

Faulkner not being outgoing is totally false as far as I'm concerned. He was glad to talk about his work. I never asked him any of those things that he's famous for not answering about his private life. Maybe that's one of the reasons we got along so well. He knew I wasn't going to ask him things like that.

RT: What about the trip you took together?

SF: Well, it was the 90th anniversary of Shiloh, so it was April 6th, 1952. They were having some kind of observance there, and it was also the publication date of my novel. So I got up early that morning, and to go by car to Shiloh I would naturally go through Oxford. So I got there at 7:30 or 8:00 in the morning. I knew Faulkner got up early, so I parked and went around the side of the house and knocked on the door. And he came to the door, said "Good morning, glad to see you." He had about a week's beard, maybe more. I said, "I'm on my way up to Shiloh. It's the anniversary of the battle, and I thought you might like to ride up there and take a look at it." He had on raggedy clothes, and after a while he said he would like to go, and if I didn't mind waiting while he got dressed, we'd go. So he went upstairs and he came back down in about fifteen minutes. He was clean shaven. He had on a natty tweed suit, and that little hat with a feather in the side that he always liked to wear. And we got in the car and drove on up to Corinth. Corinth was the county seat, with a courthouse square in the middle. We got there and I said, "We're going to have to get a drink somewhere, but it's Sunday; God knows where we're going to get any whiskey on Sunday morning." Mississippi, of course, was still dry. We were parked on the square, looking just inside the door of the old Corinth Hotel. There was a shoeshine stand there, and a young man getting his shoes shined. And Faulkner said he could find us some whiskey; anybody getting his shoes shined on Sunday morning would know where it was. I said "I don't think so. I think he's probably on his way to church." Faulkner said, "Why don't you step in there and ask him." So I went over, and the shoeshine boy was polishing his shoes. I said, "Excuse me. My friend and I are strangers here, and we were wondering where we could get a drink. Could you tell me where a bootlegger is?" And he said, "Well I was fixing to go out there myself. If you could give me a ride, I'll show you the way."

RT: I guess that shows Faulkner was a good judge of men.

SF: Yes, Faulkner knew what he was talking about. We got in the car, drove out to the bootlegger's, and got us a pint of Old Taylor, with cokes for chasers. We took two drinks, and when it got time for what I considered a highly desirable third, he said he didn't want any more. So I took my drink. He didn't take a third. So much for Faulkner as a heavy drinker, at least on that occasion. I enjoyed going around the fields with him, though. Shiloh is one of the most difficult battle sites in the world. You can get turned around on your fiftieth trip and not know where you are. I had studied it so hard, I knew it pretty well. And it amazed me how quickly he could grasp the geographical factors and the military factors.

RT: If you had to single out one particular thing you admire about Faulkner's writing, what would that be?

SF: I've always said that Faulkner's number-one ability, which nobody pays any attention to and which Faulkner himself condemned in his Nobel speech, is his ability to communicate sensation, the actual texture of things. It goes beyond any writer I know. And I'm speaking advisedly. I'm talking about Shakespeare or anybody else you want to name.

RT: You're probably bored to death with being asked about the relationship between fiction, which would seem to be an act of the imagination, and historical writing, which would seem to rely on facts—

SF: Keats said a long time ago, "A fact is not a truth until you love it." And old Francis Butler Simpkins, a great historian who has been dead about twenty years now, said that a historian can't make a more serious mistake than to equate facts with truth. It's what you do with them that counts, the order and manner in which you release them. When the facts are put together properly, they add up to the truth, and any distortion is destructive. But history can be plotted just as well as fiction. In fact I think plotting is more important in history than in fiction. I don't think there's much truth in a book of twenty essays about the Civil War, one chapter dealing with slavery, one dealing with military things, usually called, "The Armies Meet," and that sort of foolishness. The whole thing ought to be telling a glowing story or it won't be true. Lincoln should not be presented in a chapter on Abraham Lincoln, and Jefferson Davis in another one. They should walk through the story and demonstrate their characters as it goes along.

RT: I remember thinking, when I read your opening descriptions of Davis and Lincoln, that that was all one would need to know in predicting who would win the war. It floors me to consider the work it must have taken to write that book.

SF: It floors me too. I can't believe I spent twenty years doing something like that; I can't believe I got all that material into that fairly small space. It's only a million and a half words. It, uh, it awes me looking back on it. It's an incredible story. You've got all the elements for the greatest thing since the Bible, you see. I think that the analogy is not false, that the Civil War as a subject is—to Southerners in any case, and I would say to the whole country—what Troy was to the Greeks. I think no one can pretend to understand the basic nature of this country unless he has some fairly profound notion of what the Civil War was about, how it was fought and what came of it. It had far more to do with the character of this nation than, say, the Revolution.

RT: Something I've noticed in my lifetime is that the consciousness of the Civil War, which was so prominent when I was a child, is fading somewhat now. We played Civil War games, we knew all the characters, we knew all the battles. We knew Pickett's Charge—in fact Barry Pickett, one of my classmates in junior high here in Memphis, was a descendant.

SF: You also had a very heavy prejudice against Yankees. And that's gone now, which is good. During the Second World War there was a pilot training thing in Greenville, and lots of those cadets married Greenville girls. And one common characteristic of Delta girls is, whoever they marry, he's going to live there. They're not going to his place. Usually because the father's got land. It's a good opportunity for the boy. But the last thing a mother and father tell a girl before the wedding is, "We like John, he's a fine boy, and you couldn't have picked better—but if you have any trouble, you know where home is."

RT: The parents' impulse is probably basically a kind one. But it's not an altogether happy situation, is it?

SF: There was a darker side to it as well—a really ugly side, which

I tend to write about. The old man's got a plantation, you've married his daughter, and you're going to work for him, or his son is going to work for him. Early on, you're out checking the crops or doing whatever you're doing, and he looks down and says, "By golly, I've run out of cigarettes. Would you run up to the store and get us a couple of packs?" And of course you say you'll be glad to. But you're the person who runs after cigarettes all the rest of your life. Nobody at that point has sense enough to say, "No, I won't. Get your own cigarettes." You can't say that. But it was a double-barreled thing. It was just greatly overdone respect for your elders, and it was greatly overdone mistrust for your juniors. So the man is not about to trust his plantation to this young fellow, son-in-law or son, who doesn't know up from down. And many of those planters wound up seventy years old with these fifty-year-old sons with nothing to do. It happened in business as well as on the plantations. There's nothing like that these days. Young people won't put up with it, and old people have been better informed about young people.

RT: You're tracing all this back to the plantation patriarchy?

SF: That was the beginning of it. You see, that was what the plantation thing was. The planter abuses people right on down the line. And he gets away with it because he tells these people who were abused, "Stand still for this because someday you're going to be where I am, and you'll be able to abuse people." And they say, "That's true, that's true." And in many cases it *is* true. But it's a wretched life, abusing people, working people all day long for a dollar. That's no good life, and whatever you get out of it, it's not worth doing that to people. Decent people would know that from the start. But the Mississippi Delta planter never had any notion that it wasn't a good life. He thought it was the very best life of all. I condemn it on other terms, too. He had no use for art. He left that up to his wife; and she had no use for it either. But it was a decent society in many ways. It had virtues. People would genuinely help each other in any kind of distress. That's nearly always true in a backward country.

RT: You've chosen to live here in Memphis rather than down in the Delta or somewhere else.

SF: Yes, I have. There are certain aspects of Memphis that I like. What I like in Memphis is when people have parties, they don't do it for any reason except to have a good time. I like it in Memphis that men don't get in one end of the room and women in the other. They mingle. I like those aspects. The thing I do not like about Memphis is its backwardness in all kinds of things. But there are things I like very much about it. And the things I don't like about it, I don't tend to talk about.

RT: I understand you work every day.

SF: Yes. Throughout the first thirty years of my writing life, I worked seven days a week, eight hours a day, and sometimes more. I discovered that if I stopped for one day it took me two to get back to work, so I stopped stopping. But now that I'm getting older I don't work on Sundays. And I take off any day I want to and don't feel guilty about it. What I did through my hardest working years was I developed so many habits that if I took off, I'd be a lot more wretched than I would be sitting at that desk sweating and fretting. So I didn't take off. I'm a very slow writer. Five or six hundred words is a good day. So I have to be industrious to make up for what I lack in other directions.

RT: Do you want to say anything about the book you're working on now?

SF: I'm working on *Two Gates to the City,* a big family novel set in the Delta. The time of the book is 1948, but it goes back into the 1870s and forward into the 1960s. It's a wild, experimental, long, crazy book.

RT: Are you almost finished?

SF: Barely started. I'm still shifting things around, doing the outlines. I'm up on a high cliff, contemplating a jump into the water. Once I go, I'm gone.

Shelby Foote

W. Hampton Sides/1986

From *Memphis*, 10 (January 1986), 38, 40-44, 49, 51-53. Reprinted by permission.

Shelby Foote, 69, is perhaps Memphis' best-known writer. He is the author of six novels: *Tournament, Follow Me Down, Love in a Dry Season, Shiloh, Jordan County,* and *September September*. Foote has also written a comprehensive three-volume history of the Civil War which was the product of over twenty years of meticulous research; *The Civil War: A Narrative* is considered by some critics to be the definitive account of the war. "What I wanted to do was to present the *look* and *feel* of the war, not just to summarize battles and movements," explains Foote.

Foote grew up in Greenville, Mississippi. He attended the University of North Carolina for two years, served as a captain of field artillery during World War II, and returned afterwards to the Delta to write fiction. He has lived in Memphis for over thirty years.

We spoke with Foote in the study of his East Parkway home, where he has lived with his wife Gwyn since 1966. He is currently working on his seventh novel, which will be called *Two Gates to the City*.

Memphis: We understand you've spent the last few years doing nothing but reading.

Foote: That's right, but I'm about all read out now. I did that for about three years, and practically wrote nothing. I would spend six months on Dante, then six months on Chaucer, and so on, through all my favorite writers from the past. I read them all, the whole damn gamut. Reading like that is a wonderful thing to do. From the ages of 18 to 23, I read like that, about eight hours a day or more. I just went crazy reading in those days, like a colt in clover. So it was wonderful to get back to some of that great literature.

Memphis: Not many people seem to have the time or inclination to read so much these days.

Foote: I said I spent eight hours a day reading during my adolescent years. Well, I now spend about four hours a day watching television. I watch the news for an hour, I watch a movie at night, I watch *As the World Turns* every day.

You can get out of the habit of reading and think it's a whole lot more trouble. But the excitement that you get from reading *The Brothers Karamazov,* for example . . . there ain't nothing that can match that still. Or read Shakespeare's plays and really absorb what he's saying. That's an experience you're not going to get off the television or radio or anywhere. You read *Macbeth* from start to finish, with an appreciation for the irony that's loaded in every other line of the play, and you see that whole Macbeth universe open up. There's nothing that's going to replace that. But God knows, people don't read anymore.

Memphis: Do you think the reading you've been doing will influence your work now?

Foote: I'm not sure anything will influence my work. I'm old and set. And when you develop a style, the better you get at it, the more you're locked in. Until finally, you can't move except in your style. I think, "Well, I'm going to write something simple and forthright." And you can't do it. You get more and more skillful, but the borders shrink on you.

Memphis: So you read more for pleasure than for influence?

Foote: Read for pleasure and—to use a really fancy word on you—for wisdom. I'm getting wise. But you know, in your early years, literature can be extremely influential on your style. I believe that literature is a progressive thing. All of the good writers I know came out of combining things that appealed to them enormously. William Faulkner, on the simplest terms, is a combination of Sherwood Anderson and Joseph Conrad. He absorbed what those two men had to give him and he came up with a third thing. Now, it's a lot more complicated than that. But basically, he found a way to combine those talents.

I once told Faulkner, "I have every reason to believe that I'm going to be a better writer than you ever were . . . 'cause you had Anderson and Conrad, and I've got you and Proust, and my writers are better than your writers." He laughed about that.

Memphis: Can you tell me anything about your new novel?

Foote: I don't ever talk about a book that I'm working on. But it's called *Two Gates to the City.* It's a big Delta novel set in a town that I call Bristol. It's based on the life that I know, so I don't have to do any research. The novel's about down home, and it concerns a family.

Memphis: How long have you been working on it?

Foote: Off and on for a long time. I first conceived it before I started *The Civil War* over twenty years ago.

Memphis: *The Civil War* was quite a detour for you.

Foote: If I had known it was going to take twenty years, I never would have begun it. But I'm glad I did it. I enjoyed the history thoroughly, the whole time. I was never the least bit doubtful about whether this is what I should be doing. But it was not an interruption. I found no difference in writing history and writing a novel. The narrative history is very much like a novel. Nothing pleases me more than when somebody asks me whether I made something up in that history. It pleases me greatly. I didn't make up anything in it.

Memphis: But do you think that the discipline of writing narrative history is any different from the discipline of writing fiction?

Foote: I really don't. There are differences, obvious ones. You can't say Lincoln's got gray eyes, unless you know that he did. And you do. But if he's a fictional character, I'll give him any color eyes I want to. But once I give him those eyes, those are his eyes. A good novelist would no more be false to a fact dug out of his head—and they *are* facts—than a good historian would be false to a fact dug out of documents. If you're not true to your facts, you've got a trashy book. You can't go being false to what you've laid down as being a man's nature. You can't have someone arbitrarily doing something that he just would not do.

In my fiction, I had always decided what color a man's eyes were, what shape his fingernails were, what kind of tie he wore. Those things were always important to me. In the history, it didn't bother me the least bit to have to look them up, instead of imagining them. So that I wound up with exactly the same approach doing the history that I had when I was doing the novels. With this added dimension: Who's going to write a novel that's got characters like Stonewall Jackson, Robert E. Lee, and U. S. Grant in it?

Memphis: Real life is richer than fiction at certain times?

Foote: Infinitely richer.

Memphis: Still, there must be plenty of academic historians who criticize your whole approach to writing history.

Foote: Oh, sure. Professional historians resent the hell out of the absence of footnotes, for instance. And footnotes would have totally shattered what I was doing. I didn't want people glancing down at the bottom of the page every other sentence. The professional historians have criticized it, but what they *haven't* done is point out any errors. I'm not saying there are no errors, but there are damn few, fewer than most history books that are just loaded with footnotes.

Professional historians resent it and creative writers don't read it. So I'm falling between two stools, you see. But that doesn't bother me. The book makes its own claims.

Memphis: Has the history done well for you?

Foote: It's done enormously well, as a matter of fact. I can live on it. And I've got backed-up royalties at Random House, plenty of them. So I don't have any worries. It's made a lot of money, and continues to.

Memphis: It's hardly one of those flashy titles that enjoys one hot summer on the best-seller list. It stays around.

Foote: Well, it now sells around 4,500 copies a year. It's been very consistent. It's in school libraries, and it's used in college courses on the Civil War.

Memphis: I imagine writing a work like that has made you a kind of resident expert on the Civil War.

Foote: Something like that. I got all kinds of offers from publishers to do the War of 1812, the American Revolution, and so on. I told them all, "Absolutely no, under no circumstances." I said, "I've got my discharge from that war, and I'm out of it." You see, I don't want to be *the* Civil War expert. The day I finished that book I stopped having anything to do with the Civil War. And I've done my best to forget it.

Memphis: But all the pressures of the mass media must conspire to make you the expert against your will.

Foote: They will do it. My God, they will do it. They will grab hold of you and squeeze you like a sponge. I might have ended up on television four hours a day every day of my life. And I'd be a shell after about two weeks of that. I'd be dead. If I had let them, they would have gotten me. There's money to be made out of me, for one thing.

Memphis: Hasn't that been especially true with Southerners? The networks will say, "Let's get some Southerner to comment on this or that problem."

Foote: Oh, yes. Some Southerner will always pop up to explain how it really is down here. Like the man that I have been seeing who is a specialist on hurricanes down there. He's on all the networks three times a day. They'll wear him out like you wear out a tire on a car. Plain wear him out. People will just say, "Oh my God, here *he* comes again. I already know what he's going to say."

Memphis: Like Carl Sagan?

Foote: Right. He's ridiculous. I mean, he's just an absurd man. They wore him out. But the problem is, they hit you where you're very vulnerable, in your pocketbook and in your desire for fame. It's a lovely thing to be known in every household in America. You shouldn't feel that way, but you do. Freud said that we write for three reasons: money, fame, and love of women. And there ain't no other. That's it. He said, "Don't talk to me about talent. That's foolishness." I think there's a lot of truth in that.

Memphis: You write for fame yourself?

Foote: Sure. I would never deny that. I don't think any other writer would either. You want to say, "Kilroy is here."

Memphis: Ever have the urge to write a best-seller?

Foote: Urge? I've been practically convinced that everything I write was going to be a best-seller. But I've never been on any best-seller list anywhere except in France, where *Follow Me Down* did pretty well. I don't think you can deliberately sit down to write one unless you are a best-seller writer to begin with.

Memphis: Someone like Erich Segal in *Love Story?*

Foote: Yes. I didn't mean it can't be done by a bad writer. It's hard to make a silk purse out of a sow's ear, but it's even harder the other way around. It's a difficult thing to try to dope the market and anticipate a need.

Memphis: In your last novel, *September September,* you set the action against the backdrop of the Little Rock desegregation crisis of 1957. Why did you choose to focus on that historic episode?

Foote: It fit into the novel as a kind of demonstration of something that has been true throughout most of the South during the period of racial unrest. Somebody said once, "If you want turmoil and real bad trouble, all you have to do is let good people relax a little bit." In Little Rock—as in other places in the South—what the good people did was turn their backs and let the trash take over. They said, "Let *them* handle it, let the Ku Kluxers and the White Supremacists take over." I'm not claiming that "the good people" were integrationists. They certainly were not. But they were not rabid segregationists. They weren't about to get out and fulminate against it. It would have been bad manners for one thing. So they just stood back and let the riffraff take over.

Memphis: In *September September*, you pay close attention to historical details. You weave in old headlines from *The Commercial Appeal*, old TV sitcoms from the fifties, reports on Eisenhower and Sputnik. What role do you think historical accuracy should play in fiction?

Foote: I believe you owe two things: the place and the time should be accurate, absolutely accurate. And there's no excuse for not making them so. The information is all there. But having said that, I do not think that the *worth* of any novel is simply in its historical accuracy. That alone won't make a great novel. You might as well write history. Still, I would disagree with anyone who thinks that history has no place in the novel. When I was writing *September September,* I kept a map of the city of Memphis from 1957 on my desk at all times, so that if someone went somewhere in a car, I made them go to the right place. I think you owe that accuracy to the book. I always think that a historical error detracts badly from a book. Not just because it's anachronistic, but because it's wrong.

Memphis: But many of the great novelists have sidestepped that issue of time and place by creating their own little worlds. Faulkner, for instance.

Foote: Faulkner was funny about that. He would not stop for an instant to look anything up. Accuracy that is achieved by research, he had no interest in. But he did try hard as hell to get into the frame of mind of those people at that time. *Absalom, Absalom!* is a lot better picture of what the Deep South was like around the Civil War than *Gone With the Wind,* which came out the same year. A lot more accurate. But not with regard to names and dates.

Memphis: Names and dates are especially important to the journalist. Have you ever done any journalism?

Foote: I worked for the Associated Press in New York for about six months. I worked on the central desk there, and I really enjoyed it. But I knew not to stay there in much the same way that I knew not to stay in school.

Now, journalism has a certain value. Names and dates, like you say. And learning how to meet a deadline is very valuable. Even if you don't meet them, you're at least conscious of them, and you know how to work under pressure. And that's good. And you learn to purify your style, if you've got a good editor. Hemingway learned an awful lot working on *The Kansas City Star.* It taught him how to write. It's a good experience. But if you stay with it too long, you have a journalist approach to life, which is too flashy for the use of a novel.

Memphis: You were raised in Greenville, Mississippi, a place that seems to have produced a disproportionate number of good writers and journalists. What was it like to grow up in a place like that?

Foote: Most people's boyhood seems rather ideal to them, I suppose, even if it was spent on the Lower East Side of New York. They'll say, "The richness of that experience . . . why, I wouldn't swap it for anything else in the world!" Well, I feel the same way about Greenville. When I grew up there, the population was between 15,000 and 20,000. We had two high schools, one for black and one for white. But in that one white high school I attended, all the white boys and girls between the ages of 14 and 18 were there together for six hours a day. So that when you grew up, you had been to school with everybody in that town. It was a particularly rich thing, because one of your best friends might have been the son of the banker; another of your best friends might have been the son of a janitor. So Greenville was a perfect place to spend those years, because I knew every person and even every dog in town. It was a wonderful, wonderful way to know all classes of society.

Memphis: Hodding Carter, Walker Percy, David Cohn, Ellen Douglas, yourself—why so many writers from Greenville?

Foote: There was something conducive going on. It was not a literary society. There was no passing of manuscripts or anything like that. But there was a thing, and the number one thing was the presence of William Alexander Percy [author Walker Percy's uncle].

Will Percy was a writer and a cultured man. One such man in a small town is enough to kick off a lot of reaction.

Memphis: Did you attend college?

Foote: Eventually, for two years. I had been editor of the high school paper in Greenville, and I spent most of my editorship attacking the principal of the school. It came time for me to go off to school, and I made application to [the University of North Carolina at] Chapel Hill. They wrote my high school for my record, and the principal went to the trouble of writing a letter saying,"By no means allow this dreadful person in your school." So I got back a letter from them saying, "We are sorry to inform you that you have not been accepted into the University of North Carolina." So I got in the car and went up to Chapel Hill on the matriculation date and got in line. I got up to the table there, and they looked in the file and said, "We told you not to come." And I said, "I know you did, but I couldn't believe you meant it." So they said, "All right, since you're here . . . "

Memphis: Did you know by then that you wanted to write fiction?

Foote: I guess I did. I certainly never had any notion of doing anything else. As for how I was going to make a living, I was perfectly willing to weight cotton in gins or work as a carpenter's assistant or anything that came along. Just as long as it didn't interfere with my work. And that's the reason that I never wanted to teach. I think it draws on some of the same resources.

Memphis: Your home is Greenville, but you've lived here in Memphis for a long, long time.

Foote: I've lived here now for 31 years. But it wasn't a move in the sense of moving to New York or Chicago or even New Orleans. Because Memphis was always just the city for me. I felt at home in Memphis all my life. Even when I was a little boy, I used to come up here with my aunt on shopping expeditions. So Memphis was just a bigger place in the Delta.

Memphis: Do you think Memphis is the social capital of the Delta anymore?

Foote: When I was a boy, there was a common saying—and it was absolutely true—that you could go in the lobby of the Peabody, and if you sat perfectly still for five minutes, you'd see at least three people that you knew from town. And you would. You see, women used to come up here and buy their shoes at Levy's. Men came up to get guns and hunting equipment. People from the Delta came to Memphis the way Japanese go to Tokyo, the way Frenchmen go to Paris. It drew people in.

But I don't think that's nearly as true anymore, for all kinds of reasons. Like the lumber industry, for instance. Memphis used to be called "the hardwood capital of the world." But so much of that Delta land is all timbered out now. And the cotton industry—it has changed so much. The government had nothing to do with cotton back in those days. Now, the price is fixed, and the brokers are not functioning the way they used to.

Memphis: So somewhere along the line, the city sort of severed its ties with the outlying rural areas.

Foote: Yes, that's true. It had something to do with the Chamber of Commerce style that first began to take hold when Crump ran the city and now has us on the road to becoming another Atlanta, another Houston. But it also has to do with a change in Greenville and all those other Delta towns. You can now get as good a pair of shoes in Greenville as you can get in Memphis. There's no need to come here. There are shopping centers in all of those little towns. The homogenization of America has changed a lot of things like that.

Memphis: Has the "homogenization of America" likewise changed the nature of writing? Critics speak of "a Southern style, a Southern voice, a Southern tradition" as if those things reflected a distinct spirit originating from a special kind of mythic locale. This Southern thing—is there anything left of it?

Foote: I don't think that "The Thing" is dead, nor do I think that the South was a very special region. I think you'll find that the northeast corner of Iowa would be a special region if you had a good writer there.

Now the publishing world in the East helps to perpetuate a certain view of the South. They're looking for sultry atmospheres and that sort of stuff. But "The Thing" is still there. We just don't have the writers. You don't get Faulkner all that often. I think that gothic novels always were inferior works, including *War and Peace*. A novel that has historical characters moving through it, saying things they never said, looking ways they never looked, is by nature a bad novel. They're not out after the truth; they're out after something else. So then the gothic novel was bankrupt to start with. A great artist could work with it and bring it off. Faulkner brought it off in *Absalom, Absalom!*, which was certainly a gothic novel. But what the hell couldn't he bring off, except maybe the French Army mutiny?

Memphis: Still, the locale must make a difference.

Foote: I have always preferred writers who had a strong sense of place. That holds for Dostoyevsky in St. Petersburg, for Proust in Paris, for Faulkner in Yoknapatawpha. But it's not that their place has made them special. It's the other way around. They have made their place special. It's the writers. It's always the writers.

Memphis: If a sense of place is important for a writer, what does the homogenization of the country do to that sense of place? In other words, if Memphis, for example, is becoming less and less distinctively Memphis, how will that affect the quality of the work of a writer who is living in Memphis and writing about it?

Foote: It need not affect it that much. There is always going to be *a place,* and there's always going to be perceptive people to write about it. I don't think the homogenization can ever be so great as to do away with the differences perceived by an artist.

Memphis: You spent over twenty years immersed in the Civil War. What do you think are the legacies from that experience here in the South?

Foote: I used to be amazed when people would say, "Americans never lost a war." Patton was famous for saying that, and yet his own grandfather was a colonel under Lee. If anybody ever lost a war, we lost that one. And few people have been so ground down after their defeat. Now here is the legacy: I think the Civil War gave us an enormous gift lacking in the rest of the country. It is a profound sense of the tragedy of life. Getting whipped is a hell of an experience. If you're a kid in a fist-fight, and you really get beat up bad one time, you learn a lot from it. I'm not talking about being scared; I'm talking about what it feels like to be really defeated. And so it is with nations.

Memphis: Do you really think people in the South still think about war in those terms?

Foote: Not consciously. I don't think young Southerners today think about having lost a war; but I think the influences have been passed down through grandparents and parents in many subtle ways.

Memphis: Do you find it necessary or even useful to keep in contact with a circle of literary friends?

Foote: No, I object to that as much as I do going to college. Now some writers thrive on that kind of thing, or seem to. Norman Mailer, for instance. I can't imagine him living outside of a literary milieu. A good friend of mine practically associated his whole life with things like writer's colonies, for God's sake. I couldn't get any work done that way.

I think that the death of American poetry, which is a very real thing, is a result of all the poets now being writers-in-residence on college campuses. They're not writing. They're bull-sessioning at night, talking about their work—what time they're not jumping the co-eds. It's not a good life for a writer. They'd be much better off out on the road, riding freight trains or driving taxi cabs or something. Anything but that. It's a very dangerous thing to talk about your work. And all the old writers knew that. Nowadays, people sit around and talk about their work all the time. They'll say, "This is what I'm doing now . . . I'm fixing to work out this problem . . . " and so on. The next thing you know, you just talk it away. It can really happen. If you solve your problems, you're not going to write about them.

People don't write books because they've got a great deal of wisdom to impart to somebody; they write books because they want to find the answers for themselves and share the search. It's not, "I have a thing to tell you," even if you say it is. It's an exploration and a discovery. And once you've found out the answer, you'd think, "Now I can *really* sit down and write another book—even better—about this same thing." But it's not in you.

Memphis: In much the same way that you don't want to become the Civil War expert and continue to write in that vein?

Foote: That's right. The old question won't engage your interest.

Memphis: So what will you do next after *Two Gates to the City* is finished?

Foote: Die, I expect. I don't care. I've got about two million words between covers now. If I don't do anything else, it's all right with me.

Seeking the Truth in Narrative: An Interview with Shelby Foote

William C. Carter/1987

From *The Georgia Review* (Spring 1987), 145-72. Reprinted by permission.

Over thirty years ago, Shelby Foote's career as a Southern novelist seemed well on its way. Five novels had appeared in rapid succession: *Tournament* (1949), *Follow Me Down* (1950), *Love in a Dry Season* (1951), *Shiloh* (1952), and *Jordan County: A Landscape in Narrative* (1954). All of these except *Shiloh* were set in Foote's homeland, the Mississippi Delta—and even *Shiloh* had a Deltan in it. The novels spanned a period of time from the late eighteenth century to the mid-1950s, and they managed to incorporate virtually all segments of the Delta society—rich and poor, white and black. At that point in his career, Foote was recognized as a fine regional writer in the best sense: his characters were firmly anchored in their own place and time and yet transcended these apparent limitations to become universal in their appeal.

During the writing of *Shiloh* (a novel that Faulkner considered to be "twice the book that *The Red Badge of Courage* is"), Foote had collected an abundance of material about the Civil War. When the novel was finished, his publisher, Bennett Cerf at Random House, suggested that he undertake a book to be entitled *A Short History of the Civil War.* Foote signed a contract that called for one volume of approximately five hundred pages, a project he assumed would take only a year or so. Twenty years (and three thousand pages) later, Foote had completed *The Civil War: A Narrative,* a three-volume set that many writers and historians have acknowledged to be one of the great creations of our time. Walker Percy called Foote's *War* "an unparalleled achievement, an American *Iliad,* a unique work uniting the scholarship of the historian and the high readability of the first-class novelist."

Writing the *Narrative* confirmed Foote's belief that the only difference between the novelist and the historian is one of method, not substance or skill. As he stated in one of the bibliographical notes to his masterpiece, both the historian and novelist are "seeking the same thing: the truth—not a different truth: the same truth—only they reach it, or try to reach it, by different routes. Whether the event took place in a world now gone to dust, preserved by documents and evaluated by scholarship, or in the imagination, preserved by memory and distilled by the creative process, they both want to tell us *how it was:* to re-create it, by their separate methods, and make it live again in the world around them." This resurrection of things past so as to cast them in significant and harmonious form has been the ambition of many a writer. Few have achieved it as convincingly as has Shelby Foote.

After the Civil War books, Foote returned to the novel form and wrote a gripping thriller, *September September* (1977). Although sales were rather disappointing in this country, the book was very well received in Europe, making the best-seller list in France. In fact, all of his major work is now available in French—except for *The Civil War: A Narrative* (which, because of its length, has not yet been translated into any other language). This has led to an ironic situation: in America, where many of his novels have been out of print for some time, Foote is regarded primarily as an historian; meanwhile, in non-English speaking countries he is known almost exclusively as a novelist. Perhaps the recent renewal of interest in Foote's work at home will alter this perception. Two of his earliest novels, *Tournament* and *Jordan County,* will be reprinted soon (joining the recent Vintage paperback edition of *The Civil War*), and Foote is presently working on a new novel.

The interview that follows is a much-shortened version of my conversations with Foote, recorded in his Memphis home during two days in September 1985. We sat in the large, book-lined bedroom/study where he works. Almost all of the numerous photographs of Civil War generals, which had lined the walls during the years that Foote was reliving the War, have been taken down. Only one portrait hangs there now: a poster of Marcel Proust, sent from Paris by Foote's son Huger. Both father and son are great admirers of the French writer, and Foote has hung the poster over the typewriter where he makes a fair copy of each day's work. Now the Parisian writer of *Remembrance of Things Past* gazes down on his Mississippi Delta colleague, whose novel-in-progress bears a title with strong Proustian resonances: *Two Gates to the City.*

During our time together, Foote talked at ease about his favorite topics: writing, history, literature, and life in the South. He has an intimate, writer's knowledge of the major literary works in Western civilization, leavened by a keen sense of humor. Foote's answers and comments flowed freely—often punctuated by laughter—as he spoke about his life and the craft through which he continues to seek the truth.

Mr. Foote, how did Memphis come to be your home?

That's really simple. Memphis is the capital of the Mississippi Delta, so whenever you went to the *city,* you came to Memphis. Almost every month of my life I've been in Memphis. Women down in the Delta would come up here to buy shoes—or used to—and men came up to buy shotguns and things. We were always coming to Memphis, so that moving to Memphis was just . . . it might as well have been in Mississippi. I'd written those five novels down home before I moved up here.

There was a four-year period in 1949 to 1952 when you published one book a year.

That's right. When I got back from the war I went hard to work and in those five years I did write five books. I finished *Tournament* before the war, in the first draft, and I took it out of the closet where I had put it during the war and began to rework it. But I wrote *Shiloh* before I finished reworking it, and *Shiloh* was submitted to Dial Press, whose editors said they liked it very much, but that they thought it wouldn't sell. Did I have anything else in mind? I said yes, I had in mind a novel called *Tournament,* and I came back home and quickly finished revising it, so it became my first novel. It *was* my first novel, but it was an accident that it came out first. *Shiloh* came out three years later.

You have never been tempted to use some of the things that have happened in Memphis? I'm thinking particularly of Martin Luther King, Jr.'s assassination and the Elvis Presley phenomenon.

I haven't. I learned something very important in writing *The Civil War.* I think if there had not been a hundred years since the war it would not have been possible to have the perspective that I had on it. Dust has to settle; the thing has to adjust itself in your memory. *Follow Me Down,* which I wrote as of 1950, was based on an incident that had happened four or five years before, so that I was able to get some kind of perspective. What writers do—I know *I* do and I think most do—is they have some idea or they have some experience or they hear some story that interests them, and it moves into the back of their minds. Something happens to it there—especially if you've forgotten it—and then it comes forward again in your memory enriched, or as Stendhal would say, encrusted with something that has happened to it while it was back there in your mind. That's one reason I like to write about things that are in the past. I am conscious of trying to cover different periods of time, most especially in *Jordan County,* which actually does cover different periods.

I was reminded of Flaubert when I read Love in a Dry Season.

Flaubert has always been one of the writers I think has taught me most. *Madame Bovary* especially, but also *Sentimental Education* and the *Three Tales* and even *Salammbô.* Flaubert's way of writing is one that appeals to me.

How do you mean "his way of writing"?

I mean his idea of the way to set a scene or recount an experience. The economy of method appeals to me enormously, as well as Flaubert's reported practice of reading over to himself, aloud, anything he had written so that he'd have the right pitch to it.

Do you do that?

I do, yes. I think that all good writing I know is based on speech rhythms. I don't know of a writer that's more true of than, say, Proust. You'd think that wouldn't be true of him, but it certainly is. Proust flows beautifully when it's spoken.

I've read that you always work from character rather than from situation.

That's right.

On the other hand, you've said that you always have a plot outline, that you always plot carefully.

A story occurs to me as a person and as a type of person, and then the story comes out of what that person is, what he's like, what he does. You take a person like Harley Drew and you put him in a town like Bristol and certain things start happening. It always occurs to me as a person first. I think most bad books are written, "How about a situation in which a man . . . ?" and good books are written, "How about a man in a situation ?" To me that really is the difference. I don't mean great books can't be written out of profound conviction—Dostoevsky certainly did that—but once he got to that point, the next thing was the characters, and then they took over. I certainly don't mean by that that the story goes anywhere it wants to. I do plot very carefully, but the plotting follows the conception of the character and the conception of what would happen. Then it's a question of giving shape to the story.

I agree with Aristotle, who said the first thing a writer learns to do is to write good descriptive things. A high-school student can write a splendid description of a sunset, really good. The next thing you learn to do is draw characters who stand up off the page and cast a shadow. The last thing you learn, and the most difficult, is how to plot. I believe in books being plotted. All my favorite books are plotted, and plotted superbly.

Do you have many details worked out in your head or do they come to you as you write?

I have the plot worked out. I know who's going to be where and when, but the details come in the writing itself and they are what bring the book alive. The other is just skill. The details are what make the book real. It's the most important thing that I can think of about writing a novel: know where you stand to tell the story. It's the whole tone of the thing, who are you, talking: what kind of views do you have of the world? It can vary from book to book. And it's extremely important.

I just read two very different novels by two German writers. One of them was Hermann Hesse's *Demian.* It's what they call an apprentice novel about a young man coming of age. He's a brilliant young man, like Joyce in *A Portrait of the Artist as a Young Man,* and he bores me with his brilliance and so does Stephen Dedalus bore me in the *Portrait.* He doesn't in *Ulysses,* but he does in the *Portrait.* On the other hand, Thomas Mann's *Magic Mountain* has a rather thick-skinned young man, not too bright, but he's just bright enough and it's perfect. There's such a difference between those two books. They both are about coming of age, but Mann has a receptive, sort-of-average young man—he's introduced to us as "an unassuming young man"—whereas in *Demian,* the narrator Sinclair is a brilliant young man who has all kinds of problems that come out of his brilliance. *The Magic Mountain* is a much better novel because of the stance and because of what it's concerned with.

How did it feel for you, after spending twenty years writing The Civil War, *to return to the novel form in* September September?

It felt strange to finish a twenty-year work. My experience was very similar to Gibbon's, who said he didn't quite know what to do with himself. But, as to returning to the novel, there was no problem there at all, because I had felt no different writing *The Civil War* from what I had felt writing the five novels that preceded it. It was exactly the same kind of writing so far as I was concerned. The only difference was I had to look up the facts instead of imagining them. But when I imagined them, they were just as much facts to me as if I had gotten them out of documents. So that I really did not feel any different. I knew I was never again going to have such characters to deal with as Stonewall Jackson and Bedford Forrest, and I regretted that, but I didn't feel any gap.

I've read that when you started The Civil War: A Narrative, *you thought it was going to be fairly fast going.*

The contract called for "A Short History of the Civil War."

If you had known in the beginning that it would take twenty years to complete The Civil War, *would you have done it?*

I thought it would take a year and a half at the most, and I never would have done it if I'd thought it would take so long. But having done it, I'm not at all sorry that I did. It's exactly what I wanted to do. I believed very much that the American Civil War is an experience central to our lives—all Americans, but especially Southerners. The

Civil War, for us, was very much similar to the Trojan War for the Greeks; the Civil War is our *Iliad.* And I think it could be written any number of times by any number of writers in part or as a whole, the way the Greeks did.

Was The Iliad *a model to you in the beginning, or did you become aware of that in the writing?*

It worked both ways. I was aware of *The Iliad* as a model when I began, but it became even more a model as I went along and became fonder and fonder of it. I think *The Iliad* is our greatest narrative poem. To me, it's an absolute model for anybody wanting to write anything, most especially history. Homer's descriptive power of the camp at night, with the horses feeding and things like that, is just absolutely incredibly beautiful, and it *communicates*—he may be writing myth, but it's very real to me. There are so many parallels between any good narrative history and Homer's *Iliad* that I think it is going to be a model whether you know it or not.

I was thankful that I lived a hundred years after the war so the dust could settle, but also so that—not reading Greek—I had Richmond Lattimore's translation of *The Iliad.* I'm convinced his translation is by far the closest thing to Homer. And I also think it's pertinent in our time. Each generation needs to retranslate the great classical works so that they are accessible to that generation, but I consider myself extremely fortunate to link the Lattimore translation of *The Iliad* to *The Civil War.*

Did you reread The Iliad *as you were working on* The Civil War*?*

I still read it all the time. I've read *The Iliad* God knows how many times—start-to-finish reading—because I truly love it. It's great. I like it much better than *The Odyssey.* Most writers like *The Odyssey* better, but I prefer *The Iliad.*

Why do you think that's so?

I don't know. *The Odyssey* is often called the first novel. *The Iliad* is not a novel—*The Odyssey* is certainly a novel, and I agree with that. But *The Iliad* to me is a greater work in every sense. It's concerned, it seems to me, with larger issues; that is, it's the Trojans versus the Achaeans. It's not Odysseus trying to outwit the Cyclops—it's something larger, and therefore on a grander scale. I can see someone preferring *The Odyssey; I* don't, but I can see someone preferring it because it's smaller, because it concerns more human things, they would say. I don't agree with that either.

You have said that the historian should bring to his task the talents of the novelist. Do you feel that you are setting impossibly high standards for the historian?

I never hesitate to set high standards for anyone. I don't see why I shouldn't. I don't think there's anything immodest about it, just as there's nothing immodest about a carpenter trying to make a good house. It's just that an artisan is expected to have a certain degree of skill. And he should want to have more than he's got. So I never hesitate about high standards. A professional historian looks askance at what he calls good writing. He thinks it detracts from the facts. I always remember a quote from Keats saying that "a fact is not a truth until you love it." And that's what I think, too. You have to have this creative fondness for the facts before they'll come alive. You can leave the facts out as readily as anything else, and still communicate the nature of the thing.

A mere accumulation of facts cannot tell the way it was?

It will not tell at all the way it was. It will mislead you into thinking that. It's the way it *wasn't.* Now don't think for an instant I'm saying it's ever all right to the slightest degree to distort a fact. It's not. But the facts alone are not enough to tell the story.

Can you describe how the room where we are sitting now looked when you were writing The Civil War?

It looked exactly as it does now except instead of notes for a novel there were notes for history. There was an outline of the whole history on the wall throughout the writing of it, and I'd do it volume by volume. I've still got those outlines just to show you how little they changed from before I ever wrote a line. I had, I guess, maybe a hundred different pictures up. They were up over here where Proust is now. There was a big wall-board thing loaded with photographs.

The Civil War was the first major war that was thoroughly photographed. How did that affect your work?

It affected it greatly. I got to know those people in a way from looking at their photographs that I could never have known them otherwise. I didn't want to use photographs or illustrations of any kind in my book, except maps. But for my purposes, they were of considerable use.

Did you discover character in the faces?

It wasn't exactly character; it was a sort of aspect. You see a photograph of someone like Ben Wade, a very tough abolitionist and politician from Ohio, and you get to looking at his face, and many of the qualities of Ben Wade that you are then going to communicate—what he was like—come at you by a process of osmosis off that photograph. You should get to know those people well, even though you don't write a lengthy description of them. You know, for example, how Lincoln moved; you read what his gait was like, a sort of shuffling plowman's walk. You learn that his height was mostly in his legs: when he stood up, he was very tall, but sitting down he wasn't much taller than anybody else. His law partner, Herndon, said that when he was sitting in a chair his knees were as high as his waist and if you put a marble on his knee it would roll back into his lap. Well, I never put that in the book but it was always in my mind—how Lincoln looked and acted. Lincoln had his picture taken so many times that I was able to say things like he had a haircut just before the second inaugural and it made him look younger. Things like that. The clothes were important, too—the way they wore them, the way they were cut, their trouser legs over their shoes, things like that. Even if you don't use them, you have them in your mind. It's like Hemingway said—a very true thing—that when you really know something you can leave it out of the story, but if you leave it out because you don't know it, it makes a hole in the story. He said it again in an interview about *The Old Man and the Sea*. He said he knew all about the mating habits of the marlin and therefore he didn't have to put it in. [*Laughs*]

I believe you visited all the battlefields to see the lay of the land.

What I did on those trips that's of additional importance, of great importance, was I always visited them at the same time of year that the battle was fought. Shiloh, for instance, if you go there in the wintertime, is a very different place from what it is in early April when the battle was fought. The trees, the greenery, all that kind of thing—the bogs that you go through—are not there at some other time of the year. The weather is very important in any kind of writing, and especially in war. Napoleon called mud the fifth element. It's very important when you're moving an army on the ground.

When I read Shiloh *and* The Civil War, *I feel that I come close to understanding what a real hell it must have been to be in that relentless hail of bullets.*

Those soldiers experienced all the fear we would feel, but they had a different attitude towards what you did with that fear. We're good soldiers today—some of those boys in Vietnam were fine soldiers—but the whole attitude has changed, at least on the surface. Nobody is afraid to admit that he's afraid anymore. All the same, they talked some about being afraid while they were waiting for the charge at Gettysburg. The men were sitting around knowing they had to cross this damn valley—they were hidden in the woods—when a rabbit jumped out of the bush and took off to the rear. And one of the men said, "Run ole hare, if I was an ole hare I'd run too." [*Laughs*]

But don't you think, because of books like yours and our experience in Vietnam, that the romantic notion of war is dead forever?

It was dead from the start. The romantic notion of war is just something written for civilians. Any soldier knows that.

What did you think of Mailer's use of the American tradition of violence in Why Are We in Vietnam?

All I can say for sure is that I think that's Mailer's best book—and no one pays any attention to it. He's crossed Browning with the funny papers or something, and he did a good job. Vietnam is never mentioned in the book, but it's a good job. I like it best of all Mailer's work.

Why do you think it kind of got lost in the shuffle?

I don't know; I don't have any idea. It may *stay* lost too. Mailer's a splendid combination of a good and bad writer. He can be truly bad and he can be truly good. There's a lot of stuff in Mailer's books that he probably would have done better to write pamphlets about.

When did the idea that the novelist and the historian both seek the same thing occur to you? Was it when you were writing Shiloh, *which I believe is your first truly historically based work, or is it a notion that you have always held?*

I always felt that way about it, even before I wrote *Shiloh*—and I followed it in *Shiloh.* No historical character in a novel should do or say anything that you don't know he said and did. You can't displace him in time, and you can't move him geographically. And you've got to be true to him. If I wrote a novel that included Billy the Kid, it would be the Billy the Kid out of history; in other words, he couldn't be the main character; he would have to be a character *in* the novel, unless somebody was wondering about him or something. I would never quote Billy if I didn't have a valid quote. I wouldn't put him in any part of New Mexico that he wasn't in at that date; I believe you owe that to historical characters. Nothing distresses me more than to see an historical character in one of these historical, romantic novels take the hero aside and give him a little advice on his love life or something. I don't think you have a right to do that with historical characters.

The only appropriate use of history in the novel, as you see it, is what you did in September September. *That is, the facts that you use from 1957—Sputnik, Eisenhower, the integration of the schools in Little Rock . . .*

Right. If you find Eisenhower quoted or Faubus quoted, that quote will be accurate. I don't think anyone has the right to distort it. I'll give Shakespeare the right, but nobody since him. *War and Peace,* I think, is badly flawed by that. The Napoleon in *War and Peace* is the Napoleon who was on St. Helena. It's not the Napoleon who was in Russia. He's a tired, fat man in *War and Peace,* which he certainly was not when he was in Russia. It's a fooling around that I don't think is ever justified.

So far as genre is concerned, you don't endorse the historical novel. You would call War and Peace *a pure work of fiction or history misused?*

I think that *Anna Karenina* is a much better novel than *War and Peace,* partly for that reason. I don't know of a modern historical instance where the truth wasn't superior to distortion every time. I don't mean the battle reports are always better or will give you a better description of a battle than Tolstoy gave you: I really don't mean that. But I do know that the closer the writer sticks to the truth the better the work will be. Now he can look at it slant, as Emily

Dickinson said. Stendhal's Waterloo is marvelous, and there aren't any facts. It's just confusion—which is okay.

I think Gore Vidal said someplace in one of his essays that there is no such thing as the novel, there are only novelists. In other words, a novel can be anything the novelist wants it to be. Do you endorse that?

I endorse it with the exception we just discussed. I think Vidal's *Lincoln* is fairly dreadful, mostly for the reason I just gave.

Can you remember your thoughts—and you must have been working on the second volume of The Civil War*—on 22 November 1963, when Kennedy was assassinated, almost a hundred years after Lincoln?*

I had finished volume two by then, and in the bibliographical note I had said how frightening the approximations can be. What I had been thinking about primarily was how similar Barnett and Wallace and Faubus were to the fire-eating Southerners who helped bring on the Civil War. The assassination of Kennedy emphasized that note, which was written before he was killed. I said I suppose it's true that history never repeats itself, but it can be terrifying in its approximations. And here came the assassination, as if I had been some kind of voice crying in the wilderness. The Civil War is our great national tragedy, and I do believe it's necessary to know it to understand this country. For someone who knows it, constant parallels are always jumping up. Santayana said that a nation that does not know its history will be obligated to repeat it.

Some people, when they heard that Kennedy had been shot, started to applaud and laugh.

Right. That's the underside of the American character. To me the most poignant were the school children in Dallas who cheered when it was announced by the teacher that he'd been shot, because they had heard their folks at home cussing him. That's the dark underside of the American character that goes with lynchings and strike-breaking—all ugly sides.

How do you account for the violence in Southern writing?

I think that it'd better be understood. If we really got the world that we pray for, it might not be as satisfying a world as we think it would be. I very much admire the work of Robert Browning, who was interested, his whole writing life, in why evil should exist, and he came up with a very simple answer that I think is quite true: without evil there wouldn't be any good. If there's no black, there's no white. And he assigned it to the whole plan of the universe. In his case, God was doing it, but it was very necessary to have that side for men to be men. If there were no death, there'd be no life.

We'd have to be very cautious if we could rearrange our genes so that we were not the way we are. I don't see how anyone could not want to remove things like the propensity towards lynchings and applauding assassinations, but if you did take them away—which you can't—you might be left with something bland and characterless. It's an interesting problem. And God knows what novelists would write about without it. [*Laughs*] I put a very high value on the injustices I saw, especially with regard to blacks, which taught me a great deal. And once again, I am emphasizing how valuable it is to be a Southerner. You had a sense of the tragedy of life—from having lost a war and other things—and you also saw an oppressed people at first hand, cooking your food and mowing your lawn.

I don't know what the Russian novel would be without the peasants. I do know that something dreadful happened to it when they freed them; aside, that is, from Chekhov, who's a sort of carry-over. I am not for an instant claiming injustice should exist in the world so that novelists will have something to write about. I am talking about the quality of life itself. It's very strange.

Do you think that we Americans are a violent people?

I think it is true that we are more violent than other people, and I think Southerners are more violent than other Americans. I can remember, when I was a very young man, being in New York with a group of people, and two men would get in an argument and somebody would call somebody else a son of a bitch and everybody'd sort of laugh and pass that off. Down home it would have been an instant invitation to step out into the yard. [*Laughs*] I couldn't get over the blandness with which insults were handed around. At home violence was considered the answer. Now I'm not defending this as a good thing, but I am saying that it does add to the complexity of life, this possibility of violence. In the New York episode, there was scarcely any possibility of violence and that is far more civilized, but it also has its shortcomings.

What exactly did you mean in the bibliographical note to The Civil War *when you wrote, "Proust I believe has taught me more about the organization of material than even Gibbon has done, and Gibbon has taught me much"?*

Along with *The Iliad,* the model for *The Civil War* is Proust's *Remembrance of Things Past.* It's the handling of multiple themes. It's tying them all into one thing, and Proust taught me that. Proust taught me so very much in so many ways, and for the same reason the writer who taught me more than anyone else is probably Shakespeare. The better he is, the more he teaches you. I'd be hard put to say where Proust's chief talents lie, whether it's the telling of a little incident or the drawing of character or looking at life as to what it's all about, or what's the nature of memory. God knows where his chief talent is. It's a broad, marvelous talent. And anybody can learn from him. I certainly did—especially, to come back to your question, in the handling of a large-scale thing. *Remembrance of Things Past* is a miracle. If I could have one wish, it would have been to give Proust four more years of life to fix up those last three volumes, good as they are.

Proust has been criticized by some of his greatest admirers for sort of losing control of the material. Many people believe that had he had four more years, we would have had an expansion of material rather than a shaping.

I think he would have had an expansion of material and any material he ever expanded he certainly improved. I'm for *The Guermantes Way* the way it is.

Proust's main influence on The Civil War, *then, was the handling and weaving of thematic material?*

Right. I said I wouldn't name his major talent, but what interests me perhaps more than anything else—on the repeated reading of it—is how he moves that story, the *whole* time. No matter how many digressions there seem to be, that story is moving forward. It may be a little incident that's nothing, whether it's looking through a window at Montjouvain or whatever little incident it is; later on you'll find out why it was there. And it's that way all through Proust. He's nudging the story forward *all the time.* And that was the thing I had very much in mind while writing *The Civil War:* keep the story moving. Proust does that and he does it superbly. And the paradox is, he's thought to depart from the story so frequently. He *never* departs from the story.

I can always read Proust. If I ever want to read anything, I'll go get a volume of Proust down and I'm absorbed right away. It's always been that way. There are several such writers, to be fair. I can do this with Keats. And Browning delights me. Browning is one of my very favorite poets. He's a great writer who has been sadly neglected, I think, in these last few years. Often because of the misconception that he was an optimist who didn't believe evil really existed. The opposite is true. He is one of the bleakest pessimists the world ever saw, and I never knew a man more conscious of evil walking the earth than Browning was. I'm crazy about Browning. Once again as a technician; he's a marvelous technician. He's very exciting, whether it's a lyric or a narrative. It's great. Browning's *The Ring and the Book* is a Balzacian or even Flaubertian novel written in blank-verse dramatic monologues. There are twelve of them. And nobody's better at that than Browning was. Alas, *The Ring and the Book* is almost unread nowadays.

It's also the technical aspect, I believe, that you admire particularly in Joyce and Proust. Is that correct?

Right. Joyce almost exclusively for the technical aspect. Proust much larger. My admiration for Proust is much greater than my admiration for Joyce, although I like both *Ulysses* and *Finnegans Wake* about as well as I do any books I know.

Many people name Proust and Joyce when they talk about the great achievements in the twentieth-century novel. If you had to add a third name to that, whom would you choose?

It would be a sort of contest between Faulkner and Thomas Mann. I do know the most influential writer of the twentieth century—and I have absolutely no doubt about it—is Hemingway. Not the best, but certainly the most influential. Nobody's writing a news story today who is not influenced by Hemingway. Hemingway's impact on the writing world is enormous, partly because his work was so popular.

Hemingway reached a great many people. The apparent clarity of it, in his early work anyhow, had a terrific influence on writers of all kinds—magazines, newspapers, everything.

Did he influence you in any way?

Surely. I think he influenced every writer since his time. He had a large influence on Faulkner.

How did he influence you?

The attempts to use the rhythms of natural speech, for one thing; the sort of clarity. And the awareness that, if you write it truly smooth—the way, say, Thornton Wilder did—it's dead on the page. Hemingway knew how to rough it up, repeat words where somebody else wouldn't. At the same time he's writing that beautiful, limpid prose, he's also putting enough hitches in there to keep it alive. It's a strange thing.

Another interesting thing to me about Hemingway is I consider him an absolutely self-made man. I don't think he had any God-given talent at all. I think he learned how to do it—which is a kind of strange thing, for him to be so successful. He seems to me to have been highly intelligent in being able to use what had come before him, to put it together into a new thing—most especially Sherwood Anderson, Gertrude Stein, and Daniel Defoe. But he made a new thing.

Would you also describe Faulkner in the same way, as a self-made man?

All writers are self-made and self-taught, and so on, but Faulkner had something Hemingway never dreamed existed, and that is something of the nature of genius, which Hemingway had no fraction of. Faulkner had a burning vitality, a real jumping thing inside him that Hemingway didn't have—or when he had it, he wrote badly.

If you write a lot about the South, this tends to label you as a regional writer?

Yeah, that does indeed happen. But it never bothered me to any degree whatsoever. I don't mind being called a Southern writer, I don't mind being called a Mississippi writer. To get back to Proust, I consider him a regional writer. Paris was his region [*laughs*] which was quite a region, but he's a regional writer and he made the most of it. And I don't see that it crippled him in the least. And I don't think it does us. I never objected to that. I know many writers who do, but—forgive me—I think that's a lack of confidence.

All writers know that if they write well enough about anything on earth, it's not going to be a shortcoming; it's going to be a virtue. Writers always work with what they have to work with. I suppose I could claim that Southerners have more to work with than other people because it seems to me they do. Small-town Southern life is a glorious opportunity to study life in all its phases, but I'm not sure that a Mississippi writer has any advantage at all over, say, an Iowa writer. It just depends on how good a writer he is. The material is always there. There's no lack of stories to tell, there's no lack of characters. And where you are I'm not sure makes much difference.

Does it bother you that the South is becoming more homogeneous with the rest of the country?

It bothers me to the extent that it means the loss of a conscious heritage. But it doesn't bother me to the extent of wanting to do anything about it, because I don't think there's anything you *can* do about it. I don't like losing values. I don't mind acquiring new ones, so long as they are not trashy.

You say that a Southern writer has so much to work with. Do you think that we're getting to the end of that?

No, I don't think that. All it takes is a good writer. You see writers that you hope are going to be good and they disappoint you. Barry Hannah is a writer I had big hopes for, but he keeps kicking the gong around. That's what they do nowadays. Of course there are some good writers now. Cormac McCarthy is a hell of a good writer, but nobody reads him.

What are some of his titles we should read?

The Orchard Keeper was his first novel; *Outer Dark* and *Child of God; Suttree*—and his last one was called *Blood Meridian.* They are marvelous novels and they go unread. They are truly Southern in every sense, wonderful books. They have a strange, weird, bloody quality to them, but they're great.

I believe Faulkner said one reason Southern literature is unusually rich is because it had been influenced so much by Shakespeare and the Bible.

I think that's true. We've always had a large appreciation for the King James version of the Bible. We've always been familiar with it, read it often, gone to Sunday School and heard it at church services. It's entered into the fabric of our lives in a way that the beauties of the Bible are very present to us, so that when we write we are aware of those beauties. And the Shakespearean thing is something else. I remember that when I was a boy, American literature consisted of a flock of New England writers, with Edgar Allan Poe sort of thrown in to leaven the lump. I was told that the great writers were Lowell, Whittier, Longfellow, Emerson—and as far as I'm concerned, with the possible exception of Emerson, those are very, very bad writers. I'm talking about *bad* writers. Their verities are lies, their scorn for the rest of the world is contemptible. It's a wonder we ever had any literature in the country, if we start out thinking that Longfellow and Lowell and Whittier are great writers. I think they've largely gone by the wayside now, and I'm glad to see them go. It's funny that the one we never paid any attention to is now the top dog up that way—Thoreau. We didn't even know Thoreau existed.

Do you think that's right—that he's indeed the one we should have been paying attention to?

I'm still not all that fond of Thoreau. [*Laughs*]

What can you say about Shakespeare's influence on your writing?

He's a giant, but there's a very small thing he can do and it's not like Flaubert's *mot juste.* He can say "Full many a glorious morning have I seen / Flatter the mountain tops with sovereign eye." Well, I don't know where flatter and sovereign came from but, Jesus Christ, if you could say a thing like that, you'd be happy the rest of your life. Just saying it over and over to yourself, "Flatter the mountain tops with sovereign eye"—my God! And that's what you can learn. The beauties are there to be discovered. What Shakespeare had was . . . "verbal felicity" is putting it way too lightly. He can take a familiar word and turn it into something that's as bright as a new coin. "Flatter the mountain tops"—that's an incredible thing to say. And yet it's just part of our language, we just skim by it. But to use that word "flatter" there, it's almost unbelievable that he could do that.

The three American writers I think of as having the greatest literary reputation in the first half of the century would be Hemingway, Fitzgerald, and Faulkner. How would you say the literary reputations of those men hold up today from your point of view?

Faulkner has held up the best, but only, I think, because his work lends itself to explication by academics. I believe the Fitzgerald reputation will probably fade. The Hemingway one will fade and come back. And I think Faulkner will always be interesting because of the complexity of his work. It gives you so much room to explore; academics will always be interested in taking Faulkner apart, just as they are in taking Dante apart. For centuries Dante has been kept alive by academics, although Dante is a much greater writer than any of these people we are talking about.

I took off three or four years recently to read again the things I liked best when I was young. I reread Chaucer and Dante and this time really studied them. It was a great experience. One of the finest experiences I ever had in my life was back about 1952. I read Shakespeare chronologically, insofar as they know the order the plays were written in, and to watch that mind grow, to watch that talent expand, is a marvelous experience. It's a good way to read a writer. Dostoevsky reads quite well that way. You watch him learn how to write. You recognize all his tricks. It's great.

One thing I notice that you and Faulkner have in common is the use of characters who reappear in different stories and novels.

Right. I like that; it gives things a relationship to each other. I would not be the least bit interested in writing a short story that wasn't tied in somehow to other things. A perfect little moment just doesn't interest me for its own sake. Even in *Shiloh*, for example, I have to have somebody from down home in the battle, Luther Dade. He's a Mississippi private and the grandfather of the main character in *Follow Me Down*, Luther Eustis.

Did the use of different voices to tell the story begin with a particular novel? For example, in Tournament *and* Love in a Dry Season *you don't, I believe, have different voices.*

At least very little; that's right. No, it's just a variation. You tell one story one way and another story another way. I was probably greatly influenced by my fondness for dramatic monologue, by my fondness for Browning and Faulkner—both of whom use it superbly.

I've read about the reception of your work in France, where you are considered in many ways to be the successor to Faulkner. When September September *came out over there the reviewer in* L'Express *credited you with inventing what he called the* "thriller au ralenti."

"The slow-moving thriller!" That amused me very much. That is exactly what I was trying to write. You might think I'd be offended by that, but I was pleased. I had wanted to write a novel that paid attention to the people rather than the events. I didn't want to write a detective thriller. In *September,* unlike *Follow Me Down,* I kept back how it was coming out, but I didn't want the emphasis on how it was coming out. I wanted the emphasis on the people, how they acted, how they thought, what they were doing incidental to that, and their own personal problems. I wanted the emphasis on the people rather than on the events. That required slow movement. If you're going to take time to look at people while they are doing these dreadful things, you have to move slowly. So the kind of reader I was looking for, I suppose, was one who would be interested in what I was interested in, rather than just how it was going to come out.

I remember the relationship between the characters and the amount of decency that you discover even in the characters who belong to the criminal element.

If you don't know about compassion, you're in bad shape. Proust would take that so far as to see that really horrendous scene at Montjouvain where he's looking through the window at the two women. Later it's going to develop that one of them saved the man's music, but even then he tries to analyze his reactions to the two people in this cruel scene he's watching. He finds one redeeming virtue in it—that at least they weren't guilty of indifference. That's reaching pretty far to find something to sympathize with, but he found it. He said that the one true and lasting form of cruelty was indifference, not what these people were doing.

I detect a lot of the same compassion in The Civil War.

I certainly hope so. That's a thing that interests me very much. There are two wonderful things about bad characters. If he's a real scamp, he'll bring your pages alive the way Uriah Heep does in *David Copperfield.* And for me Stanton—Lincoln's secretary of war—was one of the scoundrels of all times, and I was absolutely delighted every time he walked into the book, because of what he could lend the book in the way of narrative drive. The other thing that interested me very much was men who failed, like Hood, or even John Pope (an extremely unattractive character), or Rosecrans at Chickamauga. I was very interested in seeing things from their point of view.

There's a Confederate general named Braxton Bragg for whom I think everyone on the face of this earth has nothing but contempt. I found great redeeming features in Bragg. There's a famous confrontation between him and Bedford Forrest in which Forrest walked into Bragg's tent and said, "If you were any kind of man, I'd box your jaws, and if you ever give me another order, I won't obey it." And Bragg, whom no one ever accused of being a physical coward, did not bring charges against Forrest for that. He could have had him dismissed from the army, but the reason he didn't do it was not that he was afraid to do it—Bragg wasn't afraid of anybody anywhere. He didn't do it perhaps because he knew that Forrest was a very valuable general to have in the Confederate army and he didn't want him thrown out—or at least that's a possibility.

I was always pleased to be able to redeem a reputation that's been run down too much. Proust taught me a lot about that and so did Faulkner. Faulkner's last, latest works were weak compared to those of his prime, but when he redeems Mink Snopes, for example, that's a hell of a redemption. Mink is a pretty evil fellow, and Faulkner put him right back on course and made him a whole middle part of *The Mansion.*

Some of the French critics say that you are persuaded of the long-term failure of the American adventure. Would you elaborate on that interpretation, if you agree with it?

I do agree with it, and I think it's an advantage that the Southern artist has, whether it's in music or sculpture or painting or writing. I'm often amazed to hear the frequent quote, "We Americans have never lost a war." You hear it all the time: "Never lost a war"—at least you heard it before Vietnam. I know *some* Americans who certainly lost a war—lost it about as thoroughly as a war can be lost, and afterwards got ground into the dirt harder than most any losers I know—and they lived in the South. That gave us, by inheritance, a true sense of tragedy. We do not believe that all noble experiments are bound to succeed. We know at least one noble experiment that failed miserably. We don't have the bright outlook that everything is for the best in this best of all possible worlds, because our history taught us differently.

And while the war was not always in the forefront of our consciousness, it operated very strongly in our unconscious and on our manners and our morals. For instance, Vicksburg fell on the fourth day of July. The Fourth of July throughout my childhood and young manhood was never celebrated in Mississippi. One year a couple was there from Ohio—why they were there I do not know—and they drove their car up on the levee, spread out their blanket, and had a picnic on the levee to celebrate the Fourth. They forgot to set the brakes of the car properly and it rolled down the levee and into the river; everybody said it served them right for celebrating the Fourth.

But this true sense of tragedy on a large scale is a very Southern heritage, whereas for a Northerner it's a true sense of triumph. Northerners believe that all the virtues conquered because they are now the virtues, but Southerners don't believe that virtue necessarily conquers because we believe strongly in the virtues of our forebears. We don't believe that government of and by and for the people would have perished from the earth if the South had won the war, although we are required to memorize those very words in school. It's very strange what power there is in literary skill. We memorize Lincoln's Gettysburg Address simply because he phrased it so well; we don't even hear what it's saying.

Do we still have any of the problems today that brought the Civil War to a head?

Oh, absolutely. It doesn't matter whether you're opposed to slavery or peonage or just segregation. They're all problems; they just vary by degrees and definition. In some ways peonage is as vicious as slavery, and in some ways it's more vicious. I think it was Thomas Carlyle who said the Civil War was an argument between people one of whom believed in hiring their servants for life and the other believed in hiring them by the week. [*Laughs*] I'm not defending slavery, incidentally.

We often hear white Southerners congratulating themselves on how well things have gone with integration. Do you agree that there is room for a fair amount of self-congratulation?

I do indeed; I don't see how anybody could deny it. If integration can work in Mississippi, then—my God—where can't it? When I was a boy I memorized, along with every male schoolmate I had, obscene doggerel about Abraham Lincoln. The war held on that long. I don't think my son feels it now, fifty years later, but we did. It was very much a part of us without our being all that conscious of it.

How do you account for the awful things that did happen?

I blame the "decent people" for most of that. They did not want integration either, but instead of accomplishing it in an orderly way—and they did know it was coming—they stepped back and said, "Let the riffraff take care of it." In place after place they did that. And wherever they did that there was big trouble, because those yahoos were very anxious to get some excitement into their lives. I think Mark Twain was right—the main cause of lynching was boredom. These people were delighted to get out and loot and burn and curse and spit. And if decent people had not permitted it, it would not have happened. You take a town like Yazoo City—a decent, good town. That town stepped back and let every yahoo in it take over during that time, believing that those were the people who were best able to deal with the problem. They were wrong. They were as wrong as they could be, and they know that now.

Was this a loss of nerve or looking the other way? Did they do it consciously?

They consciously shared many of the beliefs of these Ku Kluxers. They weren't Ku Kluxers and never could be, but they wanted the same thing the Kluxers wanted. They wanted to keep segregation, and they believed that the Kluxers might be able to keep it regardless, but they should have known they were wrong the day they thought about it. Finally they did know, and they put these people back where they belonged, that is, within the law. And it was a sad thing—it always happens. It happened in Reconstruction; we had a good chance then, a really good chance; our grandfathers had a great chance to do the thing right. But it was a missed chance. They held the Negro down and left him for us to deal with when he finally busted out.

Did you not say that many of the worst fears about blacks being integrated into the society have been realized?

Yes, I think that many of them have been realized. The disruption is just as great as it was expected to be. It took a different form, but I was for letting the blacks up from the beginning—I said when the whole thing started we ought to bring the Marine Corps out and knock everybody in Mississippi in the head with the butt of an M-1. I thought that would be the solution to the whole thing, so I was for it all-out, the day it began. But the consequences have been dire, and they might have been expected. You can't hold people down for two hundred years, and then all of a sudden let them up and not expect them to celebrate being let up. And they celebrated it in some pretty strange ways. Memphis is the rape capital of the United States today. There's more rape per thousand people in Memphis than any place in the United States. And that's a celebration. It's not a sex act; it's an act of violence, a protest and a celebration. The muggings that occur are mostly done—around here anyhow—by blacks, and that's a form of celebration. You do what you can, and when you can't do anything else you go to crime. It's a perfectly natural thing to do. And the presumption is that the people who have been let up and are celebrating will get tired of celebrating and become more civilized in all kinds of ways. I'm glad that they've been let up, but certainly there's a price to be paid.

In September September *there are social risers—for example, the black bourgeois couple, the Kinships, and the rich grandfather, Theo Wiggins. Do you see more blacks making progress now and becoming bourgeois?*

Yes, I do and I regret what they lost in the process of rising. Walker Percy said it best. He said this whole thing is to develop to the point where blacks just like whites can watch *Bonanza* every Saturday night. [*Laughs*] And that's equality, you see.

What do you think of Gone With the Wind as a Civil War novel?

I don't have much thought about *Gone With the Wind* as a novel. I liked it all right, but I don't think it amounts to anything. It came out about the same time as *Absalom, Absalom!*, which is a really good novel about the Civil War. It's the great favorite nowadays with so many Faulkner scholars, but I find that about midway it shifts gears and breaks into a high falsetto.

Can you pinpoint that moment?

Yeah . . . when Quentin and his roommate Shreve got to tossing the story around. Faulkner's point is that art is the most interesting thing in the world—the chances and speculations and everything else. I like the first half of *Absalom, Absalom!* so much better than I do when Quentin and Shreve start kicking it around.

You think at that point it gets a little contrived and that Faulkner is pulling too far back from the immediacy of his characters?

Yeah. Now he did that on purpose. He was very interested in the telling of this story so he winds up with it being told in various versions by two people; speculation and this and that and the other. And he wanted to do that, and I think it's wrong, that's all.

In what way did Faulkner influence you most, as a Mississippi writer or just as a writer?

It's very easy to say. He influenced me most by his excellence—now we can set that aside. The first good modern novel I ever read was in 1932 and it was *Light in August.* I did not know that there was any such thing as the modern novel until I read *Light in August,* which was a hell of an introduction to the modern novel. But even more important, he was writing about something I knew at first hand, and I said, "My God, you can write about what you know."

How do you account for the fact that writers like Faulkner and you and Eudora Welty and Walker Percy were all living and writing at the same time in a state like Mississippi? Is that just a coincidence, do you think?

I think things do go on in areas at times. I can really branch afield and tell you that I've noticed time and time again that country after country turns out superb motion pictures. They do about twelve of them and then they're through. Right after the war the Italians made the best movies you've ever seen and then all of a sudden they stopped making movies, and it switched over to Japan. They were making the great movies. Then the new wave hit France and they were making the great movies. There's something going on, there's a fever in the air.

A powerful current flows through certain places on the face of this earth at times, or it certainly seems to me to be so. Elizabethan England is a good example of that. Things just happen; there's a ferment or a power or something that you draw on mutually. I think something like that happened in Mississippi; over that period of time, in that area of Mississippi, something was going on. And usually the reason given—and it'll do—is Faulkner's talent. Just as Will Percy's being present in Greenville, Mississippi, made Greenville have a lot of writers, so I think the quality of Faulkner's talent encouraged Mississippians to work. If Faulkner had been an Iowan, maybe Iowa would have been the hotbed of production.

What was Faulkner really like when you were with him?

There appear to have been many different Faulkners. The one I knew was a genial, outgoing, amusing companion. He had his silences and his reticences, but they coincided with my own. His reticence mostly was with people who wanted to pry into his private life. And I was not interested in prying into his private life, nor would I be into anyone else's private life, and he knew that. So there wasn't any problem there. We enjoyed each other's company. Certainly I enjoyed his.

Do you consider him to have been a genuine eccentric as he is often described?

No, I don't. In fact, he took a good deal of trouble not to be an eccentric. He dressed more carefully than most people. You see photographs of him in ragged clothes. You hear about him going barefoot all the time. I'm sure he did those things, but he was a rather spiffy little gent most of the time.

You describe somewhere being at his home once when, during a conversation, he abruptly cut everything off and fell silent.

That's the only time he ever did anything like that. His step-daughter Victoria and I were engaging in this youthful badinage across the dinner table, and he got exasperated and stood up and threw his napkin on the table and walked off. I think—God knows this is speculation—I think he was mourning his lost youth or something. Cho-Cho said, "What got into him?" And Estelle said, "You know I've long since given up trying to understand Pappy." [*Laughs*] After dinner I went over in the room where he was, and he was sitting there perfectly content with himself. I told him, "I thought that was a good meal," and he said, "I'm glad you enjoyed it."

How did going out to Hollywood change Faulkner?

I think that he got ideas about several things. It was a fallow period for him anyhow, and—now this is all supposition—he sort of took stock of his work and saw that there were certain gaps that had to be filled, certain areas that should be corrected. And he proceeded to do that all the rest of his life. It might have happened no matter where he was, but I think of him engaging in this real jump in film scripts. A good writer can learn anywhere, even in Hollywood, but I think it tilted him in a direction, somehow; that the plots, the film sequences, all those things got into his work. I don't know what changed him from having an utterly bleak view.

Do you think that Faulkner's going out to Hollywood represented a sort of selling out as a writer for a while?

I wouldn't call it a selling out. What he did was he entered into it the way he did anything that he'd agreed to do. If he was going to paint a house, he would learn how to paint, which is what he did at one time. So when he went out to Hollywood, he learned how to do it. He never did it very well, but he learned to do it. I think it got into his work.

Faulkner insisted a great deal at the end of his life that he really wanted no biography, nothing that would detract from his books. Do you feel that way about your work?

Faulkner didn't feel that way either. The main thing you can always depend on: when Faulkner speaks for publication, he's lying; always—no exceptions. He had a way of dealing with journalists—he came out flatly and said it one time when he came back from getting the Nobel Prize. He was met at the airport here in Memphis by a bunch of reporters, and they had some questions to ask him. One of them said, "What do you think is the most distressful thing about modern life?" and Faulkner said, "What you're doing now." [*Laughs*] He came out with it there, but his usual way of dealing with it was just to lie to them. "If you are so rude as to ask me questions I don't want to answer, I simply will answer you with lies," which disposes of that.

Was he that way from the beginning or was it some bad experience that turned him against the press?

I didn't know Faulkner as a young man because he was that much older than I, but I've always had the theory—and that's all it is—that he talked his head off one time and made a fool of himself and resolved never to do it again. [*Laughs*] But I'm not sure of that. I think he probably was that way from the outset. I've heard Ben Wasson say—he was a close friend of Faulkner's at Ole Miss and they were about the same age; Ben was a little younger—that the Faulkner he knew back in the early days was by no means reticent. He would like to turn out the lights and play Beethoven and things like that.

I have read in several different places that since September September *you have been working on a long family novel called* Two Gates to the City. *You say that it's about a family in the Delta, and it's not historical. You have referred to it as sort of a Mississippi* Karamazov.

It's a family novel in the sense that *The Brothers Karamazov* is a family novel. In other words, it's not a saga; it's concerned with what goes on in a family. I'm also interested in the grandfather and the father. The situation is a very strange one. There are three cousins, all only children of three daughters, and their grandfather has remarried and had a child in his old age who is younger than they are. So they have an uncle who is younger than they are—this is not unheard of. The book opens with the suicide of this boy and they've all come back to the town. They are together in a family situation, the grandfather dying of cancer and the women doing this, that, and the other, and a whole lot goes on, lots of swapping partners. But it's very complicated. It's laid in 1948, it goes forward to 1963 and back to 1872, and it's all happening at the same time. It's a madhouse. [*Laughs*]

When you write, do you revise extensively afterwards?

No. I revise as I go along. At the end of the day, I've got my 500 or 600 words, and I make a fair copy of it and put it on the stack.

And there's no going back?

Almost none. Oh, I get a lick at the typescript and change this, that, and the other. Take a comma out and put one in, a few things, but very little. And never any extensive revision. That's one reason I think I gain time by working slowly; 500 or 600 words is a good day's work. Seven days a week—that stacks up.

Do you keep notes?

No, I've never kept notes. I believe in what D. H. Lawrence said: if you take notes, you short-circuit this process that Stendhal calls crystallization; that is, you freeze it. If you take anything like detailed notes, you've frozen it; this thing—crystallization—won't happen in your head. Some poet once told me that he never typed a poem until he'd finished writing it and he was perfectly satisfied with every revision he was going to make, because once it was sitting there in type, it was inviolable. So, you see, it's something like that.

What advice would you give to a young writer starting out today, particularly to someone living in the South?

Read hard and work hard—that's enough. That's it. And it wouldn't necessarily be Southern, just any writer. Read voluminously. Dickens will teach you how to write, if you'll just read him. And read critically. I'm not saying don't give yourself over to the story, but also learn what Dickens is doing. The main way you learn how to write is through *re*-reading. When you know where he's going, you can better appreciate how he goes about getting there. Rereading is the most valuable thing a writer can do.

Index

D

E

F

G

H

I

J

K

L

M

N

O

P

T

U

V

W

Y

Z